WESTVIKING
FARLEY
MOWAT

The Ancient Norse in Greenland and North America

Douglas & McIntyre

Copyright © 2024 Farley Mowat Ltd.
First edition 1965

1 2 3 4 5 — 28 27 26 25 24

All rights reserved. No part of this publication may be reproduced,
stored in a retrieval system or transmitted, in any form or by any means,
without prior permission of the publisher or, in the case of photocopying
or other reprographic copying, a licence from Access Copyright,
www.accesscopyright.ca, 1-800-893-5777, info@accesscopyright.ca.

Douglas and McIntyre (2013) Ltd.
P.O. Box 219, Madeira Park, BC, V0N 2H0
www.douglas-mcintyre.com

Indexed by Colleen Bidner
Cover illustration by Kim LaFave
Cover design by Libris Simas Ferraz / Onça Publishing
Text design by Dwayne Dobson
Maps and drawings by Claire Wheeler

Printed and bound in Canada
Printed on 100% recycled paper

Douglas and McIntyre acknowledges the support of the Canada Council for
the Arts, the Government of Canada, and the Province of British Columbia
through the BC Arts Council.

Library and Archives Canada Cataloguing in Publication
Title: Westviking : the ancient Norse in Greenland and North America /
Farley Mowat.
Names: Mowat, Farley, author.
Description: Includes index.
Identifiers: Canadiana (print) 20230621120 | Canadiana (ebook)
20230621147 | ISBN 9781771624077
(softcover) | ISBN 9781771624084 (EPUB)
Subjects: LCSH: America—Discovery and exploration—Norse. |
LCSH: Vikings—North America.
Classification: LCC E 105 .M89 2024 | DDC 970.01/3—dc23

For Claire

CONTENTS

ILLUSTRATIONS

MAPS

FOREWORD

MOST OF MY BOOKS have been accidental, in the sense that they have never followed the carefully calculated course I planned at their inception. But this book is more accidental than most. It took its genesis from a desire to write the story of the sea-girt, cod-redolent island of Newfoundland. I made the island my home and, after some years there, decided I was ready. I began my story at the beginning—with the appearance of a handful of Greenland Norse men in the gray waters off the northern coast.

I intended to give the Norse one chapter at the most. But they ended up pirating the entire book right out from under me—an act which is perfectly consistent with Viking character.

As I delved deeper into the accounts of the Norse voyages across the Western Ocean I found myself faced with hundreds of conflicting reconstructions and interpretations of the voyages. In order to synthesize all of them I concluded I would need to spend several years in close company with an educated computer.

The alternative was to reconstruct the entire tale myself. This was a somewhat intimidating prospect, since I am no specialist in the arcane field of Scandinavian scholarship. But was this such a frightful handicap? A fresh look at the Norse story through the lenses of diverse studies, including climatology, seamanship, anthropology, zoology and many others, might prove more revealing than the results which had been achieved by subjecting the subject to the single-eyed scrutiny of Norse scholarship. And I possess a working knowledge of a great many fields which bear upon the problem of reconstructing the voyages.

I am a northerner by nature and by residence if not strictly so by birth. When I was thirteen I made my first venture into the subarctic tundra and I have been back many times since then—usually as an unencumbered wanderer, and always seeking understanding of that immutable world. I have sailed no Viking ships in northern seas, but my father began teaching me seamanship when I was old enough to walk, and I have sailed (and still sail) an antique schooner in the cold waters which hunger at the shores of Newfoundland. I know the sea well enough to comprehend something of its mysteries; and I know many seamen of an earlier age (my friends and neighbors in Newfoundland) well enough to lift my admiration for them to the level of a sustained affection. The sea and the north—and the men of both—move me as little else does. I have written extensively about both.

There are a number of minor facets of knowledge and experience which have helped me too. In my youth I trained as a biologist and I have studied many of the beasts whose lives closely impinged upon the lives of the Norse. I was, for ten years, a volunteer observer for the Canadian meteorological service. In the waste of war I learned about cartography and came to value the knowledge locked in maps and charts. I am an amateur anthropologist who has lived with and written books about the peoples who really owned the north—the Inuit. As for the Norse, their proud and violent ghosts have haunted me since I was old enough to lift a book, or turn a page. Beyond that I possess a scepticism which is my bane, and my strength. I am constitutionally unable to accept apparent facts without an investigation of my own.

Whether these attributes have been enough to meet the need is something else. To me they seemed sufficient.

There is no point in pretending modesty about what I have attempted. I have made a reconstruction of the Norse voyages which follows no previous book (except the original saga sources) and which is at variance with most, but which I am convinced is closer to the truth than any previous attempt. In detail I believe I have resolved a number of outstanding problems, including the degree of Celtic participation in the westward thrust; the real scope of Erik the Red's explorations; the geographical concepts of the ancient Norse as these applied to the western regions; the conflict between the two main saga sources dealing with the western voyages; the identities of the several native peoples the Norse encountered; the detailed tracks followed by all the voyagers; the identity and location of the landfalls, havens and settlements; the major factors which prompted, shaped, and sometimes doomed the efforts of the westward venturers; and many lesser matters.

In making my claims I do not pretend that I am always first in the field, for I have been anticipated on a number of points, as I acknowledge in the text. Nor do I ignore the possibility that future writers may find it possible to consign some of my answers to limbo. But if I have been able to clear away some of the deadwood of outmoded concepts which has obscured the true story of the voyages, and so assist someone else to find better answers than mine, I shall be delighted.

This book does not work in quite the usual way. Because I have had to re-examine and analyze every available piece of information connected with the voyages and wring dry, one corner at a time, many obscure bits of evidence, some academic tedium in the text became inevitable. But I wished this book to be read for the sake of the story, and so I have tried to minimize the fault by relegating as much as possible of the supporting evidence to that section of the appendices titled "Analytical." Here it can be read or left alone, depending on whether or not the reader requires to see the proof of every plum in the pudding. Also, since I did not want to slow the narrative more than was absolutely necessary, I have collected much of the relevant background material dealing with such things as ancient climate, Norse ships and navigation into a series of essays which form the "Descriptive" section of the appendices. Although it may be unorthodox, I suggest that the reader would do well to browse through these descriptive essays before starting on the text.

My prologue is a rapid gallop through the history of European voyaging to the west from prehistoric times to the beginning of the Norse venturing. The balance of the book is divided into three sections which deal minutely and chronologically with events between about 960 and 1010 A.D. Most chapters open with the relevant section of the original saga accounts. In the Epilogue I show the unbroken continuity of westward voyaging from the cessation of Norse voyages to the beginning of modern times, and suggest that there was no considerable gap and that the Cabots and Columbus were following old trails.

Endnotes have been kept to a minimum and are almost exclusively devoted to illuminating the text. There is no bibliography because I have made sparse use of other authors' commentaries. When I have drawn upon someone else's work I have acknowledged the fact in the text.

A word of explanation regarding my use of excerpts from the sagas. There are a great many English translations of the several existing saga transcripts and these vary considerably in detail. Rather than adhere slavishly to any single version I have compiled a composite translation, and where conflict between the versions exists I have based my choice on specific linguistic research, the logic of the passage, and my knowledge of the conditioning circumstances. For those who are interested in reading an independent and eminently modern translation of the whole of the relevant sagas I suggest *The Norse Atlantic Saga* (Oxford University Press, 1964) by Gwyn Jones.

ACKNOWLEDGMENTS

I am extremely grateful to the following people for much help in a variety of ways: Mr. Percy Saltzman of the Canadian meteorological service; Professor Gwyn Jones of the University of Wales; Mr. Harold Horwood, St. John's, Newfoundland; Dr. William Taylor of the Human History Branch, National Museum of Canada; Dr. Elmer Harp of Dartmouth University; Mrs. Evelyn Stefansson and the staff of the Stefansson Collection, Dartmouth University; Jane Davison, Mary Macdonald and Esther S. Yntema.

F.M.
Burgeo, Newfoundland

PROLOGUE

The Forerunners

THE BEGINNINGS OF the story of man's conquest of the vast
sea barrier which separates Europe from North America is lost
in the fog-chilled darkness of the Western Ocean. In the nature
of things, we can never know when that restless, groping and
grasping unfurred mammal who is ourself first crossed the
Western Ocean from east to west. He left no mark of his passing
on the faceless waters of the North Atlantic, nor did he raise any
beacons on the farther shore which historians could recognize
as proof of his accomplishment. He is a shadow out of time, yet
he is not without substance. Centuries, and perhaps millennia,
after he had vanished, men who were his brothers of the Neolithic Age not only crossed the Western Ocean but spanned the
abyss of time itself to land upon the shores of medieval Europe.

They came from west to east. History preserves the records
of several such "discoveries" of Europe from America, and there
were doubtless more now lost to knowledge. These voyagers
were true Neolithic men. Some of them were Inuit who made
the crossing in skin boats called umiaks, surviving examples of
which can carry forty passengers on extended voyages. Some
seem to have been nomadic peoples who may have crossed in
immense bark canoes. Examples of these canoes, paddled by
twenty to thirty Beothuk men, were still being encountered

by European fishing ships far at sea off the eastern coasts of Newfoundland in the seventeenth and eighteenth centuries.

These strangers out of time and space had the assistance of the prevailing westerly winds and currents in the middle reaches of the North Atlantic; but those who were their peers in northern Europe in dim antiquity had an advantage to offset this. They possessed a line of island stepping-stones reaching out from the British Isles by way of the Shetlands, the Faeroes, Iceland, Greenland and Baffin Island. Nowhere along this route was there an open-water crossing of more than four hundred miles, and in the higher latitudes, currents and prevailing winds favoured rather than retarded westbound voyaging.

THE CELTS AND THE PICTS

The Shetlands and Orkneys, and perhaps the Faeroes too, were reached and settled by a sea-going race of such antiquity that they were dead and gone before the Golden Age came to the Mediterranean. Of the west-voyaging of these prehistoric people we know nothing, but we must credit them with at least as much competence upon the unquiet waters of the North Atlantic as was possessed by the Inuit and Indigenous peoples who voyaged eastward in our time. At any rate we know that the Celts and Picts, who supplanted the earlier island dwellers in the north, were seamen born and bred and had long been familiar with the cold Western Ocean when what we are pleased to refer to as the "historic period" on the northern seaboard of Europe began, about the year 330 B.C.

It was then that a Greek mathematician, astronomer and geographer named Pytheas set sail from the colony of Massilia (Marseilles) to put certain geographical theories about the northern regions to the test. Pytheas's ship sailed out past the Pillars of Hercules (Gibraltar) and worked northward until she came to a Scottish port. Here Pytheas encountered local sailors who told him of a land lying six days' distance to the northward in the wilderness of ocean. With their aid Pytheas went to seek that land, and when he came to it he called it Thule. We call it Iceland now, but the name by which the Pictish mariners of twenty-three centuries ago knew it is now forever lost.

Most of the maritime history of the Picts, and of their close neighbors, the Celts of Ireland, is lost. Only tantalizing fragments remain. We know, for instance, that as early as A.D. 232 the Desi, a Celtic people from southern Ireland, were making extensive seaborne raids on the coasts of Cornwall and Wales, while during the same period the Picts of Scotland were so efficient on the seas that they were successfully challenging Rome in British waters.

It is believed that they continued to visit Thule even during the severe climatic conditions which prevailed between the fourth century B.C. and the fourth century A.D.[1] They probably made no permanent lodgments in Iceland during these centuries, being content to use it as a summer hunting and fishing ground, for the Icelandic climate from Pytheas's time to about A.D. 400 would have discouraged attempts at settlement. Nevertheless, third-century Romano-British silver coins which have been unearthed at two localities in eastern Iceland suggest that there were visitors from the British Isles.

Even if the Picts and Celts had made only occasional voyages to Iceland, one or more of their vessels would eventually have strayed within sight of the Greenland coast, whose range of visibility from seaward averages about sixty miles, with a maximum of nearly a hundred miles.

Written evidence exists to substantiate the view that natives of the British Isles managed to sail more than halfway across the Western Ocean early in the Christian era, or even before it began.

In the literary mélange which he called "The Face of the Moon," Plutarch, who lived between A.D. 40 and 120, describes an "island"[2] called Ogygian lying five days' sail to the westward of the British Isles. Plutarch goes on to add that the natives of Britain reported knowing of three other "islands," equidistant from Ogygian and from each other, lying in the direction of the setting sun. Then, in the dialogue entitled "The Silence of Oracles," he speaks more specifically of one of these western islands and this time gives his source—a Greek named Demetrius who was a government employee of the Romans in Britain during the first century A.D.

Reporting on conversations between himself and natives of the British Isles, Demetrius told Plutarch of the existence of a large "island" which lay at a considerable distance westward from Britain and which bore a native name that sounded, in Demetrius' ear, like Cronus. Demetrius was naturally familiar with the Mediterranean Cronus myth, and we can imagine his surprise and curiosity at this apparent evidence that the natives on the Atlantic seaboard shared the Cronian legend, and even believed they knew the location of the land where the Titan, Cronus, was imprisoned.

There are good grounds for the belief[3] that the land whose name sounded to Demetrius like Cronus was identical with Greenland. It is a fact, at any rate, that for some centuries after the time of Pliny the Elder, geographers applied the name Cronian Sea to the waters lying beyond Iceland and bounded on the west by Greenland.

During the fifth and sixth centuries A.D., coincidental with the beginning of a long-term improvement in North Atlantic weather conditions, the navigation of the Britons, Picts and Celts began to loom large in written history for the first time. According to a recently published study of shipping and commerce in

Northern Europe, the ships of these peoples came to dominate the waters of the Channel, the North and Irish seas, and even more northerly waters, as far as the coasts of Norway. Furthermore, they were apparently making more or less routine voyages to Iceland, where they procured eiderdown feathers, sea-mammal products and other exotica, some of which eventually reached Mediterranean markets.[4]

The vessels they used were proper ships, ranging in type from the carvel-built wooden vessels favoured by the Picts and Britons to the hide-covered curraghs of the Celts.[5] An example of a fourth-century Romano-British ship recovered from the bed of the Thames gives us some idea of what the wooden vessels of those times were like. She was 60 feet long, had a beam of 16 feet, and her mast was 10 inches in diameter at the butt. Her lines were those of a sea-going ship, and she was probably not much inferior to schooners of equal size which were sailing regularly between Newfoundland and Europe well into the twentieth century.

Nor were the Celtic curraghs inferior to the wooden vessels of the Picts and Britons. The fact that they were covered with ox hides, instead of being planked with wood, did not detract from their seaworthiness. Fifth- and sixth-century curraghs were big, sturdy, sea-kindly ships which carried crews of up to twenty men and were able to freight considerable cargoes between Ireland and the coast of Spain. As was the case with the vessels of the Picts and Britons, the curraghs were propelled by squaresails, with auxiliary oar power for calms or for navigation in narrow waters.

The use of squaresails does not imply that these vessels were unhandy and could only run before the wind. Such acknowledged experts as Alan Villiers (not to mention innumerable masters of square-rigged ships) have demonstrated that square-rig is nearly as efficient as fore-and-aft rig, and will enable a well-designed ship to go to windward quite successfully.

The sixth and seventh centuries witnessed the full flowering of Celtic and Pictish maritime activity, with regular trading voyages being made all the way from mid-Norway to Nantes in France, and with occasional voyages to points both farther north and farther south.

It was during this period that the accounts of the voyages of the Celtic priest, St. Brendan, were composed. The Brendan story suffers from the imagination of the Irish, and it has been dramatically overcoloured. Nevertheless it unquestionably preserves the memory of at least some actual voyages to real places. It is particularly explicit in its description of northern landfalls, and it demonstrates a working knowledge of navigation to Iceland, Greenland, and perhaps even to Jan Mayen Island.

During this period the Picts were trading regularly to Norway and into the Baltic. They were also firmly established on the Orkneys, Shetlands and Faeroes. In the last quarter of the sixth century, Picts of the Orkneys embraced Christianity. They and the Celts may have had semipermanent hunting and fishing settlements in Iceland by this time, for the climate there was steadily growing more amiable, coincidental with a general improvement in the weather of the whole North Atlantic region. But permanent settlement by Picts or Celts was probably still at some distance in the future since Iceland, despite the phenomenal fishing and sea-hunting which it offered, was a long way off and there was as yet no shortage of land at home in either Ireland or Scotland. Nor had these countries as yet been subjected to population pressures great enough to set an emigration wave in motion.

Up until this time the Scandinavian peoples apparently did not possess either the knowledge or the ships with which to engage in deep-sea voyaging. They were, in fact, late-comers to the open sea. Although there have been a number of archeological finds of Scandinavian boats which were built earlier than the seventh century, there are no truly ocean-going ships among them, and there is nothing to show that the Norse were capable of making deep-sea voyages before the latter part of the seventh century. Prior to this date their maritime activities seem to have been limited to coasting and fishing voyages, or to short trading trips in the relatively narrow and protected waters of the Baltic. Their trade was largely land-directed toward the Germanic regions to the south, or toward the Russian regions to the east. They had little need of deep-sea seamanship and ships, and had developed neither.

But during the later part of the seventh century a rising internal turmoil was beginning to trouble the Scandinavian countries. The Northmen were developing an appetite for luxury goods and were liberating themselves from a life of hard simplicity. Celtic and Pictish trading ships from Britain not only helped to feed and to increase this appetite but, by their mere existence, must have suggested to the Norse a means by which they could burst out of their constrained northern regions and so be able to seize what they wanted from the rich aliens to the south. The sea was a path many men could travel, and for many different reasons.

There seems to be little doubt that the Northmen began their deep-sea venturing in ships patterned after the hull models of Pictish and Celtic vessels, and that they made their first major open-water voyages along the routes to Scotland, Ireland and the Outer Islands[6]—routes which had been pioneered by the elder seamen of the British Isles.

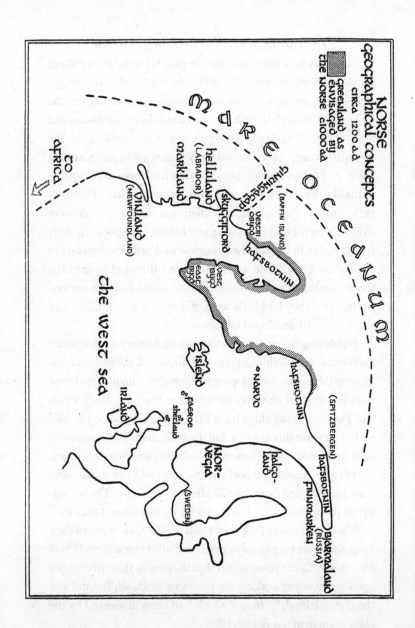

NORSE
GEOGRAPHICAL CONCEPTS
CIRCA 1200 A.D.

▨ GREENLAND AS
ENVISAGED BY
THE NORSE C1000 A.D.

MARE OCEANUM

TO AFRICA

the WEST SEA

GRŒNLAND

HELLULAND
(LABRADOR)

MARKLAND

SKRÆLINGELAND

 OESTRI OBYGD

(BAFFIN ISLAND)

HAFSBOTNIN

VESTRI BYGD

EASTRI BYGD

VINLAND
(NEWFOUNDLAND)

ÍSLAND

HAFSBOTNIN

NARVO

(SPITZBERGEN)

HAFSBOTNIN

ºFAEROE
ºSHETLAND

IRLAND

NOR-
VEGIA

(SWEDEN)

HALOGO-
LAND

FINNMARKEN

BJARMALAND
(RUSSIA)

The Norse were quick students. Furthermore they had independently developed a type of ship construction, based on the clinker-built wherries and skiffs they had used for fishing and coasting since late Neolithic times, which lent itself admirably to the building of ocean-going ships.

The times were also on the side of the Norse. Early in the eighth century socio-economic changes in Europe brought about a rapid decline in the seafaring activities of Ireland and Scotland. Internal troubles hastened the decay so that by the end of this century the mercantile fleets of the Celts and Picts had all but vanished from the seas. At the same time as this decline and collapse, the north was boiling up with an immensely vital ferment which was to send the Viking hordes spilling out over most of Europe, eastward into the far reaches of Russia, southward to the Caspian and Mediterranean seas and, eventually, westward to America.

The population of ninth-century Norway, Sweden and Denmark was composed of two disparate elements: the aboriginal inhabitants, who were an amalgam of peoples of the long-headed Neolithic type, overwashed by many diverse waves of forgotten immigrants; and a "master" race, originally known as the Aesir or Eastmen, who conquered the entire Scandinavian region at about the time of Christ. The Aesir (whose ruthless qualities have been so much admired in modern Germany) resisted the effects of racial assimilation with such success that in the ninth century their recognizable descendants still remained the aristocracy of Scandinavia. It was these men who, in the main, comprised the true Vikings and who organized and led the seaborne raiders who terrorized the littoral peoples of Europe for three centuries.

However, even before the Viking terror began, there were already sailings south from Scandinavia as small but stout clinker-built trading vessels, modeled on Celtic ships and manned by the elder Norse, began reviving the use of those sea routes which were being abandoned by the Picts and Celts. Late in the seventh century small groups of these plebeian Norsemen had begun to arrive in the Outer Islands—in particular the Faeroes and the Shetlands—where they intermingled with Pictish inhabitants and with Irish Celts who had settled there as early as A.D. 600. During the next century this trickle developed into a steady flow which lapped at the shores of northern Ireland and Scotland, since not only were the narrow agricultural lands of Norway becoming badly overcrowded, but the depredations and aggressions of the Vikings upon each other's homelands and peoples were becoming unendurable to many ordinary folk.

These yeomen Norse were true immigrants. Besides engaging in farming they took part in and probably greatly improved upon the local fisheries in their adopted lands, since fishing was a trade at which they were unexcelled. Many of them even gave up their pagan beliefs and accepted Christianity.

The native people of the Outer Islands, the Hebrides and northern Ireland, were passionate Christians who followed a Celtic variant of the Roman faith and often lived in semi-religious communities. These colonies of papas, as the Norse called them, were not comprised solely of monastic ascetics, although this is the way they have usually been represented. Because there was as yet no rule to bar men of the cloth from leading normal sexual lives, most of the clerics were married men with families. Ascetics did exist, of course, and some of these individuals chose to live the life of starving hermits on barren islets and bare rocks where they could mortify the flesh in high medieval style; but those islands which were capable of providing a decent livelihood held much more rational Christian communities, where the cry of the newborn lamb mingled with the cry of the newborn acolyte.

While the early Norse immigrants seem to have had no particular dislike of the papa societies, and to have intermingled with them on good terms, the Vikings had nothing but contempt for Christians; and Viking contempt was usually fatal to those who earned it.

THE VIKING SCOURGE

Following in the sea paths traced by the emigrant Norse, the Vikings began raiding the outlying islands early in the eighth century. The islands were easy targets, and relatively rewarding ones. The Christians tended to lavish much of their resources on church furniture of gold and silver, and Celtic, Pictish and Norwegian settlers alike possessed valuable herds of sheep and cattle. From about 750 onwards, the Outer Islands were seldom free of Viking marauders. The scope of these raids was rapidly extended until by the turn of the century coastal Ireland, the Hebrides, northern Scotland, the Orkneys, Shetlands and Faeroes had all become singularly unhealthy havens for those who cherished the quiet life and worshipped Christ.

Many of the residents of the exposed mainland coasts of Ireland and Scotland fled for safety to the interior of their countries, although even there they were by no means secure. But the Christian Norse-Celtic-Pictish populations of the islands had no interior regions into which they could retreat. We are told that the islands were abandoned to the Vikings, who established pirate strongholds on them until new waves of pagan Norse from western Norway eventually moved in and occupied the abandoned farmsteads.

The question of what happened to the displaced islanders has seldom been posed, let alone answered. One thing is certain—they would hardly have sought refuge on mainland Scotland or Ireland, which by this time had become the main magnets for Viking attention in the west, if they had been able to find a safer sanctuary somewhere else.

And a safer refuge did exist. It lay only four or five days' sail westward from the Shetlands and Orkneys, and only two days' sail from the Faeroes.

It is hardly open to dispute that the peoples of the Outer Islands must have known for centuries of Iceland's existence, and that they knew how to reach it and had the means to do so. The climate of this era was so genial that Iceland would have offered excellent conditions for stock farming as well as for fishing and sea-hunting. It was still effectively out of reach of the Vikings, whose longships (unlike the Norse trading vessels) were notoriously unseaworthy. Furthermore, the Norse of this period did not even know of Iceland's existence.

Iceland would have been a veritable paradise for a maritime people seeking a safe refuge where they could lead quiet, pastoral lives and devote as much time as they liked to religious activities without fear of interruption or attack. And there is sufficient evidence (which is examined in the first part of Appendix I and in Appendix J) for us to conclude that some if not most of the fleeing islanders did make their way to Iceland and established permanent settlements there during the early decades of the eighth century.

By the beginning of the ninth century the Viking terror lay over most of western Europe, and was still swiftly spreading. There were few countries bordering on the North Atlantic which were not being savaged by the Norse hordes. Most of Ireland was in Viking hands, as were the northern counties of Scotland, together with the Outer Islands.

Iceland was still untouched, but its days were numbered. The secret of its existence as a Celtic sanctuary could not have been kept indefinitely from the Vikings, who by this time had penetrated deeply into the fabric of the shattered Celtic society in Ireland, and the Pictish-Scottish societies of northern Scotland. Celtic and Pictish slaves, renegades or concubines serving the new master race must frequently have let the secret slip. In all likelihood the Vikings knew about Iceland for some decades before they did anything about it. As long as there were more rewarding targets to be found along the continental coasts of Europe, the Norse raiders would not have been much tempted by the remote fishing and farming settlements in the far western island. Furthermore, it was not until early in the ninth century that the Vikings, after suffering some appalling losses due to the unseaworthiness of the longships, began to appreciate the advantages of building vessels after the models of the plebeian merchant ships in which Norse traders had been successfully sailing the open ocean routes for many generations.[7]

THE NORSE REACH ICELAND

The surviving Scandinavian accounts of the first Norse voyages to Iceland, which took place in the middle of the ninth century, imply that the Norse discovered the island entirely by accident of wind and weather. But this contention is highly suspect in view of the fact that all of the early Norse visitors to Iceland were professional Vikings, which is to say they were pirates and sea raiders.

One version gives the credit for the initial visit to Naddod the Viking, who was supposedly storm-driven into the Western Ocean until he encountered Iceland. According to another version, first place belongs to Floki Vilgerdarsson, "a great Viking" who apparently sailed from Shetland, but who (so we are told) *knew* where he was going. Ingolf and his foster-brother Hjorleif, both pirates, are also listed as having been early arrivals. Before settling in Iceland, Hjorleif "went harrying in Iceland . . . he harried far and wide, winning great wealth there and taking ten slaves captive. . . ."

Although the Norse sources do not admit that Iceland was first visited by Vikings who were engaged in purposeful voyages of reconnaissance, this is probably the correct explanation of how and why they first appeared off Iceland's coasts. Certainly the subsequent actions of these first Norse visitors are hardly what we would expect from mariners who had been accidentally blown off course and who would have presumably been anxious to regain their intended ports. Naddod, for instance, remained in Iceland until after the first autumnal snowfall. Gardar Svavar, a Swedish Viking (and another of those who is credited with the first "discovery"), is supposed to have been blown there while making a voyage to the Hebrides to claim his wife's inheritance. If this was true, he could have been in no hurry to collect it, for he leisurely coasted the southern part of Iceland, wintered in the west, and completed a circumnavigation of the island the next summer.

Floki Vilgerdarsson took his departure from the Faeroes, and we are told that he knew where he was going. He and his companions spent two winters in Iceland, although there is nowhere a mention that this was intended as a settlement voyage. Floki and his companions returned to Norway, and it was not until some years later (when King Harold Fairhair was making it difficult for independentminded Vikings to remain in that country) that Floki or any either Norsemen came out to Iceland as settlers.

We will probably be close to the mark if we envisage increasing numbers of Vikings in a new kind of vessel (one which looked far more like a merchant ship than a longship) descending on the Icelandic coasts and "harrying far and wide" until they had filled their holds with stolen cattle, slaves, and whatever else they could seize from the luckless Christian settlers whose next to last sanctuary in the west this was.

In accordance with well-established Viking precedent when overwintering in the lands of their victims, the raiders sought out remote and lonely havens which were easily defensible, where they could sit out the winter months free from the dangers of reprisal attacks. This is why men like Gardar and Ingolf deliberately eschewed the many welcoming havens Iceland offered, and which they undoubtedly saw, in favour of wintering at some of the worst places on the coasts. Karli, who accompanied Ingolf, makes the point when he grumbles, "to an evil end did we pass through goodly countrysides, that we should take up our [winter] abode on the outlying cape."

The first Vikings probably did not care to risk wintering in the "goodly countrysides" because these were still occupied by Westmen,[8] who outnumbered the raiders and who would have taken a sharp revenge on any Viking they could catch. Hit-and-run raids would have been the Viking order of the day, at least until the number of raiders grew large enough so that the inhabitants could be swept away by main force.

The fact that several of the first Norse arrivals overwintered suggests another common Viking practice. When a man was outlawed from Scandinavia, with everyone's hand against him, or when he fled from it to avoid blood vengeance, it was often the custom for him to spend his time of exile buccaneering.[9] Individual exiles who owned their own ships sometimes joined forces with other Vikings in order to take part in raids on rich but well-defended territories in mainland Europe; but often they operated independently on less well protected if less rewarding coasts, such as Iceland in the 860's would have had to offer.

There is no reason to suppose that the pattern of events in Iceland was any different from that elsewhere in the Norse-dominated area. First came isolated raids which increased in intensity as word of a new source of loot spread. Then, when the ability of the inhabitants to offer any real resistance had been destroyed, came occupation. Most histories of Iceland state that although the island was reputedly discovered by the Norse about 860, no settlement was begun until 874. This hiatus becomes explicable when we interpret it as being the raiding period during which the local population was decimated or driven out.

NORSE SETTLEMENT BEGINS

The first Norse settlers seem to have been that same Ingolf and his foster-brother Hjorleif who had made a previous voyage to the island sometime in the 860's. By about 874 these two had managed, after committing a series of killings, to make even Norway too hot to hold them, and they were forced to look for homesteads somewhere else. Since the Outer Islands, north Scotland and Ireland were already crowded with Norse pirates and freebooters, they decided to try their luck in Iceland. Most of the other early Norse settlers were also men who, for one reason or another (usually murder), were unable to remain in Norway, or even in the Outer Islands. These seem to have been such super-Vikings that even their peers could not tolerate them. Numbers of them followed hard on Hjorleif's and Ingolf's heels.

These outlaw's outlaws were the vanguard of a great wave of Viking settlers which began to break over Iceland around 880 as a result of the attempts of one of their own number to unify all Norway under his personal rule. This man, King Harold

Fairhair, had no scruples about using Viking methods on his own kind. When the local chiefs and jarls proved reluctant to accept his suzerainty, it was his summary practice to put them and theirs to the sword.

Since the Viking aristocrats were dedicated to freedom (by which they probably meant much the same thing most of us mean when we use the word today; that is, license to do what we please without interference), they reacted fiercely to the threat of any restrictions being placed upon their enterprising natures. The struggle which ensued was brought to an end when the Viking fleet was decisively defeated by Harold at the battle of Hafrsfiord in 885. After that there was nothing left for freedom-loving Norsemen but to flee the country and find new homes elsewhere. Iceland seemed just the place to go, and go they did in such numbers that within fifty years they had occupied all the land worth having.

THE WESTMEN FLEE AGAIN

The Celts and Picts in Iceland would have realized that the appearance of the first Norse ship heralded the inevitable approach of an armada of Viking raiders who would be followed by Viking land-seekers. Those Westmen with well-developed instincts for survival would have fled the island. But where could they have gone?

The Faeroes, Shetlands, Orkneys and Hebrides were ruled out because these were completely dominated, and mostly occupied, by Vikings. Most of northern Scotland was in Norse hands, or subject to constant raids. Almost all of coastal Ireland was under Norse control, and the raiders were making incursions deep into the central parts of that country. The Viking scourge was now at its worst, and there was precious little safety from it even in England or in France. But, there was still the west. There was, in particular, that land which we now call Greenland and whose existence was known to the Irish as early as the sixth century. It would have been even better known to the Westmen settlers of Iceland in the ninth, since it is unthinkable that they could have lived in Iceland for any length of time without gaining some familiarity with the neighboring land.

Possibly the earliest Westmen to make the crossing of the by then ice-free Denmark Strait had been anchorites seeking ultimate seclusion. Archeologists have found a number of small stone cells along the southeast Greenland coast which are strongly reminiscent of anchorite cells in the Orkney Islands. Some of these are sited in the most inhospitable surroundings imaginable—just the sort of places which the masochistic ascetics preferred.

At the time of the Norse invasion the Icelandic Westmen may no longer have possessed enough ocean-going ships to have enabled them to transport their people, goods and cattle on the long ocean passage to the nearest eastern lands. They would have had little need for such large craft, particularly if, as was evidently the case, they were being kept in contact with their onetime homelands by merchant ships sailing from south Irish or from British ports. However, they would have had numbers of small craft of the curragh pattern which they used for fishing and sea-hunting. These were adequate for the 260-nautical-mile crossing of the narrowest part of the Denmark Strait to Greenland.

Fleeing Westmen would hardly have chosen to resettle themselves on the barren and forbidding east Greenland coast. It offered little or no pastoral land and, besides, it was far too close to Iceland for safety. With or without advance knowledge to guide them, they would have coasted south, rounded Cape Farewell (or passed through one of the sounds separating it from the mainland) and turned north searching for an area suitable to their pastoral needs and one which also offered a reasonable degree of security against discovery by the Vikings. They would have found ample lands in southwestern Greenland at the bottom of the deep Julianehaab fiords. For reasons which are set out in the second part of Appendix I and in Chapters 1 and 2, it seems clear that this is indeed where many of the fugitive Westmen went.

ICELAND BECOMES NORSE

The flood of Viking immigration into Iceland which began soon after the year 870 slackened only slightly after King Harold Fairhair's death, for he was succeeded by another ambitious warlord who was determined to perpetuate the concept that Norway should be a unified and single kingdom. By A.D. 900, barely thirty years after the arrival of Ingolf and Hjorleif, Iceland had a population of nearly twenty thousand people; and by 930 this had apparently increased to nearly forty thousand.

In addition to the main wave of Scandinavian Vikings there had also been a great influx of Vikings from Ireland, Scotland and even England. After being held in subjection to the Norse for generations, the native peoples of those lands were now rising against their overlords, and many Viking settlers who had long ago seized land in the British Isles (and were themselves often of mixed blood as the result of their ancestors' free intercourse with native women) were finding it hard to hang on either to lands or lives. Many of them set sail for Iceland, preferring safety and lean times there to fat times and flames at night in the lands which would not stay conquered.

In the entourage of these British Vikings were numbers of native slaves as well as upper-class Celts and Picts, and even some Britons, who for one reason or another (usually expediency) had thrown in their lots with the Northmen, and who could expect little mercy from their compatriots if they remained at home. By 950 as much as 20 per cent of Icelandic blood lines may have been non-Scandinavian. It is certain that, far from being the gigantic, flaxen-haired, blue-eyed people of heroic legend, the Icelanders tended to be small in stature, at least by modern standards; and many of them were dark-haired people who were more Celtic than Nordic in appearance.

Thus there were many diverse elements in the Icelandic population to dilute the Viking strain, a blessing for which modern Icelanders have not, perhaps, given thanks enough.[10]

ICELANDIC SOCIETY

Icelandic society was divided into three classes. There were the aristocrats—primarily composed of Viking champions—who held most of the land. Below them was a larger group of less wealthy and less powerful yeomen who held part of a chieftain's lands in fief, or else owned small properties nearby and lived under his protection. Finally there was a large class of slaves, thralls and nominal freedmen, some of whom had been taken captive on raids as far afield as the Mediterranean.

In 930, when the first Althing, or national assembly, was convened on the gloomy plains of Thingvellir in southwestern Iceland, there were about four hundred chieftains who had parceled all habitable Iceland out among themselves. They were a supremely touchy, arrogant and independent lot who were united in only one thing—their fierce determination to resist any real diminution of their individual freedoms. It was this set determination which gave birth to what has often been called, if somewhat loosely, the first western democratic republic.

Whether it was democratic or not (or even a republic) depends on the interpretation of the words. The chieftains foregathered every spring on the plains of Thingvellir and here they "legislated" the laws under which the island lived. But these laws were unwritten, frequently unenforced, and often unenforceable, since there was no law-enforcement agency of any kind. Disputes were legion, and if a chieftain was not actually engaged in bloody skirmishings with his neighbors, he was almost certain to be taking judicial action against someone. These disputes were theoretically settled at the Quarter Courts, or local Things. However, an award of damages, of compensation against an aggressor, or even a judgment of outlawry against a malefactor had to be enforced by the person who had made the claim or lodged the charge.

In many cases justice was evaded by the use of legal trickery or massive bribes, or, if that failed, the supporters of the accused could draw their weapons and either drive the accusers into the hills or so cow the assembly that proceedings would be discreetly dropped. There was little security of life, limb or property except that which could be provided and defended by force of arms. Blood feuds perpetually swept the island like brush fires. The concept of individual honour had become so highly refined that a derogatory remark could lead to the destruction of the offender and his entire household by fire.

When one searches the Landnamabok, a contemporary Icelandic history which lists almost every man and woman of importance who lived in Iceland during the first decades of its occupation by the Norse, it is difficult to find references to more than a handful of men who died natural deaths. The majority seem to have died violently at the hands of their fellows. The accounts of murders, ambushes, burnings, human sacrifices and general mayhem are on such a scale that it is a little difficult to understand how the Icelandic race survived at all. Fortunately it was fecund.

A single quotation from the Landnamabok will give the flavour of the times.[11]

Thorodda married Torfi, the son of Valbrand, the son of Valthjof, the son of Orlyg . . . Torfi slew the men of Kropp twelve of them together. He also especially promoted the slaughter of the Holes-men, and he was at Hellisfitar, with Illugi the Black and Sturli the Godi [priest] when eighteen cave dwellers were slain there. They also burned, in his own house, Audun the son of Smidkel at Thorvardsted.

These cave dwellers, by the way, may have included remnants of the Westman population who had sought refuge in the lava caves of the interior instead of fleeing the country.

The general contempt for life if not for law was reinforced by a steady influx of outlaws from Scandinavia, where the rudiments of order were being forcibly imposed by a series of short-lived kings. By 900 it had become the custom for a man outlawed from the mainland to flee to Iceland. Manslaughter, a euphemism for murder, was then about as common as fist-fighting is today. Nor was it considered particularly reprehensible—except perhaps by the victim's kin. The records of the times make it clear that a man was not thought much of unless his battle-axe, heavy sword, or two-handed javelin had let out the life of at least one human being. The victims did not need to be foreign enemies; in fact the killing of a doughty neighbor could bring more renown than the killing of an alien warrior in a distant land.

The lives of men or of prized livestock could be bought and paid for with almost equal facility. Every free man had his value depending on his rank and connections. If his killer was rich, and agreeable, compensation could be arranged in cash.

But if compensation went unpaid or if the judgment of the peer court went against the murderer, a sentence of outlawry was usually mandatory.

A man who had been outlawed had to remove himself from the community, or from the country, depending on whether the sentence was one of local or national exile; otherwise anyone could split his skull without fear of having to pay compensation. However, if the outlaw could muster sufficient strength he could and often did stay home, surrounded by armed retainers, and ignore the sentence. Outlawry was not a punishment as we understand the term; it was primarily intended as a means of giving tempers time to cool, in the usually fruitless hope that a blood feud would be prevented.

This was Iceland during the final decades of the tenth century. This was the springboard; these were the people; and the west lay waiting.

1

THE WESTWARD THRUST

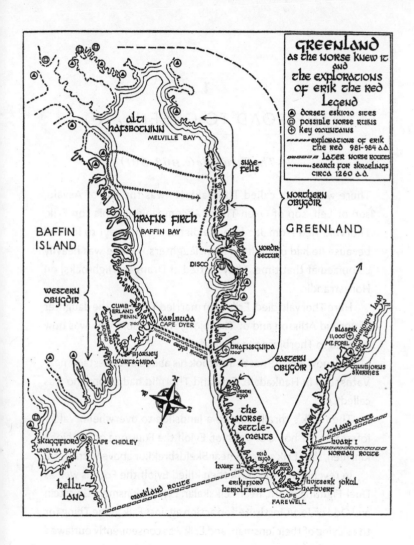

GREENLAND
AS THE NORSE KNEW IT
and
THE EXPLORATIONS
OF ERIK THE RED
Legend
▲ DORSET ESKIMO SITES
◙ POSSIBLE NORSE RUINS
⊕ KEY MOUNTAINS
------- EXPLORATIONS OF ERIK
THE RED 981-984 A.D.
□□□□□□ LATER NORSE ROUTES
········· SEARCH FOR SKROELINGS
CIRCA 1260 A.D.

ALTI
HAFSBOTNINN
MELVILLE BAY

SNAE-
FELLS

NORTHERN
OBYGÕIR

GREENLAND

BAFFIN
ISLAND

HRAFNS FIRTH
BAFFIN BAY

NORÕR-
SETTUR

DISCO I.

WESTERN
OBYGÕIR

CUMB-
ERLAND
PENIN.
7100
KARLBUÕA
CAPE DYER

VESTRI BYGÕ ROUTE

BLÁSERK
11,000
MT. FOREL

ÕÕ ÓJÖRÚLFS LAND

BJORNEY
HVARFSGNIPA

HRAFNSGNIPA
1300

EASTERN
OBYGÕIR

GUNNBJORNS
SKERRIES

VESTRI
BYGÕ

THE
NORSE
SETTLE-
MENTS

ICELAND ROUTE

HVARF I
NORWAY ROUTE

SKUGGIFIORD
UNGAVA BAY
CAPE CHIDLEY

MID
BYGÕ

ØSTRI
BYGÕ

HVARF II
MARKLAND ROUTE

ERIKSFIORÕ
HERJOLFSNESS
CAPE
FAREWELL

HVITSERK JOKUL
HAFHVARF

HELLU-
LAND

25

1

THE ROAD TO GREENLAND

The Saga Tale (c. 963–981)

There was a man called Thorvald. He was the son of Asvald, son of Leif, son of Oxen-Thori. Accompanied by his son Erik, Thorvald fled from Jaederen [a district in Norway] to Iceland because he had committed manslaughters. Iceland was heavily colonized at that time. They settled at Drangar [Highrocks] on Hornstrandir.

Here Thorvald died. Erik then married Thorhild, the daughter of Jorund Atlisson and of Thorbjorg Ship-Bosom who was now married to Thorbjorn the Haukadaler.

Erik now left the north and took his abode at Eriksstadir near Vatnshorn in Haukadale. Erik and Thorhild had a son who was called Leif.

Then Erik's thralls caused a landslide to overwhelm Valthiofsstadir, the home of Valthiof. Eyjolf the Foul, one of Valthiof's kinsmen, slew Erik's thralls near Skeidsbrekkur above Vatnshorn.

In revenge for this, Erik then killed Eyjolf the Foul as well as Duel-Fighting Hrafn, near Leikskalar. Eyjolf's kinsmen, Geirstein and Odd of Jorvi, instituted an action against Erik at the Thing for the slaying of their kinsman, and Erik was consequently outlawed from Haukadale.

Erik then took possession of Brokney and Oxney [islands] but dwelt at Tradir on Sudrey the first winter [after being banished].

At this time [when he left Haukadale] he lent Thorgest [of Breidabolstad] his dais-posts.

After [wintering at Tradir] Erik went to Oxney and dwelt there [again calling his home] Eriksstadir. He demanded the return of his dais-posts but did not get them. He then went to Breidabolstad and carried away the dais-posts, and Thorgest gave chase. They came to blows a short distance from the farmhouse at Drangar and there two of Thorgest's sons, as well as certain other men, were killed.

From this time on each of them retained a large body of armed men with him at his home. Styr Thorgrimsson, and Eyjolf from Sviney, together with the sons of Thorbrand of Alptafirth and Thorbjorn Vifilsson, took Erik's side. The Thorgesters were backed by the sons of Thord Bellower; Thorgeir of Hitardal; Aslak of Langadal and his son Illugi.

Erik and his followers were outlawed at the Thorsness Thing.

A ship was made ready by [or for] Erik in Eriksvag; but Erik himself was concealed by Eyjolf at Dimunarvag while Thorgest and his supporters were searching for him amongst the islands.

[SOURCES: Erik the Red Saga, Karlsefni Saga and the Short Saga[12]]

ERIK THE RED AT DRANGAR

ONE FOREIGN OUTLAW who chose Iceland as his sanctuary was a Norwegian named Thorvald Asvaldsson, who made a hasty exit from the Jaederen district near modern Stavanger about the year 963, "on account," as the saga primly puts it, "of manslaughters." We know little about Thorvald except that the sagas accord him the kind of sonorous genealogy which was reserved for important members of the aristocracy. We do not know the details of his crime either, but since it resulted in national outlawry we can assume it was a satisfactorily bloody one, and no such minor peccadillo as a simple case of murder.

Thorvald seems to have brought along his daughter and a redheaded son of about fourteen years of age named Erik. Other members of the family, about whom nothing has survived in history, may have accompanied the trio, together with a few of the indispensable thralls or slaves.

Thorvald was a late-comer to Iceland. Well before the time of his arrival all the good land had been taken up, leaving little except the lava deserts of the interior and the bleak and forbidding stretches of rocky land along the northern shores. He was forced to settle at a place called Highrocks on the barren and desolate coast of the northwestern tip of the island.

We are told nothing of the life the Thorvalders lived under the cold shadow of Drangar glacier, but from what we know of conditions on the smaller holdings in Iceland during this period we can guess at what it must have been like. The farmhouse would have consisted of one rectangular room whose low, thick walls were made of layers of peat interspersed with layers of stones to give them weight and stability. There would have been a single low door at one end of the structure, and no windows at all. Light entered through a smokehole in the roof, or through skylights which were shuttered over in the wintertime. Big timber was scarce in Iceland even then, and roofs were built without large beams. Rows of posts supported an extraordinarily heavy sod thatch by means of a system of small cross-rafters. The overall appearance of such a house was somewhat similar to that of a primeval burial mound.

Two rows of posts down the centre of the room divided it into three narrow naves. The centre nave contained a long, open fireplace. The two outer naves were largely occupied by built-up earthen platforms. Benches and tables stood on these during the daytime. At night they were removed and the members of the household slept upon the platforms. Halfway along one platform stood the high seat of the master of the house, flanked by ornately carved dais-posts. Opposite, on the other platform, stood a less pretentious chair for the use of the guest of honour. Members of the family, friends, freedmen and slaves sat on benches to left and right of these central chairs, their distance from them being determined by their rank and importance.

A number of small outbuildings surrounded the farmhouse. These included a kitchen, pantry, bathhouse, occasionally a privy, and the byres and stables for the half-wild sheep and goats, scraggy little cattle, pigs and ponies.

The entire economy of the farm turned on meat and dairy products, since few grain crops could be grown in Iceland even during the best years of the warm epoch. Milk formed the staple food. It was fermented to make a sour curd called skyr which, together with butter and cheese, was stored away against the winter months when the starving cattle went dry.

No one lived by farming alone. Fishing was vital to survival and so was the hunt for seals, porpoises and small whales. Bread and even gruel were luxuries, and since most grain had to be imported, there was seldom the solace of beer.

Life on small holdings such as Highrocks was not much better than a bare existence. To such exiled aristocrats as Thorvald and his son Erik it must have seemed a far cry from the relatively luxurious and well-fed life enjoyed by the well-to-do Vikings in southern Scandinavia. When in due course Thorvald died, Erik wasted no time bettering his lot. He promoted a most advantageous marriage with a girl named Thorhild Jorunsdottir whose mother bore the imposing name of Thorbjorg Ship-Bosom. The girl's stepfather seems to have been a wealthy landowner in the fertile farming district of Haukadale in the western marches of the island.

After the marriage Erik abandoned the miserable Highrock holding in exchange for a farm in Haukadale—a farm which was almost certainly part of his wife's dowry. Here he prospered for a while. Then one day a neighboring farmer named Valthiof was buried alive with all his family under a landslide triggered by Erik's slaves. There must have been reason to suspect that the slaves had been acting under Erik's orders. At any rate Valthiof's relatives drew this conclusion, and one of them, Eyjolf the Foul, retaliated by murdering the slaves.

Erik made no attempt to take this killing to law, a fact which strengthens the suspicion that he was the instigator of Valthiof's death. Instead he took revenge by slaughtering both Eyjolf and his companion, a champion known as Duel-Fighting Hrafn. This exploit gained Erik a champion's reputation but it also got him into serious trouble. He was cited for manslaughter and an action was started against him at the local Thorsness Thing.

Erik had stirred up a real hornet's nest, and the array of enemies against him at the Thing was strong enough to secure a conviction and a sentence of local banishment from the Haukadale district. By the rules of the game his life was now forfeit to anyone who cared to try to take it, so long as he remained in Haukadale. Erik fled in haste, doubtless suspecting that he and his family stood a good chance of being "burned in," as the saying went, in one great conflagration of house and people. He departed so hurriedly that he did not even take his dais-posts with him, but left them behind in the care of a neighbor named Thorgest.[13]

Erik and his family fled first to Tradir, on westward-facing Breidafiord, where they spent the winter. In the spring they moved out into the fiord to the island of Oxney—a choice which presumably owed more to the tactical value of living on an isolated island than to the good qualities of the land. Once established at Oxney, Erik made a necessarily surreptitious journey back to Haukadale to reclaim his dais-posts. Thorgest refused to part with them, perhaps because he felt that Erik was in such bad odor locally that he could not enforce his claim. But Erik had no intention of going home empty-handed. The likelihood is that he pretended to depart from the district but actually hid with his followers in the birch forests until Thorgest and the bulk of his retainers departed on some journey or another. Erik then raided the farm and seized his posts.

Erik would have anticipated a pursuit and, in time-honoured Viking style, doubtless arranged an ambush and waited for the angry Thorgest to ride into it. Two of Thorgest's sons and several of his supporters were killed in the ensuing mêlée and Erik was able to proceed triumphantly homeward, his reputation much enhanced by the affair.

This new slaughter brought both the Breidafiord and Haukadale districts into the fray, and for the next year or two there must have been great skirmishings, both with weapons and words, between the opposing factions. The home farms of both principals became armed camps, while Erik and Thorgest each sought by bribery, cajolery and threats to gain the support of as many powerful men as possible.

Erik was able to muster a good deal of support—but Thorgest was able to rally even more. In the spring of 981 Thorgest's party was strong enough to force an action at the Thorsness Thing, and since Erik had not the strength either to break up the assembly or to defeat Thorgest in open battle, he could not prevent a verdict of manslaughter. This time it was more serious. He was outlawed from Iceland for three years.

What the verdict meant in fact was that Thorgest and his followers were strong enough to take summary vengeance on Erik anywhere in Iceland—if they could catch him. But Erik still had friends. He and his family hid with Eyjolf of Sviney on that worthy's island stronghold, while a ship, which Erik had probably purchased some time earlier against just this eventuality, was hurriedly made ready for sea. Haste was of the essence, since Thorgest and his men were already out among the islands of Breidafiord searching for Erik's hiding place. The Thing would have been held quite early in the spring, and we can assume that by midsummer Erik and those of his supporters who did not dare remain behind were ready to flee into exile. But exile where?

Erik had made his decision. Like his father before him, he intended to sail west.

ERIK'S PREDECESSORS
The Saga Tale (981)

When Erik was ready he said to them [his friends and supporters] that he intended to look for that land which Gunnbjorn Ulf Krakuson saw when he was driven westward across the sea and found Gunnbjorn's Islands.

[SOURCES: Erik the Red Saga, Karlsefni Saga and the Short Saga]

Although most authors appear to believe that Erik was the first Norseman to visit the mainland coast of Greenland, the probabilities are overwhelmingly in favour of there having been a good many previous voyages during the century or more between Gunnbjorn's accidental voyage and Erik's intentional one.

From references in the Landnamabok it would appear that Gunnbjorn discovered some offshore islands and saw the Greenland mainland behind them, not very long after Gardar is said to have discovered Iceland—perhaps as early as 877. There are many references to Gunnbjorn's Skerries (Islands) and Gunnbjorn's Land scattered through the Icelandic sources, and from the casual manner in which they are usually mentioned, they seem to have been well known. Their exact location is not certain now, but the modern consensus is that they lay in the vicinity of Angmagssalik, almost due west from Breidafiord.

It seems certain that Gunnbjorn's discoveries had served, from a very early date, as landfalls for Icelanders bound for Greenland to take advantage of the excellent hunting to be found there. By the end of the ninth century the steadily warming climate of the North Atlantic region had brought about a pronounced northward retreat of the populations of walrus and pelagic seals off Iceland's coasts; whereas the icy waters of the polar East Greenland Current had preserved the sea mammal hunting grounds on the east Greenland coast. An abundance of polar bears, large pelagic seals, walrus and other sea beasts would have been more than sufficient incentive to ensure that enterprising Icelanders would make regular voyages to that region across the narrow Denmark Strait.[14]

THE VOYAGE OF SNAEBJORN HOG

Gunnbjorn's Skerries are specifically mentioned in connection with two Greenland voyages of which Erik's was the later one. The first was made by a man named Snaebjorn Hog, circa 980. What follows is a free version of the story of this voyage, taken from the Landnamabok.

A man named Hallbjorn married Tongue-Odd's daughter Hallgerd. The young couple spent the first winter of their marriage at Tongue-Odd's house and there was little love lost between them.[15] Snaebjorn Hog, who was a first cousin of Tongue-Odd, was also there that winter.

In late May, which was moving time in Iceland, Hallbjorn began to get ready to move out of his father-in-law's house. When Tongue-Odd saw this he hurried off to the hot spring near Reykholt where his sheep pens stood. He did not want to be around when Hallbjorn left because he suspected that his daughter Hallgerd did not want to leave home and that there would be trouble. Odd had already spent much time trying to mend matters between the couple.

When Hallbjorn had saddled the horses he went to fetch Hallgerd from where she was sitting in her bower. When he called upon her to get up and come with him, she neither said anything nor did she move. Hallbjorn called her three times without result, then he sang a snatch of a pleading song, but this did not move her either. At last he twisted her long hair in his hand and tried to drag her out of her chair, but she still would not budge. Thereupon he drew his sword and cut off her head.

When he heard about this, Odd sent a messenger to Snaebjorn Hog asking him to ride in pursuit of Hallbjorn. Snaebjorn did so, accompanied by twelve men. They caught up with Hallbjorn near some small hillocks, and three of Snaebjorn's men and both of Hallbjorn's companions were killed. Then someone sliced off Hallbjorn's foot and eventually he too was killed.

In order to evade blood vengeance from Hallbjorn's kin Snaebjorn set off on a voyage in a ship of which he was half-owner. Rolf the Redsander owned the other half. They each took twelve shipmates. Snaebjorn's companions included his foster-father Thorodd and Thorodd's wife. Rolf's main companion was Styrbjorn, who after a dream sang this song:

> The bane I see
> Of we two fellows.
> Frightful are all things
> To seaward, to the northwest.
> Frost and cold
> And fearful wonders.
> Such things tell of
> Snaebjorn slaughtered.

They sailed away to find Gunnbjorn's Skerries and [after that] they reached land where Snaebjorn would not let them go ashore by night. But Styrbjorn left the ship and found valuables hidden in a grave mound. Snaebjorn hit him with an axe, and knocked them out of his hand.

They made a stone hut for themselves and they were soon snowed in. In the spring they dug themselves out.

One day while Snaebjorn was working on the ship and his foster-father Thorodd was in the hut, Styrbjorn and Rolf killed Thorodd. Then the two of them slew Snaebjorn.

They sailed away after that and reached Halgoland [in the north part of Norway], from whence they returned to Iceland, where Rolf and Styrbjorn were killed by Sveinung, who in turn was murdered by Thorbjorn.

As is the case with most of the snippets of history contained in the Landnamabok (most of which are primarily intended to illuminate what is essentially a massive genealogy of the early settlers of Iceland), mention of this voyage is incidental to an explanation of what happened to the people who were involved in it. Still, we must be grateful for what little we are told.

No reason is given why Snaebjorn should have chosen north-eastern Greenland as a place to go while he waited for things to cool off at home. But except for the purpose of hunting walrus, narwhals, polar bears, white foxes and seals, it is hard to think of any reason why the party should have sailed first to Gunn-bjorn's Land and then northward to a region which Styrbjorn's verse—the oldest and most reliable part of the tale, since it is a surviving snatch from the original oral tradition—tells us lay to the northwest of Iceland and was remarkable for frost and cold. They must have gone a fair distance north too. The climatic conditions they encountered suggest it, and so do the winds and currents which took them to northern Norway after their departure from Greenland.[16] It is not unlikely that they wintered in Scoresby Sound which as late as the nineteenth century was noted for an abundance of walrus and polar bears.

The finding of the grave mound may have taken place soon after they reached Greenland and need not have happened in the north. The grave may have been the relic of some forgotten shipwreck; but on the other hand it may have been the burial place of some earlier voyager from Iceland, either Norse or Westman.

It is inconceivable that Erik would not have heard all the details of such a gloriously bloody affair within a very short time after Rolf's return to Iceland; but it is unlikely that the news added anything to his knowledge, or had any bearing on his plans. He knew about Gunnbjorn's Land and it is clear that a voyage to that locality was no novelty for Icelanders of his time.

Early voyages to northeastern Greenland by Icelandic hunters would have been one source of information for Erik to draw upon, but there could have been another and more valuable one. By 980 Iceland was full of Irish and Scots, both slaves and freemen, together with a good many Norse immigrants from the British Isles who had Celtic or Pictish blood in their veins. These people must have had much to tell, no matter how vague their information may have been, of the lands to the west which had been visited by Celtic mariners and which were variously known to the Icelanders as Albania, Hvitramannaland, or Irland Mikkla.

There is also a strong likelihood that Erik had specific knowledge of, and interest in, one particular Celtic discovery lying to the westward of Iceland; and he may have had a decisive personal reason for setting out in search of it when he went into exile.

This was Hvitramannaland (White Man's Land) or Irland Mikkla (Greater Ireland) as it was often called.

ARI MARSSON FINDS GREATER IRELAND

Ult the Squinter, son of Hogni the White, settled the whole of Reykness between Godfiord and Goatfell. His wife was Borg, the daughter of Eyvind Esstman and the sister of Steinholf the Lowly. Their son was Mar of [Reyk] Knolls, whose wife was Thorkatla,[17] the daughter of Hergils Hnappraz.

Their son was Ari, who was blown over the ocean by heavy gales to Whiteman Land [Hvitramannaland], which some call Greater Ireland [Irland Mikkla] and lies off westward in the ocean adjacent to Vinland the Good; it is reported that one can sail thither from Ireland in six days. Ari could not get back from this country and there he was baptized.

The first account of this was told by Rafn Hlymerksfari [Rafn the Limerick-farer] who had spent a long time there [in Limerick?].

Thorkel Gellirsson said that Icelanders who had heard Earl Thorfinn of Orkney tell the tale, avowed that Ari had been recognized in Whiteman Land and that he was not able to get away but was held in much regard there.

[SOURCE: Landnamabok]

Although no dates exist for Ari Marsson, it is possible to obtain an approximation of them from the relevant genealogical information found in the Landnamabok and in the various versions of the Erik the Red Saga. A genealogical table drawn from these sources reveals that Ari Marsson and Erik the Red were not only contemporaries, although Ari was some years older than Erik, but were related by marriage through Erik's wife, who was Ari's first cousin.

Both men fathered three sons. One of Ari's sons, Thorgils,

was a prosperous chieftain in the western districts of Iceland at the time of the Norwegian Thangbrand's missionary visit to Iceland at about 997. Thangbrand's friend and champion during this visit was Gudleif, another of Ari's sons, who had previously spent some years on the continent as a soldier of fortune. It is reasonable to conclude that both brothers were born between 960 and 970. This would suggest a date for Ari's birth of around 940, and such a date conforms with the genealogy of his wife, Thorkatla.

There is no certainty as to the date when Ari was blown off to Greater Ireland; but since it must have been after the birth of his three sons it could hardly have occurred much before 965. On the other hand, since Greater Ireland was evidently a locality in Greenland originally inhabited by Westmen,[18] but which had been abandoned by them before Erik made his voyage in 981, Ari, who spent some time in Greater Ireland, could not have arrived there much later than 975.

Assuming that he was westbound for Iceland at the conclusion of a trading voyage to Europe, and that a polar nor'easter struck him and disabled his ship, wind and current would then have carried him to the vicinity of Cape Farewell, from which point the Greenland Current could have swept his ship around the cape and northward up the west coast, as it does driftwood to this day. His vessel may have been wrecked on one of the off-lying islands near the Julianehaab Bight, conceivably on the same ones where an Icelandic trader named Thorer was wrecked in Erik's time. The crew may have drowned or else failed to survive prolonged exposure on the skerries. Ari may have been rescued by the local inhabitants.

Who were the people he encountered? They were a Christian people and they were certainly not Norse. They could only have been Westmen, either refugees from Iceland or immigrants who had come to Greenland direct from the British Isles.

Wherever they came from, one would expect that their fear of Norsemen would have been at least as great as their Christian capacity for forgiving their enemies; yet they spared Ari. If he was the sole survivor they may not have felt that he posed enough of a threat to necessitate murdering him. But an even more likely explanation is that Norse merchant traders were often tendered a type of immunity, even by people who were violently antagonistic toward Vikings. Ari may or may not have actually been held captive. Our version of the Landnamabok suggests that he was; but the author of an ancient Icelandic geography transcribed by Bjorn Jonsson[19] implies that Ari remained in Hvitramannaland without restraint, and says that he became a leading figure in the community. Ari became a Christian, perhaps married a local woman, and settled down.

The question remains of how word of his whereabouts reached Iceland; but there need be no real mystery about this. We know from the Landnamabok that there were sailings between the British Isles and Iceland during the time the Westmen held that island. There is no reason to think that communications between the Irish at home and in the west were severed because the open-sea distance had been increased from a passage of five or six days to Iceland, to one of eight or nine to Greenland. Mariners who could sail direct from southern intervening islands (which were held by the Norse and infested by Viking pirates) would certainly have been capable of sailing on to south Greenland. Furthermore we know from the old Icelandic geography already mentioned that there *were* sailings from Ireland to Hvitramannaland, not only by Irish mariners but by Norsemen as well.

We are told that Rafn, a Norse merchant trader living in Limerick, was the first to report the news. Rafn may have obtained it from some other Norse trader working out of Ireland, or he himself may have been one of the Norse traders who visited Hvitramannaland.

The question may be asked: Why did the Westmen permit Norse traders to visit them, thereby jeopardizing the secret of the existence and whereabouts of Greater Ireland? The answer is to be found in two circumstances. First, the times were changing and the rapid decline of Viking power in Europe may have somewhat eased the terror in which Norsemen had been held by the Westmen in their homelands. Second, Norse traders living abroad in Ireland and in Great Britain seem to have been akin to many modern businessmen in that their prime allegiance belonged to that country which offered them the best opportunity of making a profit. It is a recorded fact that after the Irish drove the Vikings out of Dublin in the tenth century, they *invited* Norse traders to come to Dublin and settle there. These traders were businessmen first and patriotic Norse a very bad last. They actually assisted the Irish in waging war against their own compatriots from the north.

Nevertheless these expatriate Norsemen were probably not permitted to visit the Westman settlements in Greenland until the Viking menace was declining. It would seem from the Landnamabok account that Rafn—or his source—did not visit Hvitramannaland until Ari had been living there for some years.

The second version of Ari's story reached Iceland at third or fourth hand through Earl Thorfinn of Orkney; but that must have been a long time after the event and probably not until the tale had become well known throughout the Scandinavian world. The prime source was Rafn, the Limerick trader. It is unfortunate that we do not know when Rafn's report reached Iceland, or in what form it was delivered. It is not impossible that it was a message from Ari himself, directed to his kinsfolk.

Ari may have explained his long absence by saying he was being held against his will, whereas the truth may have been that he liked Hvitramannaland, was quite contented there, and had no desire to go back to his original family or to the brawling society of his fellow Icelanders.

In whatever form the report of Ari's sojourn in Greater Ireland reached Iceland, it would have caused a sensation, particularly among Ari's kinsfolk. And Erik the Red was one of these by virtue of his marriage to Ari's first cousin.

WHAT ARI'S STORY MEANT FOR ERIK

The time came when, like Snaebjorn Hog (and for very similar reasons), Erik had to get out of Iceland. The sagas tell us that he decided to sail west for Gunnbjorn's Land, but they do not tell us why, nor do they tell us where he intended to go from there. We know he did not go north from Gunnbjorn's Land, as Snaebjorn had done, and so we can assume he was not intending to spend his time of exile as a hunter. He actually went south instead, where game was scarce. But why? Men of his time did not undertake extensive voyages unless they had a specific and usually eminently practical purpose. They simply did not sail out into the blue just to see what lay beyond the horizon.

I suggest he had a twofold motive. In the first place he may have intended to find and rescue his kinsman, Ari; but his most compelling reason for sailing west was probably the prospect of raiding the previously untouched Westman settlements of Greater Ireland. It was still the fashion of his time for Vikings who had incurred sentence of outlawry to use their period of exile harrying wherever there might be a chance for gain. But by 981 the opportunities available to small Viking raiding parties in European waters were becoming very slim and the risks disproportionately great, a fact of which Erik would have been aware.

This explanation of his intentions does not exclude the possibility that he also intended to keep a weather eye peeled for good new lands to be had for the taking. But essentially his was a buccaneering voyage—one which was destined to be followed in due time by land-taking and settlement. The centuries-old pattern of Viking expansion was repeating itself once more.

When we envisage Erik setting out from Breidafiord we would do well to discard the stereotype image of him as a noble and lofty-minded visionary consumed with the desire to push back the frontiers of the unknown. Erik was, as his personal history clearly shows, a ruthless, capable and hard-bitten realist. He was a Viking setting out on a Viking voyage—with all that this implies. Moreover, he knew where he was going.

2

ERIK GOES WESTVIKING

The Saga Tale (987)

Erik told his friends that he would come back if he succeeded in finding that country.

Thorbjorn, Eyjolf and Styr accompanied Erik out beyond the islands and they parted with the greatest friendliness. He said if they ever needed similar support from him, and it was in his power to give it, they should have it.

Erik sailed to sea from Snaefells Jokul and found that land [Gunnbjorn's Land] ... He arrived at that ice-mountain [formerly] called Midjokul but which is now called Blaserk. He went from there southward along the land to see if there was any habitable place [in that direction].

[SOURCES: Erik the Red Saga, Karlsefni Saga and the Short Saga]

NOT MUCH AFTER MIDNIGHT dawn begins to break over the inner reaches of Breidafiord and the red sun, which has rested for only an hour or two, begins to lift above the northern horizon. The dark islets, scattered like drowning behemoths about the fiord, begin to take on shape and substance. From the high crest of one of them a watcher sweeps the silent waters with his gaze, in search of shifting shadows which might resolve themselves into the seeking shapes of Thorgest's ships. When he is satisfied that nothing moves across the ochre-coloured fiord, lightly riffled now by a dawn breeze from the northeast, he turns northward and looks the morning in the face. For a long time he stands unmoving, then he picks up a pole-axe from the ground beside him and makes his way down the rocky slope toward an almost landlocked cove below.

The cove seems overcrowded. It is so small that the four vessels lying there fill it almost to its narrow mouth. These are big ships, appearing even larger in the long light of dawn. They are lovely ships with a great sweeping sheer rising at bow and stern into sweet curving lines. Their yards are lowered and swung lengthwise along each vessel's centre line, leaving only the heavy mast and tracery of rigging to show that they are vessels of the wind.[20]

The world beyond this cove may still lie sleeping, but there is no sleep here. Now that the light is breaking, small fires are winking into life along the shore. They are carefully tended so that no plume of tell-tale smoke will lift into the yellow skies. Each is surrounded by a restless knot of men waiting for pots of gruel to cook. More men begin to emerge from tent-roofed shelters higher on the beach. They come out spitting, coughing and stretching their arms; and their voices sound thickly, as is the way with waking men.

A boat emerges from the shadows alongside one of the anchored vessels, and such is its resemblance to the parent ship that it looks as if it might just have been delivered from its mother's broad belly. It is rowed by six men. A seventh steers it, standing erect in the sternsheets with his face turned to the wakening breeze and his nostrils twitching. Like the oarsmen, he wears no cap, and his auburn hair is rough-cut and unkempt.

This is the way it might have been on the day in the early summer of 981 when Erik the Red began his voyage. We can take it for granted that the day was fair, for good visibility was essential so that at land-leaving they would be able to set and hold a course for Gunnbjorn's Land. They undoubtedly waited for a day with a favourable wind, perhaps a quartering breeze from the northeast.

Convoyed by the ships of Erik's friends until she was safely clear of the islands and of the danger of being surprised by Thorgest's fleet, Erik's vessel sailed out along the north coast of the Snaefells Peninsula. Leeward of her the long spine of the peninsula ran westward to its outermost cape, where Snaefells Jokul, 5000 feet in height and glacier-capped, stood sentinel on the verges of the western sea. Snaefells was the ideal departure landmark, since it would have served to hold the ship on course long after the rest of Iceland had dropped out of sight below the eastern horizon.[21]

The saga tells us nothing of the composition of Erik's crew, but we can assume that it consisted of about twenty men. Among them we can number one or more of the Thorbrands-sons; perhaps Thorkell Farserk, who was Erik's nephew; and almost certainly Thorhall the Hunter, who was Erik's foreman and right-hand man. The roster of the first settlers who later went to Greenland no doubt includes the names of several other men who were members of Erik's crew, in particular a man named Hrafn, who may have been Erik's sailing master.

Except for a few head of cattle and sheep intended to provide fresh meat on the outward voyage, the ship would have carried no livestock. She would have been well stored with kegs of skyr, salted butter, cheeses and dried fish. A few bags of meal probably completed her provisions. For the rest, her people would have expected to supply themselves by fishing and hunting—and by looting.

They would have gone well armed. Each man had his sword, pole-axe, spears and perhaps a battle axe. Wooden shields covered with ox-hide would have stood ready to be slung over the bulwarks if the need arose to repel an attack on the vessel herself. Some of the men may have been armed with bows, although the Vikings did not think very highly of the bow as a warrior's weapon. They considered it more manly to engage the enemy in close combat, where brute strength rather than skill would win the victory.

The ship would have carried spare running gear in the form of coils of walrus-hide rope. A roll or two of wadmal cloth for repairing sails or clothing as required, some simple woodworking tools, and a keg or two of seal-tar would have made up the bulk of her bosun's stores. The crew probably took the barest minimum in the way of personal gear: a skin sleeping bag, and a leather bag containing a few pieces of spare clothing would have sufficed.

ERIK'S COURSE TO GREENLAND

The fact that Erik took his departure from Snaefells Jokul shows that he did not choose the shortest and most direct run to Greenland, which would have been between Horn, the northwest cape of the island, and the Blosseville Coast of Greenland. Instead he sailed west on a course for Midjokul (the Middle Glacier) which was evidently associated with Gunnbjorn's Land.

In later years, so the saga tells us, this landmark at the western end of the run across the Denmark Strait was known as Blaserk (Blackshirt), and here we see a logical evolution in the refinement of the description of a landfall as mariners became more and more familiar with the passage. In the early stages the landfall was an undifferentiated stretch of coast of considerable extent called Gunnbjorn's Land. But by Erik's time the landmark which one was to look for was being more explicitly described as a prominent glacier in Gunnbjorn's Land, a glacier which must itself still have been of considerable extent. Finally the prescribed landmark became a single feature of this glacier. In this case, by analogy with a mountain in Norway which bears a similar name, it was evidently an unmistakable mountain peak.

The designation of Erik's landfall as Midjokul is of particular interest, since if a middle glacier on the Greenland coast was known to mariners of his time, there must have been at least one other known glacier to the south, and another to the north. This is corroborative evidence to demonstrate that the Norse knew a considerable amount about the east Greenland coast at the time when Erik made his voyage.

The identifications of Gunnbjorn's Land, Midjokul and Blaserk do not present any great problems. The nearest part of Greenland to Snaefells is that portion of the coast about Angmagssalik. The course from Snaefells Jokul to this nearest part of Greenland is west by north, which would have involved only a small and easily acceptable northerly deviation for anyone intending to coast south once he had reached Greenland.

The coast between Angmagssalik and Gustav Holm is fronted by a range of mountains through which the gargantuan inland ice sheet thrusts several immense, corrugated tongues to lick the edge of the sea. These tongues are part of the mighty Kronprins Fredericks Glacier, which lies just behind the coastal range and which stretches from Angmagssalik north to Aggas Island, a distance of 130 miles. This must be the glacier which was known to the Norse as Midjokul. Gunnbjorn's Skerries are evidently the islands in the vicinity of Kap Dan at Angmagssalik, and Gunnbjorn's Land would be that stretch of coast running to the north from Kap Dan, including the coast fronting the Kronprins Fredericks Glacier.

Thrusting upward through the mile-thick Greenland icecap are occasional mountain peaks called nunatakers; and the black crests of these all but buried giants are one of the weirdest and most spectacular sights in Greenland. It so happens that one of the greatest of the nunatakers—the 11,000-foot pinnacle of Mt. Forel—thrusts its peak up through the ice of Kronprins Fredericks Glacier to form a great black patch which shows up sharply against the gleaming inland ice behind it. Although Mt. Forel is fifty miles inland it can be picked up from the bridge of a vessel eighty to a hundred miles to seaward of the coast. An officer of the Royal Navy who spent some time in these waters during the last war reports that Mt. Forel was the most visible and useful landmark along the whole of the west coast of the Denmark Strait. It would have been just as visible, and far more useful, in Erik's time; and it is to be identified with Blaserk.

Assuming that he had good weather, Erik would have made the crossing to the vicinity of Angmagssalik in about three days, of which less than a day would have been out-of-sight-of-land sailing. Those authors who attempt to make an epic voyage out of this leg of his journey demean the Norse, for their ships and seamanship were of a quality which would have made the crossing of the Denmark Strait a simpler affair than a voyage from Bergen to the Shetland Isles.

It has been claimed that Erik's ship was in great danger from drift ice; but this is nonsense. At the time he made his voyage, during a particularly warm climatic era, he probably did not even see drift ice, let alone experience difficulty with it.

SOUTH FROM ANGMAGSSALIK

From Angmagssalik south the voyage would have presented no problems. There were any number of fiords into which the vessel could have put for shelter in case of storms, and—as seamen say—Erik had "bold water," which means a steep shore with deep water up to the land, so that there would have been little danger from off-lying reefs and shoals. If the weather held good Erik would have been able to make the run to the southern tip of Greenland in three or four days, assuming that he followed the usual practice of anchoring or of lying hove-to off shore during the brief period of darkness.

Some authors have asserted that he searched the east coast looking for possible sites to plant a settlement, but this is improbable. Although the saga appears to say that he was looking for "habitable places," this may also be translated as meaning places which were inhabited. The saga indicates that Erik expected to find such places to the south; but there is no reason to believe that he would have expected to find them on the forbidding and inhospitable eastern coast. One close look at this coast would have shown him the error of holding such a hope.

In all likelihood he made his way down the barren east coast as rapidly as possible. He probably rounded the southern tip of Greenland by sailing through Prins Christians Sound rather than going outside to weather the infamous Cape Farewell with its reputation as a place of storms and foul weather. In sailing through this sound he would have passed close under the face of the most prominent glacier in southern Greenland—a wall of ice which abuts on the north shore of the sound for a distance of more than fifty miles and which is one of the most spectacular features of the southern district. This is doubtless the southern glacier of the trio of which Midjokul was the central one. It was named Hvitserk (Whiteshirt), and references to it appear in a number of accounts of later voyages to the Greenland colonies.

Having passed through the sound and the maze of channels which lie beyond it, Erik's ship would have emerged into the Labrador Sea on the southern verges of the great complex of deep fiords which comprises the Julianehaab Bight, and which still contains by far the best pastoral lands to be found anywhere in Greenland.

The frigid East Greenland Current which crowds close to the eastern coasts, chilling the narrow band of ice-free lands until they are little better than a desert (from the point of view of a pastoral farmer, at any rate), does not have the same effect upon the quiet inland waters of the Julianehaab fiords. Along this short stretch of south-facing coast, the country lying between the great fiords (which penetrate as deeply as fifty miles into the land) and the ice-free mountains beyond contains broad stretches of arctic prairie even to this day. In the tenth century, when the Little Climatic Optimum was approaching its peak, this land must have had a seductive ability to fill the heart of any pastoralist, whether Norseman or Westman, with a lust to possess it for his own.

In reaching it, Erik had arrived at that "habitable" land which he was seeking; but he had arrived too late to reap a full reward.

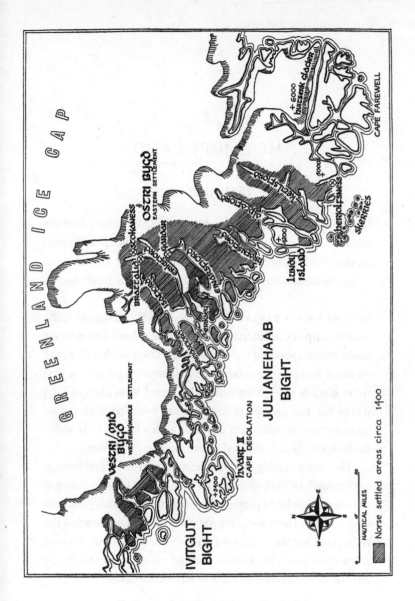

GREENLAND ICE CAP

IVITGUT BIGHT

VESTRI/MID BYGÐ
WESTERN/MIDDLE SETTLEMENT

HVARF II
CAPE DESOLATION

+2400

JULIANEHAAB BIGHT

OSTRI BYGÐ
EASTERN SETTLEMENT

BRATTALID
KOKKONESS

ERIKSFJORD
EINARSFJORD
GARÐAR

+400

EINARSFJORD

INDALSFJORD

SIGLUFJORD

HERJOLFSNESS

SKERRIES

CAPE FAREWELL

+6000
HUSSEEK GLACIER

+5000

HERJOLFSFJORD

[Herjolf]

HUNGI ISLAND

0   15   30
NAUTICAL MILES

N E S W

Norse settled areas circa 1400

The Norse settlements in southwestern Greenland

3

THE EMPTY LANDS

The Saga Tale (987)

[Erik] passed that first winter at Eriksey [Erik's Island] near the middle of the Eastern Settlements. In the following spring he proceeded into Eriksfiord and selected a site there for a homestead.

[SOURCES: Erik the Red Saga, Karlsefni Saga and the Short Saga]

BEFORE ERIK'S VESSEL cleared the islands and sounds at the southern tip of Greenland, the Norse would have begun to see lands which appeared eminently good. Deep hidden from the winds of the open ocean by ice-free mountains, even these first inner sounds held the occasional low and level plots of land where the tall grasses of midsummer mingled with tufted cotton grass to make rich pastures which lacked only men's flocks upon them to make the pastoral scene complete.

The ship probably emerged from the Farewell archipelago not far south of Herjolfsfiord, and as she turned northwestward she would have had a protected passage inside the many islands which fringe the coast. Her people would have crowded the rails, straining their own eyes while they waited for the lookout at the masthead—the keenest-sighted man aboard—to cry the electric news that he saw signs of human life ahead.

Weapons would have been ready and bright-shining, and those who had been on Viking raids in other years would again have felt the surge of old emotions compounded of the lust for fighting, of fear unrecognized, and of a brigand's greed. Nevertheless, they would have proceeded cautiously. The Westmen were no cowards, and they could put up a sharp resistance when they had a chance. One Viking ship and crew would have been too small a force to overawe them.

The need to achieve surprise would have been paramount in Erik's reckoning. Probably he anchored under the lee of successive islands and sent his afterboat on ahead to scout the land before proceeding. The tension would have grown as the long days dragged and the land stayed empty. No smoke rose from behind distant hills. No small dark specks on far waters resolved themselves into fishing boats or curraghs. And yet, with each day that passed, the land grew steadily more desirable. Picking their way cautiously into Ketilsfiord, or Alptafiord, under the lee of great Lundey Island, or into Siglufiord or Hrafnsfiord, the Norse would have beheld increasingly broad stretches of sweet, well-watered meadows, and they could not have helped but think that very soon they must find men as well. One day, perhaps, a group of them went scouting in the afterboat, rowed cautiously into one of the fiords near the mouth of the Julianehaab Bight and suddenly paused on the oars and held them motionless while the water ran off the blades and dribbled unheeded down their arms.

Perhaps they saw before them, around a bend in the fiord, and standing silent in a yellow meadow, the eyeless bulk of a sod house with low stone walls veined out from it to mark the shape of one or two small fields.

THE HOUSE AT BRATTALID

During the 1920's Scandinavian archeologists excavated a building at Brattalid on Eriksfiord. They described it as the "earliest house known in Greenland."

It was of sod-wall construction, but the walls were enormously thick—as much as twelve feet thick in places. It consisted of a single room whose interior dimensions were by no means consistent with what we know of tenth-century Norse houses. Although the room measured just over fifty feet in length, it was only slightly more than fourteen feet wide. It could never have contained the two broad platforms which ran down the side walls of typical Norse halls of the period. In fact the archeologists found no traces that there had ever been anything in the nature of raised platforms in the room. The floor, of beaten earth with some gravel and a few flagstones, was level throughout its length and width.

There was no sign of a central fireplace of the usual Norse type. There was only a small, rectangular floor fireplace of stone set against one of the long walls. Instead of being placed in one end of the structure in the normal Norse manner, the entrance was in the side. There are no indications of how the building was roofed, but the roof construction evidently did not follow the usual Norse design, for there were no signs of holes for the rows of posts which normally supported the broad roof span of a Norse house.

This building, which archeologists accept as having been a habitation, has no single feature about it which is diagnostically Norse. On the other hand, it possesses one peculiar feature which has not been reported from tenth-century Norse buildings in Iceland or in Scandinavia. It had running water, laid on. The water system was crude but effective. Water from a spring in a cutbank which abutted against the back wall was led through a stone-formed conduit to a stone basin set in the middle of the floor. The overflow was carried off by another conduit and disposed of under the front wall of the house.

The house is sited only a short distance from a multiroomed ruin which is identified as having been the home of the Eriker clan, and which is typically Norse in all its aspects. This large structure shows evidence of having gradually developed over a period of many years—if not centuries—from a single large skala or living hall of typical tenth-century Norse design which may well have been the original structure erected by Erik when he settled at Brattalid in 985.

The archeologists who excavated the site have refrained from offering any identification of the older structure, except to say that it "might have been the first house built by Erik, as a temporary measure, when he arrived in Greenland." This identification is not convincing. The amount of time and labour which must have gone into the raising of the tremendous sod walls of the old structure does not suggest a temporary home. Furthermore, the archeologists conclude that the house was occupied over a prolonged period of time.

Few artifacts have been recovered from this ruin, and none of these are specifically and undeniably Norse. On the other hand, floor plans of a series of tenth-century farmhouses in Ireland, which are not Norse in origin, are identical with the floor plan of the building at Brattalid in all essentials, including the location of the door, fireplace and other internal structures, as well as in the ratio of length to width. One of the salient features of these Celtic structures, and a feature which continues to be characteristic of cots in Northern Ireland and Scotland, is the extreme narrowness of the buildings in proportion to their length.

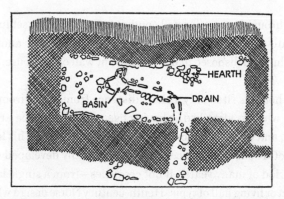

Floor plan of the ruins of the oldest habitation at Brattalid, Eastern settlement.

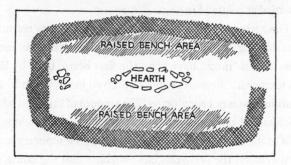

Floor plan of a typical stone-and-sod-walled Norse long house of the tenth century.

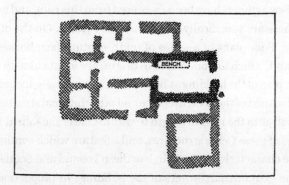

Floor plan of the Norse house at Brattalid possibly begun by Erik the Red.
The outline of what may be the original structure is shown in heavy hachure.

THE HOUSE AT NARSSAQ

Excavations of another ancient site at Eriksfiord have recently been undertaken. This is a house ruin near Narssaq. It consists of the remains of a four-room structure of twelfth- or thirteenth-century Norse design; but it includes within its walls the remains of a much earlier building which archeologists believe must have been in existence at least as early as the turn of the tenth century. This was a single-room house which, although not as large, bears a close resemblance to the old house at Brattalid. Its internal dimensions are approximately thirty-seven feet long by fifteen feet wide, and what remains of the original turf walls average between six and seven feet in thickness. It too had a built-in water system consisting of conduits covered with stone slabs which led into, and then away from, a well-like basin in the floor.

A wide variety of artifacts have been recovered from the Narssaq site as a whole, including a rune-carved stick which has been dated to the early part of the eleventh century and which establishes Norse occupancy of the general site at that period. However, since stratification is not well established, it has not been possible to date most of the other artifacts. A number of them, including some household tools, are indistinguishable from artifacts found on Celtic sites. They can be indisputably termed Norse only if it is proved that no one but Norse settlers ever occupied this site.

The artifact collection includes a number of bone and antler weapon points. These are similar in shape to iron weapon points of the Viking period from Norway and Iceland as well as to iron points from tenth-century Celtic sites. The existence of these bone points suggests that even the very early occupants of Greenland were short of iron and were forced to use bone and antler as substitutes. But Scandinavian historians have established the fact that the Norse settlers in Greenland did not begin to experience a serious shortage of iron (for the manufacture of weapons, at least) until the thirteenth or fourteenth centuries. It seems possible, therefore, that some or all of these bone points were fashioned by people who had been living at Narssaq for some time before the arrival of the Norse and who, due to poor communications with European sources of supply, had run out of iron.

The presence of the internal water systems at Brattalid, Narssaq, and one other similar Greenland site near Hvalsey (water systems which do not occur in Greenland Norse houses of later periods), together with the extraordinarily thick walls of these early houses, has caused some archeologists to speculate that these features may have been intended to give the houses the advantages of simple fortresses which would have been capable of withstanding an attack, or a short siege.

But if these very early structures were in fact built by the Norse, we must ask from whom it was that they had to defend themselves.

There were no Inuit in Greenland then, and none reached the settlement areas until the thirteenth century. So far as we know, the early Norse settlers were never threatened by human enemies.

If the archeologists drew the correct conclusion in suggesting that these may have been fortress houses, the case for identifying them as being of Celtic origin is considerably strengthened. Westmen who had been driven out of Iceland would have had no reason to believe that they would be permanently secure from attack in Greenland, and it would have been common sense for them to have taken whatever measures they could to defend themselves against the eventual arrival of Viking raiders.

Erik may have discovered "human habitations"[22] in what was later to be known as Eriksfiord—but the builders themselves were gone. The shores of the fiords were devoid of any living people.

And yet the Westmen could not have abandoned Greater Ireland so very long before Erik's arrival. Perhaps Erik did not fail in his intended Viking purpose by more than a few years; but that he did fail is certain. Greater Ireland lay empty when he came upon it.

There were good reasons why its people should have left it. By the middle of the tenth century the original *raison d'être* for a Westman settlement in Greenland no longer existed. The Viking scourge had lost most of its bite. Much Viking-held territory in the British Isles had been wrested away from the Norse by the local people; in Ireland the Norse had suffered such a devastating series of defeats that the majority of them had either been forced to flee or to acknowledge the overlordship of the Celts. By the middle of this century fugitive clerics and other Celtic refugees were streaming back to Ireland in large numbers, and the country was undergoing a considerable renaissance.

Word of this happy improvement in Irish affairs would have reached Irland Mikkla with the trading ships which appear to have maintained communications, no matter how tenuous, between the two lands throughout Greater Ireland's existence. In all likelihood some of the Greenland exiles had begun returning to Ireland aboard these ships during the middle years of the tenth century. As more and more people departed to their ancestral homeland, those who were left behind would have felt less and less inclined to remain in that isolated western settlement.

We can only speculate at what life was like in Greater Ireland; but by analogy with the conditions which the Norse had to endure when they established settlements there, we can draw some conclusions. We know that it never proved practical to grow grain in Greenland, and consequently there was a perennial shortage, and often a total absence, of meal for the making of bread and beer. In later years the Norse also suffered from a severe shortage of iron and pottery, and despite the relative proximity of a friendly Iceland with its European contacts, they had to turn to stone or bone for the manufacture of tools and utensils. Within two or three decades after the establishment of the Norse settlements there was already a serious shortage of building timber, and had it not been for the early discovery and exploitation of Markland (Forest Land) in Labrador, this shortage would have become critical. The Greenland environment was, in fact, by no means as generous to European settlers as many authors have suggested.

Greater Ireland would have suffered from all these disabilities, with the addition of an even more important one—the difficulties of maintaining adequate communications with Europe. That ships made the passage is stated in the sources; nevertheless it must have been a long, hard voyage, and shipping losses must have been relatively high. The Outer Islands, Iceland and the Hebrides remained in Viking hands and so could not have been used as way stations. Ships departing from Malin Head in northern Ireland would have had to sail about 400 nautical miles to the north-northwest in order to reach the latitude of south Greenland while at the same time avoiding the danger of encountering Viking pirates operating out of the Hebrides. They would then have had an additional 800 nautical miles to sail down a parallel of latitude—the only way they had of maintaining direction during long voyages—until they raised the Greenland landfalls.

Although the Celtic and British sailors of the times (to say nothing of the expatriate Norse traders) were undoubtedly good seamen and had good ships, such a prolonged voyage as this would hardly have been undertaken frequently. Communications must have been uncertain at best, and if Greater Ireland was in fact being progressively depopulated by emigration back to Ireland, the incentive for traders to make the long voyage would have progressively decreased.

We know that after communications between Norway and Greenland began to break down in the early fifteenth century, the Norse settlements in the far western outpost rapidly disintegrated. A similar situation must have begun to make life in Greater Ireland increasingly uncomfortable during the first half of the tenth century.

The possibility, which has been suggested by some authors, that the Westmen may have been forcibly driven out of Greenland by Erik and his followers, and that they then sailed across to the mainland of North America and established colonies there, is not borne out by any evidence. To pursue it is to pursue a most insubstantial wraith.

Whatever the facts of the matter may have been, one thing is sure. The flow of Celtic people which had trickled west from Ireland, Scotland and the Outer Isles to Iceland, Greenland and—just possibly—beyond, was at an end. This westward drift, which seems to have begun before the time of Christ and to have continued, if spasmodically, through nine or ten centuries, recedes and disappears into the darkening wastes of Ocean off forgotten Cronusland, even as the next wave rolls westward heralded by the dark-hulled ship of Erik the Red.

Erik and his companions probably felt sharp disappointment as the days passed and they encountered no human beings. In their imaginations, if not in actual report, Greater Ireland had doubtless appeared as a populous and comparatively wealthy land, well worth a Viking's time. But scattered and already crumbling ruins of mean sod houses, fragments of hide-covered boats, broken pots and abandoned utensils carved rudely out of stone or bone—none of these things would have smacked of a prosperous Celtic settlement.

There would have been little else for the Norse to find, for the Westmen would assuredly have taken away everything of any value. It is unlikely that there were even any half-wild cattle or sheep upon the lush green meadows. What the departing settlers were unable to take with them on the hoof, they would have slaughtered for the hides.

Frustrated, and perhaps growing somewhat apprehensive as the mystery deepened, the Norse saw the end of summer come while they were still somewhere in the extensive maze of the Julianehaab fiords. Winter was approaching and there would have been much to do in preparation for it. Their ship had to be hauled out and roofed over as a protection against ice forming inside her and spreading her planks during the bitter months ahead. Huts had to be built for the men. In lieu of Westman cattle, food in the form of fish and the fat and meat of sea mammals had to be procured and preserved. Fuel had to be gathered, and the ship's gear stowed away in safety.

And here we come upon a revealing fact. The sagas tell us that Erik chose to winter on an island near the middle of the settlement district. Although he must have examined any number of attractive mainland sites deep in the well-protected hinterland, Erik eschewed them all and chose an island. What is more, he did the same thing during his second winter in Greenland, on still another part of the coast.

Eriksey has been identified as one of the string of small and comparatively barren islands which stretches southwest from the entrance of Eriksfiord toward the open sea. These islands are not habitable now, except by the Inuit, and probably never were suitable for European habitation. Archeologists have found traces of only one small complex of Norse buildings (which apparently represents a summer fishing station) on one island, and no traces of permanent occupation on any of the others.

Considering the hospitable nature of the sheltered inner fiords, Eriksey could have had very little merit as a wintering place except for one thing: being an island it offered a high degree of security against attack. It seems obvious that Erik chose to winter in such an exposed place for the same reason that Viking raiders with small forces had always chosen similar sites when they had to winter on a coast whose inhabitants were known or presumed to be hostile. The Vikings bore the consequent physical discomforts stoically enough in exchange for the relative safety which such places offered during the season when their ships were useless to them and flight impossible.

Erik's choice of an island site was doubtless dictated by fear that the vanished people whose empty houses stood upon the shores of the fiords might return unexpectedly, or else because he believed himself close to, but not yet arrived at, that Hvitra-mannaland which he was seeking.

When the subarctic night drew down and the bitter winter winds blew over Eriksey, Erik and his companions must have huddled close around their fires and spent long hours discussing the summer's voyage. They probably talked at length about the fine land they had seen, for these men were raiders only by avocation—by vocation they were farmers. As the short days of the long winter slipped past, the idea of land-taking probably took root, for here was a country as good as, or better than, any they had known in Iceland; and if earlier settlers had claimed prior rights to it, they were not present to defend their claims.

One can see a dream beginning to take form in Erik's mind as the talk went on through the interminable hours. It may well have been upon that wind-whipped island that the Norse Greenland settlement was first conceived.

ERIK CHOOSES A HOMESTEAD SITE

Soon after the fiord ice cleared away in the spring of 982, the knorr, recaulked, was launched into the cold waters. When she was rigged and stored and ready for a voyage, her people went aboard. Her great yard was hoisted up the mast, and as the wind filled her sail she picked up way, not toward the open sea, but toward the entry into the deep fiord which stretched inland from Eriksey.

Erik had doubtless examined this fiord the previous year, and having by then seen most of the other fiords in the district, he would have known that this one offered the best site for a homestead. So the vessel steered her course until an arm of the fiord turned north, and here, on the western side, Erik went ashore with his companions.

Around them lay a freshly verdant land rolling gently back to the foot of the mountains. Streams purled down to the salt water, and in them swam salmon and many trout. The sprouting grass gave promise of pastures which would feed scores of cattle and hundreds of sheep; and far back toward the mountains there were thickets of scrubby trees, sufficient to keep the cooking fires burning for some years to come.

It was here that Erik took his land by having some of his men march around its boundaries carrying burning brands, and lighting smoky fires at the more distant points. This was the way the Norse were used to hallowing new land unto themselves, and this was the way it would have been on that spring day.

And it may well have been that Erik stood beside a half-collapsed sod building on the higher ground, where he could overlook most of the fiord as far as its southwestern bend, and chose this as the place where he would some day raise his hall.

4

THE WESTERN WILDERNESS

The Saga Tale (982)

That summer Erik explored the Vestri Obygdir,[23] remaining there
a long time and giving many local names there.

[SOURCES: Erik the Red Saga, Karlsefni Saga and the Short Saga]

HAVING SELECTED A HOMESTEAD by the side of the south
Greenland fiord which was later to bear his name, Erik went
aboard his vessel and sailed away to the Western Wilderness.
Now if he had spent the best part of his three-year exile engaged
in an evaluation of the Greenland coasts and had *then*, on the
basis of his acquired knowledge of the country, selected and
hallowed land in the best locality, his actions would have been
in accord with the accepted theory that he undertook the
Greenland venture solely to find and settle new lands.

But Erik did not do this. *He first chose a homestead site, and
then went off on a voyage which was to keep him away from
the selected site during the balance of his period of exile.* Those
were years which could have been put to excellent use at Eriksfiord if settlement had been his original intention. Buildings
could have been erected, homefields laid out and fenced, and
the surrounding countryside explored in detail with a view to
making the most of its potentialities. There were innumerable
pioneering and preparatory tasks which a party of twenty or

more men could have accomplished in advance of the arrival of women, children and livestock. Yet nothing of the sort was undertaken. Erik sailed away instead.

ERIK'S SEARCH CONTINUES

Whatever signs of human habitation he might have found along the fiords of southwest Greenland would hardly have tallied with what rumor had likely described as a flourishing Celtic community which possessed sufficient wealth to attract merchant traders all the way from Ireland. And having failed to recognize the fact that he had actually found Greater Ireland, it would have been natural for Erik to conclude that the place lay still farther on—either to the west or to the southwest.

A reconnaissance party sent by Erik to scan the country from one of the 4000-foot coastal mountains in southwest Greenland would have been able to assure him that there was no more land to the southwest, but would have reported that the Greenland coast north of the Julianehaab Bight ran off in a westerly direction.

Setting out from Eriksfiord, Erik would have held his course westward along this coast in the hope that it would sooner or later lead him to the land he sought. Even after his knorr had poked her head out past Cape Desolation on the Nunarsuit Peninsula, where the coast swings northerly, the Norse would have had no reason to guess that it would continue to run north indefinitely. They would have hoped that it would again swing westward. And there was only one way for them to find out—go and see.

Erik's progress northward was undoubtedly slow. There were innumerable fiords along the way, and he probably investigated many of them, at least until he had drawn blanks enough times to conclude that nobody could, or would, live in their desolate inner reaches. These were not like the fiords of the southwest coast. Apart from the Ivitgut fiords, their shores were terribly abrupt and almost barren; and grassy patches—when they occurred at all—were too small to have been of much use to a pastoral people.

Day after day the knorr sailed along the base of the dark mountains. Occasionally she would have passed the white wall of a sea-front glacier projecting out from the inland icecap. Hopes that this coast might yet lead west and even south again to Greater Ireland might have been kept alive by the fact that the general trend of the land was well to the west of north.

Perhaps a week or ten days after leaving Julianehaab the ship would have rounded the headland of Narssaq[24] and entered a complicated maze of fiords wholly contained behind the wall of the coastal mountains. The Godthaab District, as it is now known, is unique in Greenland. Its maze of quiet waterways is so well protected by the encircling mountains that it has a climate all its own. A few miles to the north and south of it the fiords are barren, windswept and steep-walled slits in the face of the coast range, inimical to men. But the land lying along some of the Godthaab fiords is low and gently sloping and in many places surprisingly well covered with grass meadows.[25]

Although it did not hold the goal Erik was seeking, the very existence of such an "oasis" on an otherwise almost uninhabitable coast could have encouraged him to continue with the search.

A few miles past the entrance to the Godthaab fiords Erik would have found himself coasting the shore of a long bight whose northerly reaches now showed a heartening trend toward the west. He and his men would have also beheld a magnificent mountain peak lifting almost from the water's edge on the far lip of this bight. They would have seen that it rose from another of the great ice tongues thrust out by the inland glacier, and as they sailed on along the coast this towering peak would have come to dominate the whole gigantic landscape.

This was by far the finest vantage point the Norse could have encountered on the west Greenland coast, and they would have realized that from its peak the world beyond would lie revealed for a hundred miles or even more, depending on whether other highlands lay at the extreme range of vision.

THE VIEW FROM THE MOUNTAIN

This 7300-foot mountain is not only the highest on the western coast of Greenland, it is also one of the most accessible. It lies only eighteen miles east of Kangamiut Island, behind which there is a small, deep fiord running to the base of the mountain. It is not difficult to climb and has been scaled several times in recent years by people with no pretensions as mountain climbers, and without special equipment.

Erik would have been able to lay his ship so close alongside that a climbing party could have stepped off the deck onto the lower slopes. Although we do not know who these men were, there is a possibility that their leader was called Hrafn and that he was one of the more important members of Erik's party. He was perhaps the same Hrafn who accompanied Erik back to Greenland on the settlement voyage of 985, and who took up land not far away from Erik's own holdings.

At a later point in the saga of Erik the Red we come to a reference to Hrafnsgnipa (Hrafn's Mountain) as well as to a body of water lying somewhere far to the north which briefly bore the name of Hrafnsfirth. In Appendix D the possible identifications of Hrafnsgnipa and Hrafnsfirth are examined, and we conclude that these were the respective names Erik's expedition gave to the great mountain behind Kangamiut, and to the northern part of Davis Strait.

While the Norse name of this dominating peak may be a matter of speculation, we know that Erik must have seen it and we have no need to speculate as to what he did about it. No sailor of his time, feeling his way into an unknown world, would have ignored its value as a vantage point.

Looking to the north, the climbers would have seen that the mountains lying between the coast and the inland icecap formed an increasingly broad fringe of ice-free lands—much broader than any such strip they had so far encountered anywhere in Greenland. Stretching from a point a few miles north of Kangamiut to the entrance of Disco Bay (a distance of 160 miles) this coastal strip remains ice free in our day to a depth of nearly a hundred miles. This would have been of great interest, but it would have been as nothing to what could be seen far out across the shimmering sea to the westward.

It so happens that the highest coastal mountains in east Baffin Island, reaching a height of 7100 feet, lie directly opposite to Hrafnsgnipa, and at the point where Baffin Island and Greenland are nearest to each other. Here, if anywhere, the possibility exists that the two lands may be intervisible.

The maximum intervisibility between a 7100-foot peak and a 7300-foot peak, as determined by the curvature of the earth, is 224 miles. The two peaks in question are actually 240 nautical miles distant from one another and, in order for them to be distinctly intervisible, two things are required: exceptional clarity of the atmosphere, and a mirage effect. As the *Canadian Arctic Pilot* notes: "Arctic air masses are pure, and visual range may be extremely great. Distant objects stand out with great clarity in shape and detail. . . ." Moreover, mirage effects are common phenomena in these high latitudes. The early Norse navigators found them very useful as an aid in locating far-distant landfalls, and they even had special nautical terms by which they referred to them. And mirage effects in the arctic frequently increase the intervisibility of massive objects such as mountain ranges and, in particular, of glaciers by as much as 40 per cent.

In order for the mountain massif behind Cape Dyer on Baffin Island and its attendant glaciers to be visible from Hrafnsgnipa, an increase in intervisibility, due to mirage effects, of only 10 to 15 per cent is required. However even without any mirage effect at all an observer on the crest of Hrafnsgnipa on a sunny day can see the diffraction loom of the land mass and of the glaciers on Baffin Island.[26]

An experienced Norse seaman would have had no hesitation in concluding that such a loom indicated the presence of a land of considerable extent.

THE CROSSING OF DAVIS STRAIT

The saga says that Erik spent a major part of this summer in the Western Wilderness, which, as we have shown in Appendix D, was part of Baffin Island. Consequently we know that at some point along the west Greenland coast Erik turned his ship's head from the land and sailed westward.

The coast close to Hrafnsgnipa would have been his logical point of departure even if none of his men had climbed the mountain or glimpsed the loom of the distant westward land, for Hrafnsgnipa had a double value in terms of Norse navigation. Not only could it have served as a vantage point; it would have served as an exceptionally useful over-the-stern steering mark which would have enabled a vessel to be kept on course for a distance of about a hundred miles in clear weather. This was a matter of particular importance to Norse mariners sailing in high latitudes during the early summer. At that season there is almost perpetual daylight to pale the skies, and the Pole Star is no longer visible to help a mariner maintain direction. Furthermore the sun is almost useless as a direction guide since it does not rise or set, but follows a wobbly course around the whole horizon.

Hrafnsgnipa was thus the ideal point from which to attempt a westward probing voyage. Even if he had possessed no foreknowledge of the existence of land to the west, and only wondered if such a land might exist, Erik could have sailed confidently out from Cape Burnil, and before the comforting peak of Hrafnsgnipa sank to the rim of the horizon behind him, forcing him either to turn back or risk losing his way, he would have raised the crest of the Cape Dyer peak ahead.

THE VESTRI OBYGDIR

As the knorr eased cautiously in from seaward the Norse would have seen that this new land had a depressingly familiar look about it. Here once again was a massive and deeply indented coast rising abruptly from the sea to a high coastal mountain range behind which stretched the inevitable fields of inland ice. Hopes of finding a gentle and welcoming coast, which might nurture fat Westman settlements, would soon have faded.

The similarities between the two opposing coasts are so striking that it is little wonder that Erik and the Greenland Norse after his day concluded that these coasts were in fact part of one and the same land which ran north up the east side of what we now call Baffin Bay, turned west across its northern reaches and then ran south again down the other side.

Nevertheless there was a difference. The climate of the western coast of Greenland is largely determined by the effect of a northward-flowing current which, although originally of arctic origin, is tempered by the inflow of warm waters from the Irminger Current. The Baffin Island coast, on the other hand, is under the frigid influence of the Canadian Current streaming directly south out of the Arctic Ocean. Even during a mild climatic era this icy stream would have made it impossible for anything except high arctic vegetation to survive in the coastal regions which it dominated. Consequently Erik would have found no grassy cattle meadows, no alpine sheep pastures, and not even a trace of the scrubby forests which graced some of the south Greenland fiords. To the eyes of a Norse pastoralist this land would have seemed to be an uninhabitable wilderness, grim and forbidding and, at first glance, utterly worthless.

By the time the knorr had coasted for a few miles under the bare basalt cliffs of the Cumberland Peninsula, Erik's hopes of finding Greater Ireland in this direction would have fallen to a low ebb. But he was a stubborn and tenacious man and so he probably continued to hold his ship on a southerly course at least until he reached Cape Mercy, where he would have found the coast bending sharply off to the northwest into what we know as Cumberland Sound but which, in his disappointment with the stark country rearing black and ugly over him, he may have been glad to conclude was the southern termination of this dismal land.

However, the apparent worthlessness of this new country was an illusion. Since the Norse were an astute and observant people, they would soon have discovered that this was actually one of the richest hunting districts in the north. They would have been quick to realize that although there were no Westman settlements to offer easy riches to a raider, there was a superabundance of animal life offering equivalent wealth to a good hunter.

The Cumberland Peninsula had—and still has—a thriving population of arctic land animals; white foxes, ptarmigan, arctic hares, barrenland caribou, muskoxen and polar bears. But the sea was where the real wealth lay. The Canadian Current kept the sea temperatures low enough so that seals, walrus, narwhals, and other sea mammals whose range is restricted to very cold waters were to be found here in immense numbers. The large whales were equally abundant (they remained so well into the twentieth century, when the vicinity of Cumberland Sound was one of the best whaling grounds in the arctic); and sea birds, including eiders, murres and a dozen other species, whitened the cliffs and islets in their myriads.[27]

Compared to the waters of the Cumberland coast, the waters of the opposite coast of Greenland during this warm climatic era must have been relatively devoid of game. The men of Erik's expedition may never before have seen, and probably could never have imagined, such an abundance of animal life both in the sea and out of it. Their hunting instincts would have been sharply stimulated even as their raiding instincts, thwarted by the failure to find victims, dulled into quiescence.

The saga says that Erik spent a long time in the Vestri Obygdir and that he gave many local places names there. This does not necessarily mean that he spent his time in exploration, which is the usual explanation of his long sojourn on this coast. He probably did very little actual exploring once he had established that this was not the kind of country where he might hope to find Westman settlements. In all likelihood he and his men turned energetically to the equally lucrative and almost as entertaining business of hunting sea mammals.

They may have ventured a short distance to the north beyond Cape Dyer, since this coast is, and presumably was then, an especially good walrus ground. Undoubtedly they gave names to the best hunting places, and some of these seem to have survived in the Icelandic sources. Bjarney (Bear Island) is one of them. Bjarney was apparently Leopold Island, lying just off Cape Mercy—a renowned collecting point for polar bears that have drifted south down the coast with the winter pack ice. Two capes near Bjarney were named Eider Duck Cape and Coal Cape, and these seem to have been located inside and on the north shore of Cumberland Sound. The name Karlsbuda (Karl's Booth or Camp) may also stem from Erik's time. It seems to have been the name given to the Cape Dyer end of the route across Davis Strait.

Erik and his people doubtless spent most of that summer collecting a cargo of oil, walrus hides and walrus and narwhal ivory. During a summer on this virgin hunting ground they would probably have done far better than if they had spent their time raiding the holdings of impoverished Irish settlers.

I have called the Vestri Obygdir a virgin hunting ground; but it may not have been quite that. Although very little archeological work has as yet been carried out on the Cumberland coast, it is known that the Thule culture occupied parts of it at least as early as the thirteenth century. This was well after Erik's time, of course, but the Dorset[28] people also may have made use of this region, and some of the things Erik was reported to have found in "the west" may have been tools or weapons of Dorset origin which he came upon on the shores of the Cumberland Peninsula.

The discovery of the Vestri Obygdir hunting grounds was of the utmost importance in the later development of the Norse settlements in Greenland. All the sources make it clear that the Norse settlers procured most of their sea-mammal hides and oil from the obygdir, as well as the walrus ivory which was their most important export product. This ivory was the major magnet which attracted trading ships from Europe, bearing the indispensable supplies of iron and other goods which were not available in Greenland, and without which the settlements could hardly have survived as long as they did.

Hunting expeditions to the Vestri Obygdir, particularly from the Godthaab settlement area, probably continued until sometime early in the thirteenth century, when a deteriorating climate led to a huge increase in the size and duration of the Baffin Bay icepack, thereby barring off the sea route across Davis Strait. The loss was not as serious as it might have been however, since the same cold weather which brought the pack ice also brought about a southward migration of sea mammals down the west Greenland coast into regions of the Northern Obygdir which were accessible to the Norse hunters.

Erik's exploration of the Vestri Obygdir did not result in the discovery of his primary objective, but it would have been an immensely successful venture nonetheless. Doubtless he was well satisfied with the results. It is unlikely that his sense of satisfaction would have been very much increased by the knowledge that he had become the first European, of whom any record still exists, to discover what was for all but technical reasons, the continent of North America.

5

RETURN FROM EXILE

The Saga Tale (982–984)

[Erik] spent the second winter at Holm near Hrafnsgnipa. But the third summer he sailed all the way northward into Hrafnsfirth to Snaefells. He believed then that he had reached the head of Eriksfirth [Hrafnsfirth[29]].

He turned back then and remained the third winter at Eriksey at the mouth of Eriksfiord. The following summer he sailed to Iceland and landed in Breidafiord.

[SOURCES: Erik the Red Saga, Karlsefni Saga and the Short Saga]

BEFORE THE FIRST AUTUMNAL storms swept down from the bleak highlands of the Cumberland Peninsula, Erik and his companions would have finished their hunting and gone in search of winter quarters.

The prospects of wintering in the Vestri Obygdir would have had no appeal to them. They would have been able to read the signs and to appreciate how bitter conditions were likely to become in winter on that bleak coast, where there would not even have been much driftwood available for their fires.

Picking a day when visibility was good and when there was a moderate westerly wind blowing, they made their return voyage across the great bay or sound (they could not have known which it was) to the coast below Hrafnsgnipa, where the conditions governing human existence were considerably easier.

Since they had doubtless acquired a good cargo as a result of their summer's work, one might expect them to have turned south and to have continued down the coast to Eriksey; but there could have been a number of reasons why Erik was not yet ready to return to the site of his future settlement. For one thing, he had not yet found any further traces of the people who had at one time inhabited the southwestern fiords. Probably he no longer expected to find Greater Ireland; but he might have been persuaded, by the great expanse of ice-free lands which observers on Hrafnsgnipa could have seen to the northward, to make one final search for the elusive Westmen in that admittedly unlikely direction.

Erik may also have wished to investigate sea-mammal hunting conditions to the northward. The remarkable hunting grounds of the Vestri Obygdir would have been a revelation. However, the Vestri Obygdir lay across a passage of two hundred miles of open water. Erik may have felt that if equally rich hunting grounds existed on the east side of the bay, at a reasonable distance to the northward of his intended southern settlement area, these might prove more convenient to exploit.

There could have been still another reason for making a voyage to the northward. Although later generations of Greenland Norse may have thought they could identify certain strange stone artifacts which had been found by Erik's party on the Baffin coasts as belonging to the Skraeling race,[30] Erik himself would not have been able to solve the mystery of their origin. He knew nothing about Skraelings, or even that such a race existed. If we assume that he found Dorset artifacts on the Cumberland coasts or elsewhere, we can be sure the discovery would have baffled him and made him uneasy. He would have had no clue to the nature of the unknown beings who had made these objects; and fear of the unknown was something to which even the Norse were not immune. Consequently Erik may have decided that it would be wise to assure himself that the coasts to the northward of his intended settlement were free of mysterious and therefore potentially dangerous people.

WINTER AT HOLM

Erik decided to winter near Hrafnsgnipa. Again he chose an island site, one variously called Holm, Holmar and Eriksholm in the saga sources. The fact that he selected an island for the second time strengthens the deduction that he believed there were inhabitants on these long coasts.

Through some quirk of the ocean currents, relatively large quantities of driftwood, which originate from Siberian rivers, are carried right across the Arctic Ocean, south down the east Greenland coast, and finally north again up the west side, to be deposited on the shores between Kangamiut and modern Holsteinsborg. Consequently Erik and his people would have had no trouble collecting fuel for winter burning, and even beams with which to roof their winter houses.

It would be fascinating to know more about the life these men led in their tiny, dark, stinking sod-and-rock shanties during the long winter months. They were a sensuous race, and they loved their drink. On Holm they presumably had no women, and they certainly had no beer. Once the winter had closed down in earnest they would not have gone out hunting, even if there had been anything much to hunt. Talk, story-telling and more talk would have occupied many of the hours. Some of them would have been fond of games (later Greenlanders were inveterate chess players). Perhaps they found emotional release in quarreling. Remembering the bloody winter spent by Rolf and

Snaebjorn on the east Greenland coast, we suspect that only the exercise of an iron-fisted discipline by the expedition's leaders could have prevented mayhem.

NORTHWARD AGAIN

In the spring the knorr was launched and readied. Most of her cargo was probably left on Holm, secured in caches. Sailing empty, and taking advantage of the almost total absence of darkness at this season of the year, Erik would have driven her north at a good pace. It is unlikely that he bothered to feel his way into every fiord, for he would by now have been able to assess their potential, as havens for human beings, at a glance.

Erik would soon have discovered that the ice-free lands to the north were savagely inhospitable, being composed for the most part of range after range of precipitous mountains whose slopes were almost bare of vegetation, and whose deep, dark valleys offered pasturage suitable only to caribou and other native beasts. He would also have discovered that the sea-mammal hunting was not nearly as good as might have been expected, considering the high latitudes into which he was sailing. Perhaps he was able to arrive at the reasons why this should have been the case. He may have noted that the ice-free north-flowing current was warmer than the southbound one which lay on the western side of the body of water he apparently named Hrafnsfirth.[31]

Erik may have sailed into Disco Bay, and out again through the Vaigat; then into Umanak Fiord and out through Karate Fiord to round the Svartenhuk Peninsula and so leave the ice-free regions of West Greenland behind him. Ahead of him at this point lay a hundred and fifty miles of coast which consisted mainly of the peaks of drowned mountains emerging from the sea as a maze of craggy islands, while behind them the inland ice crowded hard against the shore.

It is doubtful if Erik lingered in this region, even though the sea-mammal hunting here would have been somewhat improved. Sailing steadily in continuous daylight, he probably proceeded just far enough to see that the entire east and north horizons had become a wall of ice—the greatest glacier face in all the world—and to watch in awe as gigantic icebergs, some of them as much as half a mile in length, calved from the ice face with catastrophic sound and fury, sending tidal waves roaring for miles out to sea.

This was no place for a small ship. Having seen enough to convince him that this must mark the end of Hrafnsfirth and, effectively, the end of the usable portion of this new world, Erik would have brought his ship about and headed south, leaving the blinding glitter of the interminable icefields, which he named Snaefells, thankfully astern.

This journey north would have been a disappointment in one sense, for it would have revealed no hunting grounds comparable with those of the Western Wilderness. On the other hand, Erik seems to have encountered no people either, and this may have been a relief to him. As his ship bore south again, his mind would doubtless have been engaged in plans for capitalizing on his discoveries by establishing a settlement in this new country.

Stopping briefly at Holm to pick up cargo, the ship continued south until she rounded Cape Desolation and regained the quiet waters of the Julianehaab fiords. There may have been some weeks of good weather remaining of this summer, and those members of Erik's company who intended to return to Greenland with him as settlers probably took this opportunity to choose their own homestead sites.

During the final winter of his exile, which he spent in the winter huts at Eriksey, Erik doubtless completed his plans for this new land. He did not envisage the future settlement as a small land-taking by himself and a few friends. He had come to think of it as a major colonizing venture which he would direct, and of which he would remain the leader.

In the early summer of 984 the Norse venturers loaded their vessel with the wealth they had obtained from the seas in lieu of the wealth they had hoped to obtain from the Westmen, and set sail for home. The first and in many ways one of the greatest of the Norse voyages into the far western reaches was at an end.

6

THE LAND-TAKING

The Saga Tale (985)

The following summer Erik sailed to Iceland and landed at Breida-fiord. He remained that winter with Ingolf at Holmlatr. In the spring he had a battle with Thorgest and his men, and Erik's party got the worst of it. Later, peace was arranged between them.

That summer Erik set out to colonize the land he had discovered and which he called Greenland because he said men would be more readily persuaded to go there if the land had a good name.

Wise men say that when Erik set out to settle Greenland, twenty-five ships [thirty-five in other sources] sailed out of Breidafiord and Borgarfiord, and fourteen of them reached Greenland. Some were driven back, and some foundered. This was fifteen years before Christianity was established by law in Iceland.

The following men went out with Erik and took land in Green-land: Herjolf at Herjolfsfiord, he lived at Herjolfsness; Ketil at Ketilsfiord; Hrafn at Hrafnsfiord; Solve at Solvedal; Helge Thor-brandsson at Alptafiord; Thorbjorn Glora at Siglufiord; Einar at Einarsfiord; Hafgrim at Hafgrimsfiord and Vatnehverf; Arnlog at Arnlogsfiord.

Thorkell Farserk, the son of Erik the Red's sister, took land at Hvalseyfiord and also [claimed] most places between Eriksfiord and Einarsfiord. He dwelt at Einarsfiord. From him the Hvalsey-fiorders are descended. He was a man of great strength. He swam out to Whale Island after an old ox and brought it from the island on his back when he wanted to provide hospitality for his kinsman, Erik, and there was not a seaworthy vessel available.

Herjolf, the son of Bard, the son of Herjolf who was the friend of Ingolf the Settler, set about the Greenland voyage with Erik and sold his home [in Iceland]. With Herjolf on board [his] ship was a Christian man from the Hebrides who composed the Hafgerdingar Drapa [Song of the Whirling Seas]. It contains this verse:

> I begged the monk-seeker [Christ]
> To give us a good voyage.
> May the King of Heaven's Halls
> Hold his hand over me.

Erik the Red dwelt at Brattalid in Eriksfiord, which he had occupied by right of settlement. He was the man held in highest esteem, and was respected by all.

These were Erik's children: Leif, Thorvald, Thorstein and Freydis who was a bastard daughter. She was married to a man called Thorvard and they dwelt at Gardar where the Bishop's Seat now stands. Freydis was very strong-willed but Thorvard was a man of little account. She was given to him mostly for his money's sake.

The people in Greenland were heathen at that time.

[SOURCES: Erik the Red Saga, Karlsefni Saga, Short Saga
with additions from Landnamabok]

ERIK'S RETURN HOME from his epochal voyage does not seem to have earned him a hero's reception. His old enemy, Thorgest, backed by the immensely powerful Thord Bellower, had neither forgiven nor forgotten, and Erik was once again forced to seek an island refuge—this time on Holmlatr, under the protection of his friend Ingolf. But by this time island life must have become almost second nature to him.

Although Erik was probably unable to move freely about the country for fear of Thorgest's men, people could come to visit him at Holmlatr, and they must have done so in considerable numbers as word spread of his discoveries in the west. There were a good many dissatisfied men in Iceland in those times: men who had arrived too late to take up good land, who had fallen on hard times, who were at odds with powerful chieftains, or who were simply fed up with a cheek-by-jowl existence in an overcrowded land. These men would have listened eagerly to Erik's descriptions of Greenland. It would not have been necessary for him to paint the country green in order to have gathered a good following.

Among those who decided to accompany Erik there seem to have been men of wealth and position who had no real need to go adventuring. There were probably some who looked with jaundiced eyes on the slow spread of the Christian religion, which was already becoming popular among the Icelandic women, although most men still considered that the religion of White Christ was a contemptible and lily-livered faith. The bloody worship of Thor and the phallic worship of Frey seemed more in keeping with the Viking spirit.

Excitement over the Greenland project must have become intense as winter drew along. By spring it would have reached a frenzied pitch. The value of ships—any kind of ships, whether they were seaworthy or not—must have skyrocketed as more and more people caught the fever and decided to sell out and join the westbound colonists. The disposal of lands and homes, the driving of livestock to holding pens near the shores of Breidafiord and Borgarfiord, the arrival of pony trains laden with household goods, the repair and equipping of many vessels—all must have contributed to a hectic activity which would have kept the western settlements of Iceland in ferment.

Erik appears to have made his own personal contribution to the excitement of the hour by leaving the security of Holmlatr. Perhaps he felt that he was grown strong enough to face Thorgest's band of champions; but if so he seems to have miscalculated. We know nothing of the details of the battle which ensued, but we know a good deal from other sources about the way such battles frequently went. A score or so of stalwarts from either side would meet at a river crossing, or on some moor, and whack away at each other with their heavy, blunt-edged weapons until they were exhausted. By then a number of human extremities would have been hacked off, and a few skulls caved in. In this case the final count of detached legs and fractured skulls seems to have given Thorgest's party the victory, although neither of the principals suffered damage. This battle was followed by a reconciliation which could have been brought about only by the payment of heavy compensation to Thorgest for the deaths of his sons. Erik may have obtained the wherewithal to make such a payment from the sale of walrus hides, oil and ivory which he brought back with him from Greenland.

As spring progressed and navigation opened, the settlers' vessels would have congregated in the haven at Borgarfiord, and in the shelter of the islands in Breidafiord. It was an imposing fleet—at least twenty-five and perhaps as many as thirty-five ships of all sizes, the largest of which may have carried twenty to thirty people together with as many sheep, goats, cattle and as much household gear as could be squeezed aboard. These crowded vessels would have presented something of the appearance of small-scale arks, with their bleating, bellowing and jabbering cargoes of men and lesser animals jammed into one chaotic noisome conglomeration.

There must have been several hundred people aboard the many ships, and an exodus on such a scale from a country as small as Iceland should have made that spring a memorable one in Icelandic annals. Yet no details of the departure of the fleet are preserved in any of the sources. It is a good example of just how little of the detailed history of that period remains to us, and of how much must be interpolated on the basis of careful reconstruction.

The voyage itself, which began when the ships departed from the two fiords in the late spring of 985, also remains almost unreported. We are told only that of the ships which set sail, not more than fourteen got through to Greenland. The rest were lost or driven back by causes which are not specified in the sagas.

THE OCEAN-WHIRL

However, from references in the Landnamabok and in the King's Mirror, a Norwegian manuscript of a later date, we learn something about the catastrophe which evidently overwhelmed part of the fleet.

Accompanying the merchant Herjolf on this voyage was a skald, or saga poet, and we are told that this man composed a song called the Hafgerdingar Drapa, of which two fragments survive into our times. These seem to be no more than standard prayers for a good journey and tell us nothing; but the title of the poem tells us a great deal.

The hafgerdingar was a fearful oceanic phenomenon which is described in the King's Mirror.

It is called hafgerdingar [ocean-whirl] and it has the appearance as if all the waves and storms of the ocean had been collected into three heaps out of which three great waves form. These so surround the entire sea that no openings can be seen anywhere; they are higher than lofty mountains and resemble steep overhanging cliffs. In only a few cases have men been known to escape who were upon the sea when such a thing occurred.

What the author of the King's Mirror is describing is no ordinary storm sea but a confused upheaval of the ocean which was most likely the result of a submarine earthquake or a volcanic eruption. Such upheavals have also been described in modern times, and in language not much more explicit than is used in the King's Mirror. They are terrifying, and frequently fatal, phenomena and they have resulted in the loss of large vessels even in recent years.

In nineteenth-century Scandinavian sailing directions we read that about halfway between Iceland and Cape Farewell, "the sea has been reported to break very strongly on occasion, and it is believed that submerged islands or else volcanic action is the cause." There are no submerged islands in this area, but there is a great deal of volcanic action in Icelandic waters. As this book is being written a new volcanic island is rising from the sea off the south coast of Iceland.

It seems clear that submarine volcanic activity is the explanation of the dread hafgerdingar. And since we are told in another entry in the Landnamabok that Herjolf himself "got into the ocean-whirl" when he went with Erik to settle Greenland, we conclude that the hafgerdingar was the catastrophe which overwhelmed at least part of the fleet, and that the now lost poem of the Hebridean skald commemorated that tragedy.

HALLOWING THE LAND

There was no initial shortage of land for the people who got through to Greenland. There were probably no more than a dozen chieftains in the group. Doubtless the bulk of the settlers were adherents of individual chiefs and so settled near their particular lords and on a part of their holdings.

Between them, these chieftains parceled out most of the southwestern fiord district. Twelve of them are in fact listed in the Landnamabok, and each seems to have chosen a separate fiord as his own bailiwick. This was no doubt a wise move since the only way such men could have avoided inevitable and often fatal friction with one another was by wide dispersal.

Each chieftain would have taken his land by "right of settlement" that is, by riding or walking around the bounds with a lighted torch in his hand and repeating the land-taking formula: "I take this land here for my own, for I see no inhabited dwelling hereabouts."

Uninhabited dwellings did not count. There may have been a number of such, and it can be assumed that the sites where they stood would have appealed just as strongly to this second wave of immigrants as they had to the first and now vanished occupants of Greenland. New homes doubtless rose where old ones had fallen, and in a matter of a very few years most of the traces of the elder inhabitants would have been obliterated beneath the works of the new arrivals.

Erik had taken a huge holding which embraced both sides of the northern arm of Eriksfiord, and here he established his hall at the place he named Brattalid. Here his ship and the ships of his immediate adherents came to land and unloaded. The livestock would have been no more delighted to be free of their cramped quarters and to be able to reach green pastures again than the ships' crews would have been to be rid of them. After a week or two at sea, the cattle must have made a stinking shambles out of the ships' holds.

All that summer Erik's people would have laboured at the beginnings of what was to become a proper jarl's estate—one befitting Erik's exalted (and by no mean unjustified) opinion of himself. The ruins of the home of the Erikers at Brattalid[32] still survive and we can trace its evolution from the one-roomed skala or hall to its final form as an eight- or nine-room structure which was still standing when the Greenland Norse settlements came to their dark end.

The single-roomed skala was home to the early Norse in Greenland. Here men gathered of an evening to talk, to wait for their meals to be made ready, and after eating to listen to old saga stories or to new lays composed by local skalds, until it was time to clear away the benches and lie down to sleep. During the daytime it was the women's domain. When they were not cooking, making cheese or attending to the chores of the farm they would sit in the skala carding wool or weaving the rough cloth called wadmal out of which their clothing, ship's sails, and many other things were made.

That first summer would have passed swiftly. Many preparations had to be made, not only for the winter welfare of the people, but for the stock as well. Not least of the heavy tasks was to cut and lay up a supply of hay. There would have been no shortage of natural hay on the pasturelands, but it must have been slow work harvesting it with only hand sickles, on such rough and uneven ground. It would have taken a man a good many hours to make much of a showing.

Fishing and hunting would have been vigorously prosecuted. Nets were probably set in the runs between the islands, and when there were a few hours to spare from other tasks, men would have rowed out over the shoal grounds to jig for fish with hand gear. While the salmon run was on, young boys and old men would have spent their time along the streams spearing or gaffing the big fish as they worked up against the current.

The women would have been as busy as the men, helping with the haying, gathering berries, drying fish, milking the cows and goats and preparing as much sour milk curd as they could get, against the long and hungry months which lay ahead.

Fuel gathering would have been a major preoccupation, for although winter came a few weeks later in Greenland then than it does today, it would have been nearly as severe as it is at present. The benevolent effects of warm cycles in arctic climates are felt during the spring, summer and autumn months, but not much during the winter.

In Greenland adequate supplies of wood for fuel were probably always hard to find. Even if we accept the unlikely assumption that the scanty local wood resources were largely untouched before the Norse arrived, the amount of available driftwood and of scrub brush which could have been cut in the dwarf copses high in the fiord valleys must have been very limited. Evidently the Norse used peat to eke out the meager wood supply; but from the earliest days of settlement it probably proved impossible to keep the houses at a comfortable temperature once winter really got a grip.

When the days grew short and the wind-filled nights brought winter to the land, it would have fallen over perhaps a score of squalid, chill, turf-built skalas scattered in terrible isolation along hundreds of miles of frozen fiords, with the great mountains hanging over them in somber silence.

It was a small enough beginning that the Norse had made, but out of it was to come a time when fully three hundred farms sheltered perhaps five thousand people in the Norse settlements of Greenland.

That was a long way in the future, but perhaps Jarl (Earl) Erik, as he had now become through his own efforts, had some intimations of it as he sat on his high seat during the long winter evenings, silent and preoccupied. The flickering light of a small fire and of a stone lamp or two played over the dirt-darkened faces of the men, women and children who composed his family, his servants and his adherents. They talked the weary hours away, played games, repaired their tools and weapons, or snored under piles of sheepskins on the platforms.

But early in the autumn of 985 one final ship had belatedly reached the new settlement in Greenland. She was a fully-laden trading vessel belonging to the son of Herjolf Bardsson. She had come from Iceland, although her course had not been direct; and therein lay a tale to stir men's imaginations through the long winter nights ahead.

7

BJARNI HERJOLFSSON

The Saga Tale

Herjolf was a kinsman and foster-brother to Ingolf the Land-taker. Ingolf granted land to the Herjolfers between Reykjaness and Vag [in Iceland]. Herjolf's son was Bard, the father of Herjolf the younger, who went to Greenland and got into the Ocean-whirl when Erik settled that land.

Herjolf [the younger] lived first at Drepstock. He was married to Thorgerd, and Bjarni was their son.

Bjarni was a most promising man. Even in his youth he loved seafaring. Soon Bjarni owned a ship and tradegoods. He was well off [then] in wealth and stood high in men's esteem.

[SOURCES: Landnamabok and the Short Saga]

BJARNI HERJOLFSSON is one of the most controversial figures in the story of the Norse voyages to the west. And this seems odd, because Bjarni was apparently a peaceably inclined and work-a-day figure in a world dominated by flamboyant and sword-wielding extroverts. He was that rarest of individuals in Norse historical sources—a quiet but effective man who worked for his living.

Nevertheless he has become the unwitting cause of an impressive amount of contention, due to his having been the precursor of Leif Eriksson in reaching the mainland coast of North

America. Some authors have forthrightly chosen to ignore Bjarni's existence. Others have disposed of him as being no more than the invention of some ancient saga-writer who was determined to rob Leif Eriksson of his full measure of fame and honour.

But Bjarni cannot be disposed of so easily. All of the important voyages subsequently made to North America by the Greenland Norse owe their genesis to him; and by his discovery of the great forests of Newfoundland and Labrador he helped to make it possible for the Norse Greenland colonies to survive for as long as they did. Bjarni deserves better than he has received at our hands, and for that reason we digress from the story of the voyages for a few pages in order to establish the historical legitimacy of this much neglected sailor.

About the year 870 Floki Vilgerdarsson[33] made one of the first Scandinavian voyages to Iceland. He carried with him three ravens which he released at intervals in order to help him locate this new land to the west; and he was accompanied by a young yeoman named Herjolf.

Herjolf was accidentally cast adrift in an afterboat somewhere near the Reykjaness Peninsula in southwest Iceland, a mishap which forced him to do a good deal of unintentional exploration in that quarter of the island before he was finally able to rejoin Floki in Borgarfiord.

At the conclusion of what was presumably a successful Viking voyage, Floki brought his vessel back to Norway, where he reported that Iceland was no fit place for a Norseman to live. However, another of his companions, Thorolf by name, was ecstatic about the place and swore that the very grass dripped butter—an exaggeration which earned him the life-long nickname of Thorolf Butter. But cautious Herjolf thought the land had both its good points and its bad ones too.

Not more than a year or two after this voyage, two foster-brothers named Hjorleif and Ingolf,[34] who came from the same district of Norway as Herjolf, found it expedient to spend a year or so away from home until a blood feud which they had started could cool down. They sailed, so the Landnamabok tells us, "for that land which Raven-Floki had visited." Unlike Floki, they needed no ravens to help them find their way, but if we conclude that Herjolf sailed with them as a pilot we will probably not be too far off course ourselves.

These new Viking visitors spent most of their time of exile on the south coast of Iceland, a district with which Herjolf would have been familiar, and where he could have acted as an informed guide. The following spring the party returned to Norway, and although nothing is said in so many words, we have the impression that the profits from harrying Icelandic coasts were getting a little thin. Doubtless there was not much left to steal.

In any event Hjorleif went off in search of richer pastures. He spent a year harrying in Ireland, where he did very well for himself. When he returned to Norway in 873 it was to find that he and Ingolf were still unwelcome there, and in fact stood to lose their heads if they remained at home. Consequently the foster-brothers and their companions sailed away for Iceland once again, this time intending to take land and settle down.

Hjorleif was killed soon after his arrival, but Ingolf hallowed land for a considerable distance along the south coast. Then, so the Landnamabok says, he made a grant of a large piece of this land to his kinsman and foster-brother Herjolf. It was probably not by coincidence that the grant was in just that corner of the island which Herjolf had explored when he was out with Raven-Floki.

Herjolf was a yeoman, a freeman without an aristocratic pedigree; but he was evidently an energetic and capable fellow, and he seems to have become a prosperous farmer, and perhaps trader too, in this new land. He evidently did not waste his time and energy feuding with his neighbors. In a way this is unfortunate, since it meant that the saga writers did not have many words for him. The Landnamabok merely says that he had a son called Bard, who in turn fathered a son called Herjolf the younger. However, in another and later entry in connection with the history of one of the celebrated Viking families of Iceland, we are told that one Eyvind Eld was the father of Herjolf who married Thorgerd; and therein lie the clues to a success story of some proportions. This Thorgerd was the daughter of Thorstein the Red, who briefly subjugated most of northern Scotland until, as the saga indignantly puts it, "he was betrayed by the Scots and was slain in battle." Thereupon Thorgerd's widowed grandmother, Queen Aud (whose husband had made himself king of north Ireland until the Irish betrayed him too) gathered up her grandchildren and made a hasty removal to Iceland. Aud was a great lady and she and her grandchildren were of such a high degree of nobility that the family is still much revered in Iceland.

Thorgerd had been married to a man named Dalla-Koll, who seems to have died shortly after the exiles reached Iceland. It is at this point that Herjolf Eyvindsson suddenly appears upon the scene and claims the widow, thereby elevating himself to kinship rank with the first family in the land.

He is not mentioned again, but one of his children, a son named Hrut who was a sometime merchant trader and owned his own ship, managed to gain the attention of the saga tellers by becoming the lover of the Queen of Norway and then getting involved in several feuds, killings and Viking raids.

Another son, named Eyvind, achieved brief mention in Njal's Saga when he inconveniently died abroad, forcing Hrut to make a Norway voyage and so postpone his nuptials for three years.

But the rest of Herjolf's offspring seem to have inherited their father's characteristics, rather than those of their mother, and their histories are obscure as a result.

There is further mention of Herjolf's son Bard in an enigmatic passage in the Short Saga which refers to Herjolf, son of Bard Herjolfsson, and his wife Thorgerd, as being the parents of Bjarni; but this passage patently confuses the Herjolf Eyvindsson and the Thorgerd who were Bard's parents, with Herjolf the younger who was Bard's son and the father of Bjarni. It is not difficult to see how such a confusion could have arisen!

In any event Bard had at least one son, called Herjolf, who lived on the family holdings near Eyrar, a small port on the southwest coast. Herjolf the younger seems to have been a merchant trader in the family tradition, and we can assume that he was a successful one, since he was evidently able to retain a skald in his personal service.

His son Bjarni, who would have been born about 950, grew up in the tradition of a seafaring family. "Even in his youth he loved to go seafaring," and he probably began accompanying Herjolf on trading voyages when he was still a boy. Bjarni may have been skippering a vessel before he was out of his teens, even as many Newfoundlanders who are still alive today were skippering two- and three-masted schooners back and forth across the Atlantic before they reached their twentieth birthdays. By 985 Bjarni would have been about thirty-five years old. His whole adult life had been spent in the merchant trading business, and it can be assumed that he was as skilled in deep-sea seamanship as any man of his times. His skill and competence are attested to by the high regard in which he was held by his contemporaries.

Seamen of all ages have much more in common across the intervening centuries than do their landsmen brothers, and we will not be far off the mark if we envisage Bjarni in terms of the undemonstrative, effective, hard-headed owner-skippers of nineteenth-century schooners out of New England, Nova Scotia and Newfoundland who sailed vessels not a great deal bigger than Bjarni's into every ocean of the world.

The resemblance between the logs and journals of those nineteenth-century merchant-mariners and the saga record of Bjarni's westward voyage is uncanny. There is nothing of romance, of an overt sense of adventure, of braggadocio in either. They are straightforward and succinct narratives of prosaic problems met and mastered quietly—and without heroics. Any seaman will instantly recognize in Bjarni's story a verbatim abstract from the account of an actual voyage. It is far too dull to have been the invention of a poet.

HERJOLFSNESS

For some years before 985, Herjolf seems to have given up voyaging and to have settled down at home in Eyrar, where he apparently ran the shore end of the family business while Bjarni took over the maritime part. It was customary for Icelandic merchant traders voyaging to Europe to spend the winter there selling their Icelandic wares and buying up a cargo of goods with the proceeds. This meant that Bjarni was able to spend only every other winter at home in Eyrar. He was abroad during the winter which preceded Erik's settlement voyage to Greenland.

When Erik was gathering his band of settlers for that voyage, Herjolf decided to go along even though he must have been about sixty years old, hardly of an age for homesteading and for the hard life which would go with it. But homesteading was presumably not what he had in mind.

The place in south Greenland where he established himself was about the last location a pastoralist would have chosen.

Herjolfsfiord lay on the outer coast, not far north of Cape Farewell. It was surrounded by great, barren mountains and its shores nurtured a minimum of usable grasslands. But although it was a very poor site for farming, it was the most logical port of entry for vessels en route to the Norse farming settlements. It had a good harbour and was relatively easy to make, even in foggy weather or during storms.

In contrast to almost all the other settlers, who went deeply into the fiords, Herjolf founded his little settlement adjacent to the harbour, right at the mouth of Herjolfsfiord. It seems obvious what was in his mind when he sold up his Iceland home and joined the first wave of colonists to Greenland without even waiting for the return of Bjarni from abroad. He had recognized the great trade possibilities which were inherent in the opening up of the new land, and with an astuteness which seems to have characterized members of his family, he wasted no time doing something about it. Thus Herjolfsness became the major port for the Greenland trade almost from the first days of the settlement's birth; and it retained this role through nearly five centuries until the last Norse Greenlander vanished from the land.

8

BEYOND THE GREENLAND SEA

The Saga Tale (985)

During the summer of the year in the spring of which his father had sailed away, Bjarni and his ship arrived at Eyrar.

The news [of his father's departure from Greenland] came as a great surprise to Bjarni. He decided not to unload his vessel, whereupon his crew asked him what he intended to do.

"I intend to sail the ship to Greenland if you will accompany me," he told them. The crew agreed to accept his proposal.

"Our voyage may be thought foolish since none of us has sailed in the Greenland Sea before," Bjarni told them. Nevertheless when they had readied their vessel they put to sea.

They sailed for three days after the land was hidden by the water [lost sight of below the horizon]. Then the fair wind failed them and changed to northerly gales. There were fogs and they did not know where they were going. These conditions lasted many days.

Eventually they caught sight of the sun and could distinguish the airts.[35] Then they hoisted sail and sailed [all] that day before they sighted land.

[SOURCE: The Short Saga]

ON ONE EARLY SUMMER'S DAY in 984 Bjarni Herjolfsson's knorr put out from her home port of Eyrar for a foreign-going voyage. Deep laden with bolts of wadmal cloth, cheeses, dried codfish, and perhaps even a few pairs of Icelandic falcons, she was bound for a European port, most likely one in Norway.

Running east before the prevailing westerlies, she doubtless made a good passage of it, so that Bjarni and his crew may have already been engaged in selling their cargo in Norway before Erik the Red's weathered vessel reappeared in Breidafiord on her return from the Greenland exploration voyage.

Throughout the ensuing winter Bjarni carried on his business ashore. This would have entailed long trips inland with pack horses to dispose of his wares or to buy those things which would be most valued in Iceland—building timber, iron billets, honey, grain and such small wares as pottery, metal tools and weapons.

Bjarni would have been in no hurry to begin his return voyage the following year, since the prevailing westerlies, which he would have had to face, blow strongly in the spring and do not begin to slacken until July. By the time he took his westbound departure the great fleet of colonists had departed from Iceland for Greenland, an event about which Bjarni would have known nothing.

If Bjarni followed the usual route he would have sailed from the vicinity of Bergen and laid a course to clear the north tip of the Shetlands, coming just close enough to them to make a landfall and to check his position. From there he would have steered to raise the high peaks of the Faeroes to the north and would have used these as stern steering marks to set him on a course to raise the 7000-foot peak near Oraefa Jokul in southeastern Iceland, from which point he could coast the rest of the way to Eyrar. This would have been a six- or seven-day voyage for a light ship in good weather. A heavily laden merchant vessel might have taken as long as two weeks, particularly if she had to sail against headwinds. It seems reasonable to suppose that Bjarni regained his home port about the middle of July.

He must have been considerably startled by the news of the planting of a new settlement in Greenland, and of his father's decision to take part in it. However, Herjolf had doubtless left Bjarni a full explanation of his actions, together with instructions urging his son to join him in Greenland with the cargo he had brought from Norway. The first shipment of trade goods to arrive in the new colony would have commanded premium prices.

Bjarni was willing enough to follow his father, but there were problems. The ship could not be sailed without her crew, and it was therefore necessary for Bjarni to persuade his men to accompany him. Their decision to go with the ship could not have been lightly taken, since if Bjarni remained in Greenland, as he evidently intended to do, they would have had to do likewise—at least until they could find transportation back to Iceland. Perhaps Bjarni's task was made easier by the afterwash of the feverish enthusiasm for the Greenland voyage which had swept Iceland during the preceding winter. Touched by this fever, many of the members of his crew may have been happy to try their luck in Greenland.

Selling up land and gear and gathering the stores and supplies necessary to set up homes in Greenland would have taken time. The ship herself would have had to be overhauled and restored with food and water. After an absence of two summers and a winter, both Bjarni and his men would have been anxious to visit friends and relatives before setting out on a new venture from which they might not return for years, if ever. It is unlikely that Bjarni would have sailed for Greenland before early August, and he may not have got away before the middle of that month.

During his time ashore in Iceland, Bjarni would have heard full accounts of Erik's exploratory voyage; and he would also have heard the sobering story of the fleet's encounter with the hafgerdingar. Perhaps it was some survivor of the giant waves who suggested that Bjarni's voyage was a foolhardy one. But Bjarni was too experienced a mariner to have been unduly frightened by such yarns. The dangers of the sea were something he was used to and with which he could deal competently as they appeared. What would have concerned him most was the problem of finding his way to the new settlement. He would have preferred to ship a pilot—this was a standard practice of Norse mariners making a long run in unfamiliar waters—but it is unlikely that any of the men who had sailed with Erik on his first voyage were available.

In lieu of a pilot Bjarni would have needed a full set of sailing directions. These would have had to specify the proper departure landmark; the course to steer from it; the distance out of sight of land in doegr—sailing days[36] —to the correct landfall in Greenland, and a description of that landfall. In addition he would have needed directions for the ensuing coasting voyage, including a good description of the appearance and nature of Greenland together with the relative latitude of the Eastern Settlement area.

All of this information must have been procured by Herjolf from Erik or one of Erik's men and left for Bjarni at Eyrar. There can be no doubt that when Bjarni sailed he possessed detailed instructions on how to reach the new settlement in the west. That he did reach it, in spite of having been blown many hundreds of miles off course into a totally unknown sea, is proof sufficient.

The course given to him was not the short sea crossing from Snaefellsness to Blaserk, followed by a long coasting passage south to Cape Farewell. The saga tells us that he sailed on his initial course for three doegr out of sight of land from Iceland, with a fair wind; and this would give a total distance of about four hundred miles from shore. Since he had not sighted land at the end of this run, we know that his course must have been southwesterly, probably from Reykjaness toward a landfall not far north of Cape Farewell. This direct route was evidently pioneered by Erik on his return voyage from Greenland to Iceland. Its use so early in the history of Iceland-to-Greenland voyaging demonstrates the confidence which Norse navigators of those times had in their ability to find their way around.

From Eyrar, Bjarni coasted to the Reykjaness headland, where he took his departure on a course about west-southwest. In half a day's sailing he would have dropped the Icelandic marks out of sight astern.

That he sailed in good weather can be taken for granted. He would not have risked beginning such a voyage under any other conditions. We are told that he had a fair wind, which could mean any wind from southeast through to northeast, but it was probably closer to southeast since northeasters in Icelandic waters generally bring heavy overcast and bad visibility.

Bjarni seems to have picked his weather well, guided by the almost instinctive knowledge acquired by generations of weather-wise seamen, and the fair wind held during the first three days of open-water sailing. By that time most of those aboard would have concluded that the worst of the passage was over and they would have been confidently expecting to raise the distant coast of Greenland sometime during the fourth day.

Bjarni may not have shared their optimism, for he would have been quick to notice the tell-tale signs of a break in the weather, and when late on the third day the wind began backing toward the north, he would probably have guessed what was coming.

By dawn of the fourth day the overburdened ship was apparently experiencing the full force of a polar northeaster, which in those waters is the most formidable wind a vessel can encounter. It is a hard wind, and it whips the waters of the Denmark Strait until the big seas run white-foaming to the south. The northern skies grow black with driven scud, and the spume flying from the crests of breaking waves reduces visibility to a few miles. Driven sheets of rain reduce it even further, and there are times when even the master of a big modern ship can hardly see the bows of his vessel from his protected bridge.

Wallowing in a rising sea and labouring under press of wind, Bjarni's knorr would have begun to drive off toward the south. With the wind northerly she would have been reaching, and because she had little keel and therefore not much hold on the water even when fully laden, she soon would have been making leeway at an alarming rate.

In clear weather, and as long as he could establish directions either by the sun or by the stars, Bjarni would have been able to allow for the wind drift and to compensate for it to some extent. But with a shuttered sky above, and storm smoke all around him he would have been able to maintain his direction only by observing the way the seas were running and the wind was blowing. If the wind continued to back, as a polar northeaster often does, he could easily have failed to make the necessary adjustments to his course. To complicate matters, he was running into fog. At the time the storm struck, his knorr would have been close to the junction of the warm Irminger Current and the icy East Greenland Current. This is a great breeding ground for fog, which drives southward ahead of northerly winds until it blankets thousands of square miles of the Greenland Sea.

The East Greenland Current would also have been having its invisible effect on the vessel's course and progress. One of the major Atlantic currents, it flows down the Greenland coast at rates of a knot or better. Ships crossing it from Iceland to Greenland have been set to the southward as much as fifty miles in twenty-four hours. Its effect, added to those of wind and sea, would have been to increase the knorr's southerly drift until she was not making good much more than a south by southwest course.

In a typical northeast storm the wind would soon have been blowing hard enough so that Bjarni could no longer attempt to keep his vessel heading across the running seas. Sooner or later he would have had to furl his canvas and let her ride before the wind. Being of a buoyant build she would have ridden well and easily, while her people sought what shelter they could find and waited for the gale to end.

Considering all the forces at work on her, Bjarni's knorr may have drifted southwestward at close to her own normal sailing speed of five knots. Such a drift, continuing for several days, would have carried her a long way south of Cape Farewell. No doubt Bjarni took advantage of every lull to set his sail again and try to claw up to windward and so regain some of his lost northing; but these attempts would have increased his westward progress without, perhaps, significantly affecting his southward drift.

A stiff northeaster is a rare wind in summer in the southern reaches of the Labrador Sea. It seldom occurs more than three or four times in the course of a given summer, and it is most likely to be met with in August. In Newfoundland it is known as the "nine-day wind" because, when it does blow, it tends to hold for several days with undiminished force and unchanged direction. These "nine-day winds" are, in fact, true polar northeasters such as the one Bjarni evidently encountered.

For "many days" the ship drove off into an unknown ocean under cloud-wracked skies. As she closed with the coast of

North America the fog would again have engulfed her, for by then she would have been entering one of the foggiest regions in the world. In August the gray shroud stretches its opaque curtain over the approaches to the western continent from about latitude 40 degrees north, across the Grand Banks to latitude 55 degrees, a distance of 600 nautical miles.

When the "nine-day wind" died down Bjarni would have been unable to lay or steer a course as long as the fog persisted. He could have done nothing more than keep his vessel jogging aimlessly about in the murk, not knowing in which direction she was sailing. But one morning her people would have stared intently into the opalescent dome overhead as the white disc of the sun showed through the thinning pall. We can imagine smiles growing on cracked lips, and salt-caked, bearded faces wrinkling into laughter at the welcome sight.

The return of the sun would have enabled Bjarni to get his bearings, and he would also have realized, from observing that the sun stood very high in the sky at midday, that he was a long way south of the latitude of the Greenland settlement.

The sail was hoisted, and with the ship close-hauled by means of her beitass-pole,[37] Bjarni would have set a course as close to north as she would point, perhaps making good a northwesterly track, while men and women hustled busily about the decks, spreading clothes and gear to dry, preparing food and generally straightening up the chaos which was the aftermath of the long storm. The man with the keenest vision would have been sent aloft, for there would have been no way of telling what dangers might lurk in this unknown sea.

As the day progressed Bjarni would have noted vast concourses of birds about him. He would have seen the familiar black and white shapes of great auks slipping through the water alongside. Out of the thinning mists fulmars, jaegers, shearwaters, gannets, murres and petrels would have come skimming across the ship's wake. The presence of the myriad seabirds which haunt the Grand Banks would have warned Bjarni that land lay close aboard.

For some hours longer the ship drove on while the last remnants of the fog burned away and disappeared. Then the cry of the lookout must have brought everyone crowding to the port rail to stare into the obscure distance until they too saw the blue loom of land.

Bjarni had made a landfall—but it was not Greenland. It was the great island which we know as Newfoundland.[38]

9

AMERICA DISCOVERED

The Saga Tale (985)

Then they deliberated with one another as to what country this might be; but Bjarni did not think it was Greenland. His men asked him whether or not he wished to sail close to the land [and he replied], "It is my opinion that we should close with the land."

They did so, and soon saw that the country lacked mountains but was wooded and had small hills.

They left this country to port and turned the sail toward the land. After that they sailed for two doegr before they saw another land.

The men asked Bjarni if he supposed this was Greenland yet. He replied that he no more thought this to be Greenland than the former country had been, for, he said: "Very large snow [or ice] mountains are reported to be in Greenland."

They soon approached this country and saw it to be flat and widely wooded.

Then the fair wind failed them and the men said it seemed best to them to go ashore, but Bjarni would not allow it. They pretended to lack both food and water but, "of neither of these are you unprovided," replied Bjarni; and for saying this he got some grumbling from his men.

He bade them hoist sail [when the wind came up] and they pointed the bow away from the land and sailed to sea with a southwesterly wind for three doegr, and then they saw a third land.

This land was high and mountainous with snow [or ice] mountains on it. The men asked if Bjarni wanted to lay the ship to shore here, but he said he would not: "because it appears to me that this is a useless country."

They did not lower the sail but continued on along the land until they saw it was an island. [Then] they again set the stern toward the land and held out to sea with the same fair wind.

But the wind freshened at once, and Bjarni ordered them to reef the sail and not to drive the vessel harder than ship and rigging could stand.

They now sailed for four doegr and saw land on the fourth. The men asked Bjarni whether he thought this was Greenland or not. Bjarni answered: "This most resembles what I was told about [habitable] Greenland and so we may steer to this land."

They did so, and they reached the land below a cape at ebb tide. There was a boat near the cape, and there [on the cape] dwelt Herjolf, Bjarni's father, and it is from him that the cape took its name and was afterwards called Herjolfsness.

Bjarni gave up his voyaging then and stayed with his father while his father lived, and dwelt there afterwards.

[SOURCE: The Short Saga]

LAND LOOMED DARKLY through the clearing fog off the port quarter of Bjarni's knorr, and it was an unknown country on the edge of an unknown sea. "They deliberated with one another as to what country this might be," but none of the men aboard ship could have offered anything except wild conjectures.

As they came in from seaward, converging with the shore, their northern eyes, which were used to the coasts of Iceland and Norway, would have looked in vain for the familiar shapes of mountains lifting into high skies. The instructions Bjarni had been given for identifying the coast of Greenland specified high mountains; but ahead of them was a low-lying land bordered by water-worn sea cliffs pierced only by small bays and harbors. Furthermore this land was covered right to the storm-spray mark by heavy forests. Beyond the coast occasional low hills mounded green above the gently rolling contours of the country.

In our time most of the coastal forest cover of Newfoundland has disappeared as a result of four centuries of cutting and burning, so that in many regions only the rotting roots of vanished trees cling to the naked rocks from which even the soil has been scoured away by wind and water. But in Bjarni's time, as in the time of the first French and English colonists, the forests of Newfoundland were a sight to make men wonder. This was veritably a "green" land that the Norse had come to, but they were not seeking a green land. They were seeking Greenland, and Bjarni knew that this could not be it.

He had no desire to make a landing on this alien shore, and here we see the workings of the mind of a properly cautious merchant skipper as opposed to that of a Viking adventurer. Bjarni had not come to this place by design—he was there by ill fortune; and he had but one desire, and one task, to find his proper port before the onset of autumnal weather trapped him in this unfamiliar sea.

The land before him could tell him nothing of how he was to accomplish his purpose. There was nothing but a black and green barrier lying at the edge of the world, and it had no interest for Bjarni, the Master Mariner. But the sky could tell him much. That night he would have watched intently for the appearance of the Pole Star—the Guiding Star of the Norse. When it showed clearly enough against the darkening sky he would have taken a sight on it; and having read his husanotra[39] he would have discovered that he was nearly seven doegr, or about 800 of our nautical miles, south of his intended port.

This knowledge would have been of great assistance to him, but there was one more thing he badly needed to know and had no way of finding out—his relative longitude in relation to the Greenland settlement. He would, of course, have realized by now that he was west of the settlement; but how far west? That he could not tell.

Perhaps as he stood on the dark deck of his ship where she lay hove-to, well clear of the now unseen shore and whatever dangers it might hold, he reasoned something like this:

"I am seven doegr south, and an unknown distance west of the settlement. It lies on a westward-facing coast; while I am lying off an eastward-facing coast. I was told that Erik found an eastward-facing coast somewhat to the north and west of the settlement. The coast I'm on certainly isn't any part of habitable Greenland as it was described to me, but it might be a southward extension of that east-facing land Erik discovered. Maybe if I follow it north it will bring me to the Vestri Obygdir of Greenland. In any case I *must* go north, and I might as well follow up this coast. I can always abandon it if it runs the wrong way. When I have regained my proper northing I can then sail east until I strike the settled part of Greenland."

Regardless of how Bjarni thought about it, he had no real alternative but to sail north until he reached the latitude of the settlements. He would have been a fool to sail on what he hoped was a direct course, since such a course could only have been based on the wildest guesswork as long as he did not know how much westing he had made. There was also a strong psychological reason why he should have decided to follow the coast. Although he did not know its location, or even what coast it was, he knew that it was solid land—a fixed thing—while if he had put out to sea, nothing would have been fixed, and in the event that he experienced another prolonged period of fog, he would again have been completely lost.

The detailed reconstruction of Bjarni's route from this first landfall on to Greenland requires a painstaking examination of the geography of the coasts, and of the wind and current patterns of the waters through which he must have sailed. Such a reconstruction can be tedious reading for anyone except a specialist, and for that reason we have relegated it to the appendices. What follows here is a subjective account of the voyage; but it is securely based upon the reconstruction which we give in Appendix K. (See map, page 116.)

The day was fair. As the knorr jogged idly in the morning calm the long light of dawn shone on the green land, dissipating some of its mystery and giving it a touch of warmth which stirred a desire to land and investigate in some of the younger men among the crew. But Bjarni was adamantinely opposed. Apart from the other problems which beset him, he was uneasy about the weather. On the eastern horizon the black curtain of the perpetual summer fog-bank hung between sea and sky, ominous and threatening. Bjarni was well aware of how quickly it could begin its swirling and inexorable encroachment on the land if its ally, the southeast wind, should come to life.

With the first cat's-paw of a breeze—a riffle from the south— Bjarni ordered the sail trimmed; but when the knorr refused to do more than loaf along in that light air, he ordered the sweeps broken out fore and aft. There was some grumbling, but it meant nothing. Norse sailors were intractable by nature, and did not take kindly to discipline. All the same, they did their work. Under the impetus of a lifting breeze and of six pairs of sweeps, the ship began to gather way.

The wind held southerly and the fog kept its distance as the ship sailed northward, slowly closing with the shore, which trended just east of north. As the morning aged, white puffs of land-cloud materialized over the glacier-rounded hills and ridges. The lookout at the knorr's masthead strained his vision. He saw many narrow bays and inlets; but nothing made by man moved over their shadowed depths. No smoke of human habitation drifted up over the veil of forests.

He did not know—and we who live almost a millennium later still do not know—why that land should have been devoid of human kind. For reasons at which we can only guess, the native peoples of Newfoundland apparently eschewed the eastern and northeastern coastal regions of the Avalon Peninsula. Almost no trace of ancient human occupation has been discovered in these regions.

The breeze freshened and at last Bjarni allowed the rowers to cease work. The knorr drove along at a good five knots, and before the sun stood at the zenith the lookout saw that the coast was coming to an end. He called to Bjarni, who swarmed up the mast to sit astride the yard.

To port the shore cliffs were rising higher, but a few miles ahead they cut off abruptly. Bjarni was both relieved and disturbed to see the end of land. Once away from its shores he knew he would have less to fear if the fog shut down upon him; but nevertheless he felt a touch of uneasiness to think that he would be adrift once more in an alien sea.

But before the knorr came abeam of the headland which we now know as Cape St. Francis, new and distant land opened again to the northward.

Clearing Cape St. Francis, Bjarni's people found themselves sailing across the mouth of an immense fiord whose inner reaches faded into a blue and hazy distance. This was Conception Bay. They watched Baccalieu Island rising, sheersided, black and massive off the seaward termination of the Bay de Verde Peninsula ahead of them to the north. The cliffwalled island was surmounted by a whirling, glittering cloud of wings. As the ship drew near, she sailed through waters which were blanketed by mighty flocks of sea-fowl that lifted in undulating flights, making their way toward the island where they and their fellows bred in millions. Bjarni brought his vessel close under the white-flecked cliffs of Baccalieu while those on board gazed up at the wheeling multitudes, delighted to see such familiar forms of life in this unfamiliar world. And beyond the cliffs, where the forest crowded down to the sea, they glimpsed the white poles of birches, familiar to them at home.

Dusk was falling as the ship idled under the lee of Baccalieu, and Bjarni ordered her headed out to sea for the night. When she had an offing he brought her into the wind and put her to sleep, jogging gently with her head to the southerly breeze and swell. It would have been far too risky to drive on through that alien sea in darkness, with the coast of an unknown land lying off to port and, for all Bjarni knew, ahead of him as well. During the night Bjarni again took a fix with his husanotra and found that he had regained about half a doegr of his lost northing. It was something accomplished.

At dawn of the next day more land was discernible far to the northnorthwest, and they laid course for it toward Cape Bonavista across the mouth of the mighty fiord we call Trinity Bay. Here too, as they closed with the land, men marveled to see hardwood forests of such a size that, had they only stood in Iceland or even in Norway, they would have represented incalculable riches.

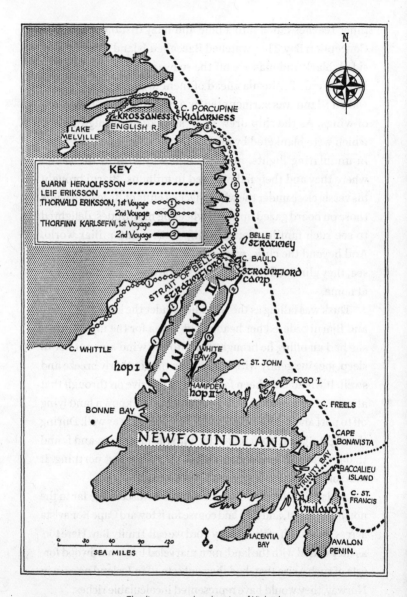

The discovery and exploration of Vinland

But they stood, instead, on the edge of the world; and they had no power to tempt Bjarni Herjolfsson.

From Bonavista no more land could be seen, and Bjarni reluctantly ordered the ship headed northward into open water. Less than an hour later the lookout once more picked up a smudge of coast to the north-northwest, and once more Bjarni altered a little to close with it. This was Cape Freels, a low, forested shore guarded by innumerable reefs, at the sight of which Bjarni ordered the helm hard over so that the vessel kept her distance from the dim line of forest. Once more the day drew to an end, and again she stood off shore as darkness fell, and jogged, hove-to, until the dawn.

The new day brought overcast skies and a wind from south-easterly. Because visibility was worsening, it was not until well into the gray morning that contact with the land was regained. This was the high mound of Fogo Island lying considerably off the vessel's course, for it bore northwest instead of north-north-west as had each of the previous capes. Nevertheless Bjarni altered so that he could come close enough to make out something of its nature.

By now a pattern was emerging. It seemed to Bjarni that the coast consisted of a number of huge fiords whose head-lands all trended northerly with some slight bias to the west. Taking Fogo for another in the chain, he made a departure from its northern cape in the late afternoon. The lookout reported seeing no land to the west or even to the southwest, but this might have meant only that the fiord beyond Fogo was of even more majestic dimensions than those which had preceded it.

They had not yet raised a new northern cape when darkness caught them, and—feeling more secure—Bjarni kept a little way on the vessel through the dark hours, for he hated to waste a good, fair wind. Dawn came, and there was still no land in sight.

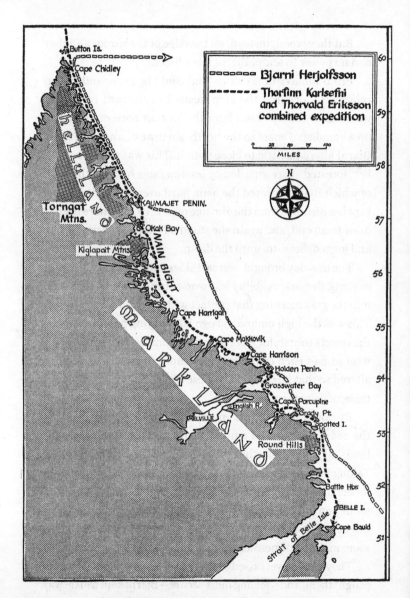

The discovery and exploration of Helluland and Markland

As the hours passed, Bjarni began reluctantly to conclude that he had finally lost touch with the new land. For a distance of two doegr they steered as close to north as wind, current and drift would let them, and their slight set to the westward from these three factors was not apparent to them. Nevertheless it was enough to bring them to another landfall.

They picked up this land as they approached the Labrador on a course almost, but not quite, parallel to it. And the land they saw was the mammary outline of the Round Hills which lie on the otherwise featureless Labrador shore near Hawke Harbour.

Bjarni's last sight on the Guiding Star had shown him that he had regained three doegr of northing, and so he ordered the vessel's head turned toward the land, intensely curious to see if it would resemble the description he possessed of the Vestri Obygdir.

He was disappointed. Once more he beheld a low, forested country with none of the great glaciers and mountains he was hoping to see.

All the same, things were going well. He had now regained almost half his lost northing, and these new lands seemed to continue in a generally northerly direction. Again he decided to maintain contact with the coast as long as it trended the way he wished to go.

The knorr coasted, keeping a good offing, to Spotted Island, then crossed the mouth of Grosswater Bay to the Indian Islands lying off the Holden Peninsula. Here she was becalmed for a few hours, and the men, increasingly curious to set foot on shore, made a concerted effort to persuade Bjarni to launch a boat. But Bjarni would have none of it. He knew that the calm would not last long, and he was determined to take advantage of every hour of daylight and fair wind to push on north.

The breeze soon revived, this time from the southwest, a perfect sailing breeze. It brought clearing weather, and since it was off the land it roused no sea. As the ship cleared the Indian Island archipelago, the lookout reported a headland dimly seen to the northwest. Confident that the coastal pattern of bays and capes would continue to repeat itself, Bjarni held to the north as darkness fell; but at dawn there was no land in sight. For three doegr there was nothing on the horizon, and before the end of this long run Bjarni concluded that he had lost contact with the unknown coasts for good.

His vessel had been crossing the vast Nain Bight. Under the influence of the Labrador Current, which not only set him back but also set him off a little to the west, Bjarni had not maintained a perfect course. No mariner of his times could have done so, for their navigation when they were deep-sea was very much dead reckoning.

Once more the cry came from the masthead, and again Bjarni swarmed up to have a look.

This time his heart leaped. Very distant on the northwest horizon he saw a mountain range with the gleam of ice or snow reflecting from its peaks. The ship's head was turned toward it, but the far peaks lifted over the horizon incredibly slowly, for the knorr had been a good half-day's sail offshore when her lookout sighted them.

As the ship closed with the land her people saw even greater mountains rising behind the outer ones; and these new ranges marched off to the northward, growing ever higher and carrying still more snow and ice.

Bjarni's third landfall was the outthrust Kaumajet Peninsula of northern Labrador, whose peaks stand 4000 feet high within half a mile of the coast, and which can be seen from as much as ninety miles to seaward. The Kaumajet, together with the nearby Kidlapait Range, marks the abrupt beginning of a portion of Labrador totally different from that which Bjarni had previously seen. From the Kaumajet northward, the Labrador is a steadily narrowing peninsula whose spine is the mountain massif known as the Torngat Range. The Torngats crowd seaward to produce some of the most grandiose, forbidding and violent scenery in the Western Hemisphere. Totally treeless, chilled by the Labrador Current, and crowned with perpetual snow and ice, the Torngat coast is a fearful wasteland where even the Inuit have been hard put to it to gain a foothold. It was no wonder that Bjarni believed this to be a new country, one quite distinct from those he had already seen.

Ignoring the now routine demands of his crew that he should make a landing, he held his course under the loom of the terrifying sea cliffs, and when full darkness came, he took a sight. It showed that he was now only one doegr south of the Greenland settlement.

Although the mountain coast trended somewhat west of north,[40] he decided to keep it in view until he had regained the last of his northing. He probably believed that it was a southward continuation of the Vestri Obygdir. As he watched the great fiords and mountains march past to the south, he felt as if he was at last re-entering the known world. It was with something of a shock that Bjarni came to the northern termination of this mountain land. It ended abruptly near Gray Strait and the Button Islands just as he was approaching his desired latitude. So Bjarni turned his back on what he now concluded must be a vast, mountainous island in the west, and set his course due east across the Labrador Sea.

It was a hard crossing. An offshore gale forced Bjarni to shorten sail and scud before it. But it was a fair wind, and so he welcomed it. Even at the height of the gale the lookout remained aloft, for no man aboard the ship could tell at what instant the land they sought might loom up out of the storm ahead.

They drove eastward for a distance of three doegr after losing sight of the Labrador. Sometime on their fourth day, land finally appeared. It loomed distant and majestic. Great, black mountains fringed the sea, and far beyond them the brilliant mass of the inland ice glittered in the autumnal sunlight. There was nothing green to be seen, and if there had been, Bjarni would have been badly worried. He had been told to look for a coast whose description fitted this ice-crowned mountain wall exactly.

So they came in toward the land they sought. They may have closed directly with Herjolfsness, although it is just as likely that they made their first landfall somewhere to the north of it and then coasted south looking for signs of human habitation. Since all the settlers except Herjolf had chosen lands well up in the deep fiords, it was only at Herjolfsness that Bjarni would have been likely to see signs of human occupation. In any event this was where he finally put in, and the great voyage ended.

And it was a great voyage, not simply because of the discovery of a new continent, but also because it represented a superb feat of seamanship.

10

HIATUS

The Saga Tale (985–c. 995)

Next it is to be told that Bjarni Herjolfsson came to visit Jarl Erik and was well received. Bjarni told of his travels when he had seen these [new] lands and he was thought by many to have been lacking in enterprise since he had so little to tell of those lands. Because of this he was somewhat derided. . . .

There was now [some years later] much talk of land-seeking voyages. Leif, son of Erik the Red of Brattalid, went to visit Bjarni Herjolfsson and bought his ship from him, and manned her with thirty-five men. . . .

Leif went to the ship with his followers. There was a southern man with them called Tyrker. They made the ship ready for sea and when all was ready they sailed out to sea. . . .

[SOURCE: Edited excerpts from the Greenlanders Story.[41] The original version will be found in Appendix L, Part I.]

BJARNI'S ARRIVAL at Herjolfsness must have been a relief to everyone concerned, but his discovery of new lands to the west does not seem to have aroused much reaction except as a curious incident in his prolonged voyage. Bjarni himself doubtless considered that his failure to raise Greenland when outward bound was an embarrassing reflection on his seamanship— a reflection which could not be entirely erased even by the consummate skill he had displayed in eventually making his proper port.

Having told the story of the voyage to his father and his father's people, Bjarni probably put the incident out of mind, for there were more important things to occupy his attention. For one thing, he and his crew would have been concerned with preparing for the winter. New houses had to be erected to accommodate his people; his ship had to be hauled out and properly secured; and the cargo of trade goods had to be stowed ashore.

When there was time for talk, Bjarni would have been far more interested in hearing Herjolf's reasons for moving to Greenland and in discussing plans for the establishment of a trading station than in talking about his own voyage.

Nevertheless there seems to have been one man at Herjolfsness that winter who saw in Bjarni's voyage an adventure worth remembering. He may well have been the Hebridean skald who had come out to Greenland in Herjolf's party and who composed the lost Hafgerdingar Drapa and who may, conceivably, also have composed a major portion of the original Old Erik Saga. In any event we credit this nameless skald with the authorship of the surviving account of Bjarni's western voyage, which forms an integral part of the Short Saga, itself a surviving fragment of the Old Erik Saga. This skald had the opportunity to hear Bjarni's story first hand, as the direct narration of a master seaman, which would go far to explaining why the account carries such an aura of credibility.

The quotations from the sagas which open this chapter are almost the only written records we possess concerning the history of Greenland during the decade following the settlement in 985. But since the ordinary events of those formative years are of importance to an understanding of the remarkable events which followed them, we have made a partial if somewhat imaginative reconstruction of them.

During the winter of 985–986 the isolation of the settlers was intense. They were widely dispersed in little groups, and the problems of caring for their stock and for themselves through the first critical winter left them little time or energy for long journeys over the frozen fiords or across the intervening mountain ranges to visit neighbors.

With the passing of the fiord ice in the spring the isolation was not much alleviated. Although boats and vessels could have begun to move about again, there would have been little time for pleasure jaunts. The fencing of the home fields, the building of livestock shelters in distant pastures, and the urgent general need to force this land to produce the wherewithal for sustaining human life engrossed everyone's attention and energy— with a few exceptions.

Bjarni and his father were not bound to the land for their living, or at least not to the same extent that the other settlers were. The livelihood of the Herjolfers depended on trade, and in their storehouses they had the entire cargo of goods Bjarni had brought from Norway, plus whatever stock Herjolf had brought with him from Iceland. These goods had to be taken to the customers if they were to be sold.

Soon after the ice cleared, Bjarni and Herjolf had one of their vessels manned and loaded. Then they set out to visit the scattered colonists. Perhaps they were accompanied by the Hebridean skald, whose task it would have been to entertain the prospective customers when settlers and visitors alike gathered around the homestead hearthfires in the evenings. The skald would have been called upon for many lays, including the Hafgerdingar Drapa and his Saga of Bjarni's Western Voyage.

One day the Herjolfers' vessel sailed around the northern

bend in Eriksfiord and came to a mooring below the stead of Brattalid, where Erik had his home. This was something in the nature of a state visit, since Erik was the acknowledged chieftain of the new land.

Herjolf and Bjarni doubtless made lavish gifts to Erik, to his wife Thorhild and perhaps to the three half-grown sons, Leif, Thorstein and Thorvald, since gift-giving by a visiting merchant was a customary way of buying the good will of chieftains.

That night there was probably a formal feast, with Erik seated on his high chair, flanked by his famous dais-posts, while across from him sat Bjarni and Herjolf. After the meal the talk could have turned to Bjarni's voyage.

It was probably rough talk and since Bjarni and Herjolf were mere traders they would have been considered fair game for the humor of men like Thorhall the Hunter, who was the black-visaged and reputedly foul-mouthed overseer of Erik's estate in winter, and his hunter and sea-rover in the summertime. It is easy to imagine the contempt which Bjarni's cautious attitude toward his accidentally discovered new lands would have aroused among such men. The prudence of a good merchant seaman would have won no plaudits from those who made a virtue out of recklessness.

Theirs was a show of disdain which Bjarni would have had to bear stoically, for there was no recourse short of resorting to the sword and axe, and Bjarni was not a dueling man. Perhaps he took his revenge by charging exorbitant prices for his wares.

After Bjarni's departure from Brattalid there must have been intense discussion of his voyage and much speculation as to the identity and merit of the lands he had seen. But at this stage the settlers were in no position to follow up Bjarni's discoveries. They required time to establish themselves before contemplating any new adventures.

Then, too, Erik himself was probably opposed to new land-seeking voyages. Anything which threatened to deflect men's energy away from the new colony would have aroused his natural and formidable ire. Greenland and Greenland alone was the scene of his ambitions. In the scale of those times it was an independent kingdom in the making, and Erik's explorations had taught him that its resources could support a population quite big enough to satisfy his own ambitions for power and pre-eminence.

At the time of Bjarni's voyage, Leif Eriksson was about fifteen years of age. The experiences of his boyhood had naturally given him a taste for the adventurous life, and with the example of his father's exploits as a land-seeker and land-taker before him, he would not have been normal if he had not dreamed of someday accomplishing similar feats.

Bjarni's tale of lands to the west provided food for such dreams. Still, there was nothing Leif could do about it for the moment. The prohibitions against undertaking any more land-seeking voyages applied to him equally with all the others. Although he was in many ways already a man, he was still under the authority of his domineering father and still too young to seek his own destiny in the mysterious western reaches of the gray Atlantic.

During the next seven or eight years, more and more Icelanders gave up their submarginal holdings on that island and took passage for Erik's colony. As the best farmsteads were taken up, the newcomers began to push farther west to the Ivitgut fiords, which then became known as the Western Settlement.[42] Farming land in this new settlement was neither as extensive nor as good as in the Julianehaab district, but it was adequate for the moment.

As both the Eastern and Western settlements became better established, and as herds and flocks grew in size, the early urgency which had forced men to work with single-minded intensity from dawn until dusk began to diminish. When summer came, the well-organized farms could be left under the guiding hands of women, older children, slaves and elderly retainers. Men in the prime of life were free to take on other tasks which were more to their tastes, such as hunting and wood-gathering journeys up the west coast, excursions far out to sea after whales, and summer-long voyages to the rich hunting grounds of the Vestri Obygdir.

Later records tell us that it became the custom for each important settler to send a boatload of men to the obygdir every spring. These excursions were of vital importance, not just to supply the settlements with wild meat, hides and oil, but also to procure the barter capital with which trade goods could be purchased from Norwegian and Icelandic merchants. Walrus tusks, in particular, had become so valuable a commodity in Europe that one good summer in Greenland's obygdir could make a hunter relatively rich. These prolonged hunting and fishing voyages seem to have led to a new development in the maritime skills and techniques of the Greenlanders—or perhaps it was a reversion to ancient Norwegian techniques.

The Greenland of the Norse was a coastal country of prodigious length, and men had little need for ocean-going vessels which were too big to be handled by small crews or to be maneuvered in the remote and narrow channels of the innumerable fiords. What was needed was something rather like the afterboat of a knorr, which itself was a survival of the ancient clinker-built skiffs and wherries that had been in use on the Norwegian coast since primeval times. Consequently the Greenland boats seem to have developed as large, double-ended rowing skiffs equipped with a sail. They drew almost no water and could be hauled out at need by their own crews. They were very maneuverable, ideally suited for whaling, sealing or walrus hunting.

No examples of them survive, but we can determine some further details about them from later sagas and other sources. They seem to have been six-oared, six-man boats of about three tons displacement. While they were primarily intended for coasting voyages, they were good enough sea-boats to be able to make regular crossings to the Vestri Obygdir.

There is no indication in the sagas of where the materials came from to build these Greenland skiffs. No natural hardwood was available in Greenland except what little might appear as driftwood. Nevertheless, good hardwood was essential to the construction of Scandinavian clinker-built skiffs, since these boats owed their strength, elasticity and lightness to the fact that their frames were very small, and their planking very thin.

Probably the first generations of Greenland skiffs were the result of a form of cannibalism. The ships which had brought the settlers to Greenland would have begun to deteriorate through lack of use, lack of care, and a shortage of hardwood to keep them in repair. Doubtless their owners chose to break them up before they rotted out, and to use the salvaged materials for building the smaller and more useful coasting skiffs.

This source of materials would have served for a while, but the presence of a minimum of several hundred settlers in Greenland would soon have exhausted this supply of timber, together with whatever usable hardwood had formerly existed in the driftwood wrack along the shores; while even the rough driftwood must have rapidly vanished into fireplaces along with a good part of the dwarf local "forests."

As buildings grew larger and more numerous, timber for rafters and supporting posts would have become scarcer, and its value would have soared. Greenland did not even have any natural softwoods of sufficient size to be of much use in this connection, consequently the settlers would have had to rely mostly on wood imported from Norway.

Lumber is a bulky substance not worth nearly as much, in terms of the cargo space it occupies, as such things as iron and manufactured goods. It is unlikely that many of the traders who voyaged from Norway to Greenland chose lumber as a cargo.

A dearth of timber, both soft and hard, must have been the first important scarcity the Greenlanders experienced, apart from the perennial shortage of grain, whose partial or complete absence they may have become somewhat used to in Iceland. It was inevitable that sooner or later men would recall Bjarni's description of the new lands to the west which were almost literally hidden under immense stands of virgin forest.

We do not know when the Greenlanders stopped talking about Bjarni's land and decided to go and see for themselves if its reputed forest wealth really did exist. But if we cannot know the date we can at least make an informed guess as to the identity of the man behind the proposal of a westward voyage.

As Leif grew older he must have begun to chafe at the limited opportunities which Greenland offered for the accomplishment of great and famous deeds. Early in the last decade of the century he was a fully grown man and, to a large extent, his own master. The ferment of ambition must have been growing hot within him. The Greenland of his father's dream had become a reality by then. Consequently Erik's initial resistance to new westward voyages had doubtless diminished. He too must have been concerned about the timber shortage. He may even have concluded that it was time for his eldest son to add something to the luster of the family name by undertaking a spectacular venture on his own account.

Leif's first problem seems to have been to find a suitable ship. The Erikers evidently no longer owned such a vessel. If they had done so, we can assume that Leif would have used it. By this time the shortage of sea-going vessels seems to have become acute throughout the settlements. However, the Herjolfers owned two ships; and since they had no use for more than one of these, Bjarni had doubtless hauled up his own vessel and placed her in storage. He was a good and careful seaman, and he would have taken care of her. She would have deteriorated but little during the intervening years providing she had been kept in a vessel shed and protected from the weather. No doubt Bjarni was glad enough to sell her, since he seems to have had no intention of going to sea again. The Short Saga tells us that after reaching Herjolfsness, he gave up voyaging and remained ashore even after his father died.

It can be assumed that part of the bargain between Leif and Bjarni was that the merchant skipper agreed to supply Leif with information concerning the western lands, including their position and the best route by which they might be reached. It is also likely that some of the thirty-five men Leif hired as his crew were former members of Bjarni's crew.

Having bought his ship, signed on a crew and put in hand the business of getting her seaworthy, Leif would have turned his attention to the navigational problems confronting him. To begin with, he had to decide which of the three lands was to be his destination. The northernmost land would have been quickly eliminated since, according to Bjarni's report, it was utterly worthless. The middle land offered possibilities, but Bjarni could have determined from seaward, without ever having effected a landing, that its forests consisted mostly of conifers, or softwoods. On the other hand, the forests of the southern land would have revealed the presence of deciduous trees, the valuable hardwoods which were in such short supply in Greenland.

Assuming that he made the logical choice and picked the southern land, Leif would next have had to decide how best to reach it. He had a choice between retracing Bjarni's entire route, which would have involved three separate departures, three landfalls, and a number of different courses or of steering a direct course from south Greenland to Newfoundland.

There was probably never any real doubt in Leif's mind as to which route he should follow. Apart from the difficulties inherent in retracing multiple courses and finding multiple landmarks, there was also the matter of pride to be considered. To have chosen to backtrack Bjarni would have smacked of timidity, particularly since Bjarni had been derided as an overly cautious, if not cowardly man.

For these and other reasons listed in Appendix L, I conclude that Leif chose to attempt the direct passage.

Bjarni may have discussed the matter with Leif somewhat in this vein:

"When I first reached that southernmost land I had no way of telling how far west of the settlement I had been blown, although the position of the Guiding Star told me how far south I was. Not knowing my westing, I could not risk laying a direct course for Herjolfsness. That is why I coasted until I had my northing, and could safely sail east.

"But after I reached Herjolfsness, it was not much trouble to work my courses and distances backward so that I could get a fair idea of how far west of Herjolfsness that southern land must lie, and of what the course to it should be. I estimate that it lies between the south and the southwestern airts (south-southwest) and at a distance of not more than six or seven doegr.

"My advice is that you should hold your course in the third portion of the southwest airt (a little west of south-southwest). It is also my advice that you wait for a northeast wind before departing. If you run before such a wind there will be less risk of making leeway and of being set off your course and, too, you will complete your voyage more swiftly.

"This also I can tell you—the mid-part of the southern land lies five and one-half doegr south of Herjolfsness (comparative latitude); but you will have to pass through a great fog-ocean as you approach the land, and then it is likely you will not be able to see the Guiding Star and so will have difficulty in determining how far south you are.

"When the fogs grow thick you must watch the birds of the ocean, and from their kinds and numbers you will know that you are nearing the southern land even though you do not see it."

Bjarni doubtless added a detailed description of the land-falls and the appearance of the land; but since Leif was perhaps accompanied by some of Bjarni's old crew, this information may not have been quite so vital.

With his ship ready for sea Leif had only to wait for a favouring breeze. One morning a gray, cold wind came blowing down across the inland ice. Perhaps Bjarni and Leif stood together on the bleak slopes of the Herjolfsness headland, their faces turned toward the northeast and the rising breeze. Perhaps, too, the older man felt the surge of an old desire within him—the hunger to know the sea-bride once again.

Below him Bjarni would have been able to see the ship—*his* ship once—lying at her moorings in the haven, her crew busy about her decks with last-minute preparations. She was ready. The wind was fair. And the young man beside him—this arrogant son of an arrogant chieftain—was more than ready.

Bjarni may still have been watching when the knorr was rowed out past the haven entrance. Her big sail was swayed up and the slat and bang of her running gear ceased as the sail bellied out and the ship began to pick up way. A bone would have begun to show at her teeth as she ran swiftly off toward the southwest reaches of the unknown ocean. Driving fast before a rising wind, she would have diminished rapidly from Bjarni's view until she slipped from sight, hull down under a gray horizon.

And now, as the saga-men were wont to put it with a succinct finality, Bjarni Herjolfsson and his father are out of this story.

2

VINLAND AND AFTER

11

THE VINLAND VOYAGE

The Saga Tale (c. 995–996)

They made their ship ready for sea and when all was ready they sailed out to sea ... before a northeaster and were out for II [U or V?] doegr before they sighted land.

They sailed to land, reaching an island which lay to the northward of the country and they went up there and looked about them in fine weather. There was dew on the grass and they touched the dew with their hands and brought it to their mouths, and they thought they had never known anything to taste so sweet.

After that they returned to their ship and sailed through the sound which lay between the island and that cape which projected northward from the land itself. They sailed westward around the cape.

There were extensive shoals there [at the place they eventually reached after rounding the cape] at ebb tide and their ship went aground. It was a long way to look from the ship to get sight of the sea.

They were so curious to go ashore that they could not wait until high water floated their ship, but hurried to the land where a river flowed from a lake into the sea.

As soon as the tide rose under their ship they rowed back to her in their boat and took her up the river and so into the lake where they anchored.

They brought their leather bags from the ship and built booths there. Later they decided to stay for the winter and they built a large house.

There was no shortage of salmon in the river or in the lake, and these were larger salmon than they had ever seen before. The qualities of the surrounding country were so good that they believed there would be no shortage of cattle fodder in the wintertime. No frost came in winter and the grass withered only a little.

The length of day and night was more nearly equal than in Greenland or Iceland. Sunset came after Eykarstad [about 3:00 p.m.] and sunrise before Dagmalastad [about 9:00 a.m.] on the shortest day of the year.

When they had built their house Leif said to his followers: "Now I will divide the company into two parts so that the land can be explored. One half of the company shall remain at home while the other half goes exploring, but not farther away than they can return in the evening, and they are not to separate."

For a while they did as he had said and Leif alternately went out with them or stayed home at the hall. Leif was a very tall and vigorous man, a brave fellow to look at, a shrewd man and careful in all things.

One evening word came that a man was missing from one of the [exploration] parties. This was Tyrker, the southerner. Leif was much distressed by this because Tyrker had been with his father and himself a long time and had been very fond of Leif during his childhood.

Leif gave Tyrker's companions a tongue-lashing and ordered an expedition to be made in search of him by twelve men, and went along himself.

They had gone only a short way from the hall when Tyrker came to meet them and was warmly greeted. Tyrker had a big forehead, restless eyes and a freckled face. His stature was low and unprepossessing but he was a man who was foremost in all crafts.

Leif said to him: "Why were you so late foster father of mine, and [why] did you leave your comrades?"

Then Tyrker spoke for a long time in his southern tongue, and rolled his eyes a lot and made wry faces, but they did not understand what he said. Finally he explained in Norse:

"I have walked not much farther than here but I have something interesting to relate. I found vines and grapes."

"Is that true, foster father?" asked Leif.

"Of course it is true," he replied, "for I was born there [in the south] where neither vines nor grapes are scarce."

Then they all went to bed, but in the morning Leif said to his crew:

"Hereafter we shall have two tasks. Every day we will either gather grapes and cut vines, or fell timber to make a cargo for my ship."

They cut a full cargo for the ship and when spring came they made ready and sailed away. And Leif gave a name to the land, in keeping with its products, and called it Vinland.

[SOURCES: The first paragraph consists of edited excerpts from the Greenlanders Story. The balance is an unaltered quotation from the same source. The original text, together with the reasons why an edited version is to be preferred, will be found in Appendix L.]

LEIF'S DEEP-SEA PASSAGE from Greenland to Bjarni's southern land seems to have been comparatively uneventful. The northeaster described in the saga account was doubtless one of the famous "nine-day winds," which would have meant that the knorr was running free most of the way, and so would have been less likely to stray from her course than if she had been forced to beat against headwinds. It would also account for the rapidity of the voyage. Furthermore, a northeaster is not generally a fog

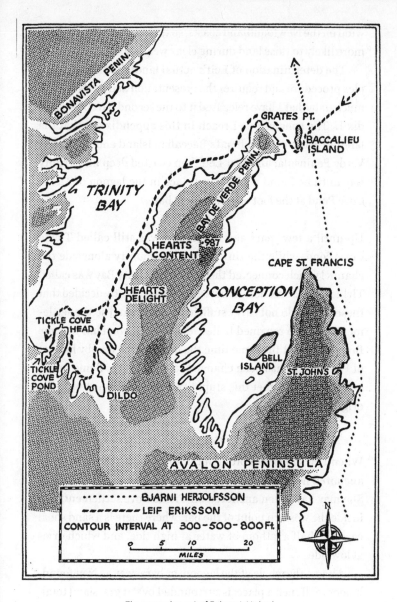

The approaches to Leif Eriksson's Vinland

The Vinland Voyage 139

wind on the Newfoundland coasts, so that Leif would have been more likely to raise land during clear weather.

The determination of Leif's actual landfall is such a complex procedure and requires the presentation and analysis of so much data that I have relegated it to the second part of Appendix L. The conclusions I reach in this appendix are that the landfall was Newfoundland's Baccalieu Island and the Bay de Verde Peninsula; and that Leif then coasted deep into Trinity Bay until he found a wintering place in the lagoon of Tickle Cove Pond at the foot of Tickle Cove Bay.

Up until a few years ago this haven was still called Tickle Cove Pond, while the tiny fishing community alongside the channel which connected the lagoon to Trinity Bay was called Tickle Cove. Some doltish bureaucrat has recently decided that these names do not carry sufficient dignity, and so the settlement has been renamed Bellevue, while the pond has become Broad Lake. At the same time the name of the nearby hamlet of Famish Gut has been changed to Fair Haven. Being under no obligation to abet this stupidity, I will continue to use the original names.

THE SITE

When Leif's men had brought their knorr into the haven they anchored her temporarily until they could explore the place. She may have been anchored off Tickle Cove settlement, just inside the western point of the bar, where there is a sand shoal carrying half a fathom of water at high tide, and which dries at low tide.

Almost the whole of the lagoon, or barasway as Newfoundlanders call such a place, is surrounded by flat grassland totalling something over three hundred acres in extent, where large

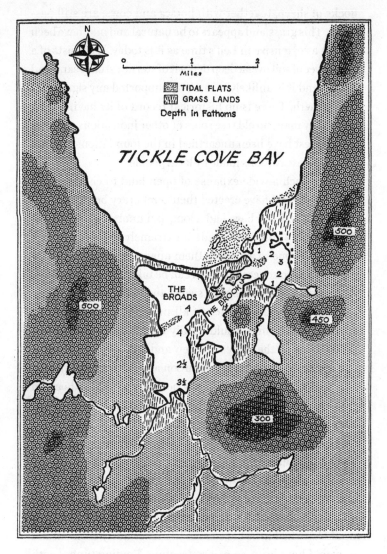

Leif Eriksson's Vinland

flocks of sheep, together with horses and cows, are still pastured. This grassland appears to be natural and may have been almost as extensive in Leif's time as it is today. It consists of a light layer of soil over a deep deposit of sterile estuary sand and gravel, and it is unlikely that it ever supported any significant tree growth. There is no historical record of its having been cleared by man; no old tree roots or other indications of a vanished forest have been unearthed in the foundations, ditches and other excavations made by local people.

With such a wide expanse of open land to choose from, the Norse could have erected their temporary booths almost anywhere and still have had a long and unobstructed field of view which would have made it extremely difficult for anything or anyone to approach them unawares. That this was a matter of deep concern to them can be taken for granted. Men who themselves lived by the sword and who, moreover, were convinced of the existence of all manner of monsters and supernatural beings would hardly have been likely to pitch their camps on the shores of a new and unknown world without taking every possible precaution against being surprised. One logical place for temporary booths would have been on the seaward bar. This grass-grown sand and gravel spit would have been secure against attack except along the narrow and easily defended stretch of beach which ran west to join the mainland.

After assessing the qualities of their haven, and finding it to their taste, the Norse decided to make it their winter headquarters and so they set about building a house, or booth. This would have had to be big enough to shelter thirty-six men, and so would have been no mean structure. Finding timber with which to build it would have been no problem. The forests which then pushed up to the edge of the grassland must have been extraordinarily lush and heavy. As recently as 1920 the timber trees which could still be found and felled at the head of the various arms of Trinity Bay were among the biggest and best to be found anywhere in Newfoundland. Leif's major problem may have been to find trees small enough for easy handling.

The choice of a house site would have depended to some extent on whether Leif had been able to satisfy himself that there was little or no danger from local denizens—animal, human or supernatural. If he felt secure enough he might have chosen to build on the mainland under the lee of the high hill which lies just behind the present settlement of Tickle Cove. Here the Norse would have found good shelter from winter winds; the forest would have been close enough so that wood gathering would have been no problem; and there would have been an excellent source of fresh water in two small streams that even now seldom freeze in wintertime. It is a notable fact that where one set of human beings choose to build their homes is very often the place selected by the next group, and the next after that. At any rate there has been continuous human habitation of the east side of Tickle Cove Pond for at least the last three hundred years.

The lack of any reference to native peoples at Leif's haven is particularly noteworthy. At that period in history most of the Labrador coast, together with the west coast of the Great Northern Peninsula of Newfoundland, was still occupied by Dorset Inuit. The rest of Newfoundland, except for the Avalon Peninsula, was populated by Beothuk, or proto-Beothuk. For some reason which we cannot as yet explain, but which was probably connected with their dual caribou-sea food economy, the Beothuk seem to have seldom crossed the narrow neck which connects the Avalon Peninsula to the main body of the island, and which also separates Trinity Bay from Placentia Bay.[43] At Tickle Cove Leif would have found no Dorsets, and it is unlikely that he would have encountered Beothuks, or found signs of them. On the other hand if his Vinland had been located at any of the alternative sites, such as the northeastern bays, he could hardly have avoided seeing signs of either Dorsets or Beothuks.

If Leif *had* met any natives, it is nearly certain that the saga would have mentioned the fact. Meetings with natives loom large in all subsequent accounts of Norse voyages to Newfoundland and Labrador. The absence of any mention of a native population, present or suspected, in connection with Leif's voyage provides strong corroborative evidence supporting the identification of Trinity Bay as Vinland.

THE CLIMATE

A problem which has bothered many authors and which has cast a shadow over the acceptability of any Vinland site north of Cape Hatteras is contained in the saga phrase: "No frost came in winter and the grass withered only a little."

There seem to be three possible ways of resolving this difficulty in connection with Tickle Cove Pond.

In the first place we can assume (as many others have done) that the meaning of the translation, or the text itself, is in error and that it should read: "*little* frost came in winter and the grass withered only a little." Another possible solution may be found by a comparison with a similar phrase in the descriptions of conditions at Karlsefni's Hop (see Chapter 21). "There was no snow and all of the livestock lived by grazing." The similarity of these two descriptions suggests that the author of the Greenlanders Story may have borrowed the essence of the phrase from the original of the Erik the Red Saga.

A case can be made for the acceptance of either of these solutions; but the saga account may be perfectly accurate as it stands. Because it is situated fifty-five miles in from the northern headlands, Tickle Cove remains almost unaffected by the cold Labrador Current, which sweeps across the mouth of Trinity Bay. But it is influenced by the weather of Placentia Bay, which is separated from it by a neck of land only six or seven miles wide. Placentia Bay, and the whole south coast of Newfoundland, has a much milder climate than the northeastern coast, since it is open to warm southerly winds blowing in across the Gulf Stream. Tickle Cove receives almost the full benefits of these mild southerly winds while at the same time remaining largely free of the fog which usually comes with such winds and which greatly reduces the amount of sunshine in Placentia Bay and on the south coast generally. Crop-sprouting times at settlements near the bottom of Trinity Bay average two to four weeks earlier than at settlements well up the bay shores. Snowfall is generally light at Tickle Cove, and frequent winter thaws tend to keep the ground snow-free much of the time. Winter temperatures seldom go more than a few degrees below freezing point, and during some winters there is very little frost at all.

These are the conditions which prevail now. When we consider how much better weather conditions were during the Little Climatic Optimum we see that there is a strong likelihood that the Greenlanders Story report of a frost-free winter may be a sober statement of observed fact. Even if it is not strictly accurate (the Norse had no thermometers), the degree of exaggeration need be very small.

It is a widespread misapprehension that Newfoundland has a cold, even subarctic climate. The truth is that the average winter temperatures of the southern and eastern coastal regions of the island are much higher than those of any other place in eastern Canada, and even of most parts of the New England states as far south as northern Massachusetts.

THE LATITUDE

A great deal of scholarly effort has been expended in attempts to establish a Vinland latitude from the saga statement that sunset at Vinland came after Eykarstad and sunrise came before Dagmalastad, on the shortest day of the year. These terms do not refer to clock times, since the Norse of this period had no clocks. They apparently refer to the azimuth directions of the sun at sunrise and sunset. The astronomer H. Geelmuyden (*Arkiv for Norisk Fiologri*, III, 128) determined the azimuth value of Eykarstad from an old Icelandic law book called the *Gragas*. He concluded that the direction was south 52½ degrees west. He then worked out the latitude where the sun would set in this direction on the shortest day of the year during the early eleventh century. The result was 49 degrees 55 minutes.

Many other attempts have been made along similar lines, and the results generally give a latitude between 46 and 52 degrees north latitude. The latitude of Tickle Cove Pond is 47 degrees 37 minutes.

THE GRAPEVINES

We come now to the one element in the Vinland description which has caused more dissension than anything else contained in all the sagas. This is the reference to vines and grapes. The antagonists whose arguments have raged (and continue to rage) about this point fall roughly into three camps.

In the first are those who believe that Leif did find authentic wild grapes. Because wild grapes no longer grow farther north than southern New Brunswick, these people insist that Vinland must be looked for south of New Brunswick, possibly as far south as Florida.

The second camp includes those who think that the Norse words vin and vinber (vine and vine-berries) do not refer to grapes at all, but should be identified with various kinds of wild berries from which wine could have been made, thereby greatly extending the northern limits within which Vinland can be sought.

Those in the third camp believe that the word vin as it was originally used in the sagas, had nothing to do with grapes or wine or berries, but was an ancient Norse word for pastures; hence, they say, Vinland should be translated as Pastureland.

As far as Tickle Cove Pond is concerned, the entire argument is academic.

Tickle Cove Pond possesses excellent pastures, and evidently did in Leif's time. If Vinland means Pastureland, Tickle Cove merits the name.

The whole of Newfoundland, and the Trinity Bay district in particular, abounds in wild berries of which wine can be made, including all the species which scholars have suggested might be identified as the saga wine-berries.

Finally, there were wild grapes in Newfoundland, and in quantity, until as late as the middle of the seventeenth century.

This last is a statement which will not please those who have insisted that Leif must have landed in New England, and whose best argument has always been that wild grapes could never have been present in the northeastern maritime regions of Canada. These authorities believe that Cartier's report of wild grapes on the Ile d'Orleans in the St. Lawrence River, at latitude 47 degrees, was a latter-day forgery, and that the same thing applies to records of wild grapes having been found in the Magdalen Islands in the St. Lawrence Gulf at latitude 47 degrees 30 minutes.

Evidence of the existence of wild grapes in Newfoundland comes from several sources. Foremost among these is a journal kept by a Plymouth surgeon named James Yonge who made four voyages to Newfoundland between 1662 and 1670 as a surgeon to the English fishing fleet. Yonge later became a Fellow of the Royal Society and published a large number of scientific papers and books, including three medical textbooks which were in wide use for many years after his death.

He was a keen observer of natural history, and his journal contains many notes on birds, mammals, fishes and plants— particularly those of Newfoundland. His identifications and comments have been checked by modern botanists and zoologists and have been found to be extremely accurate.

Yonge also travelled widely in the Mediterranean and was a surgeon on a ship engaged in the wine and raisin trade, so he was not likely to have been in much doubt as to what grapes looked like. In describing the animals and plants on the Avalon Peninsula, of which Trinity Bay is a part, Yonge had this to say: "Here are beaver, otter, and deer plentiful; for fruits strawberry, raspberries, whorts, and wild grapes incredible."[44]

Further references to the occurrence of wild grapes in Newfoundland are found in L. A. Anspach's *History of the Island of Newfoundland*, published in 1827. Anspach quotes one Patrick Gordon in a work published in London in 1772 as stating that those parts of Newfoundland held by the French (of which Placentia Bay was one of the main regions) produced wild grapevines in abundance. It is also stated that a series of severe winters in the late eighteenth century destroyed the wild grapevines in Newfoundland and that they never reappeared. This is consistent with recent climatological studies, which show that there was a period of very adverse weather in the western regions of the North Atlantic beginning about the middle of the seventeenth century.

There is therefore nothing surprising in the existence of wild grapes in Newfoundland in the tenth century. This was the period when the Little Climatic Optimum dominated the entire North Atlantic region. Climatologists have shown that between 1000 and 1200, vineyards in western Europe were being cultivated 4 to 5 degrees of latitude farther north than their present limits. This is a distance of 240–300 nautical miles. The present northern limit of wild grapes on the eastern American seaboard is about 45 degrees north latitude, or only 157 nautical miles south of Tickle Cove Pond.

One further point merits attention both in this connection and with reference to the general excellence of the Tickle Cove area. At the present time the districts at the bottom of Trinity and Bonavista bays are the only places in Newfoundland where fruit is produced commercially. Damsons, apples and blue plums are commonly grown. The climate of most of Newfoundland is suitable to these and other domestic fruits, but the orchards of Bonavista and Trinity bays exist because the bottomlands of both bays contain the best soil to be found in all eastern and central Newfoundland. These are the same soils which once produced the luxuriant hardwood forest which was still in its virginal condition in Leif's time.

THE PRODIGAL LAND

Tickle Cove on a summer's day in the twentieth century is as lovely a place as one could wish to see. It could have been no less attractive in the tenth century. We can imagine Leif's men rowing out on the Broad to fish for sea trout and salmon; or see them walking across the wide meadows, marvelling at the tall grass swaying about their knees and thinking greedily of what they could do with land like this. As the tide fell some of them might have gone to the great curving sickle of the outer beach to gather clams, blue and brown mussels and other shellfish for roasting or boiling over great open fires. Dry firewood—a luxury in Greenland—would have been present in huge quantities, windrowed above high-tide level on the beach.

If they chose they could have taken their boats out through the tickle into the waters of the open bay, where great pods of pilot whales followed the squid and herring almost to the landwash. It would have been no trick to kill as many of these harmless mammals as they desired. The Norse of Leif's time, who are known to have been expert whalers, might have used a method familiar to their ancient ancestors. Rowing small boats, and making a great racket by shouting and water splashing, the old Norwegians used to drive panic-stricken schools of the smaller species of whales into the ends of bays where the beasts would strand themselves in scores or hundreds. If Leif's men did this at Tickle Cove they would only have been anticipating a whale fishery which still flourishes there and which still employs this ancient technique. But whether they bothered to go whaling or not, the Norse would have been impressed by the vast numbers of pilots, or potheads as they are known in Newfoundland, which crowd into the bay—a limitless supply of meat and oil waiting to be harvested.

The sea hereabouts was full of wealth, but the land was by no means niggardly. As is attested by the writings of the first arrivals in the colonial period, this part of Newfoundland was once alive with caribou. The Norse would have been familiar with the beasts, for they were found in Greenland too; but they probably had never imagined that caribou could exist in such numbers as inhabited this new land. Even today, after four centuries of continuous and heavy slaughter, it is still possible to see a thousand caribou in the course of a few days' excursion into the isolated central parts of the island.

Black bears, wolves, foxes, otters, beaver and martens would also have been abundant; and the protected waters of the Broad and of the nearby lakes would have held great flocks of ducks.

As summer waned and the berries and fruits began to ripen, Tyrker and the others would have found much more than wild grapes to amaze them with the prodigality of this land. The berry barrens on the spine of the isthmus between Trinity and Placentia bays would have been hazed with a purple wash of blueberries. Cloud-berries, those oily groundfruits beloved of all northern races, would have spread a golden glow over the surface of the muskeg bogs, interspersed with crimson bursts of cranberries. The list is almost endless: raspberries, crowberries, whortleberries, loganberries, elderberries, squashberries—all these, and more, still grow abundantly in the Trinity Bay region. And on the edge of the forests there would have been wild cherry and hazelnut trees, the fruit of both of which might have been foreign to the Norse, but most acceptable for all of that.

And the forests! Men who were used to the stunted birch thickets of Iceland and Greenland would have marveled at yellow birch trees (witch hazel, the Newfoundlanders call it) growing to heights of over a hundred feet and measuring three feet across the stump; or white birches almost as large, if somewhat less numerous. They would soon have discovered, as their axes lost their edges on the witch hazel, that here was a hardwood almost as tough as oak.

The forests were—and still are—of mixed composition. Those at the bottom of Trinity Bay include two kinds of maples as well as birch. Of conifers there are white and red pine, red, white and black spruce, balsam fir and tamarack. There was wood here to build countless ships, and the proper kind of wood for every part of a vessel: tough tamarack for ribs, witch hazel for keels and planking, and tall pines for spars and yards. There was, in fact, enough timber in this region to keep a major shipbuilding industry alive through more than three centuries of later European occupation—an industry which is not dead even now. Wooden ships are still being built at the yard in nearby Clarenville.

Each evening as the exploring parties returned to camp they would have brought reports of new and greater riches which this land held, until the day came when Leif put an end to their explorations and ordered them to get down to the serious business of turning these potential riches into usable wealth.

Felling, trimming and hewing a shipload of hardwood would have been a heavy task for these men, equipped as they were with indifferently tempered iron axes and adzes. There would have been little enough time that winter for wandering about, or for anything except hard labour. Perhaps small parties were occasionally sent off hunting for venison, but the majority of the crew must have worked like slaves at lumbering.

When the spring came the knorr must have been loaded deep with as valuable a cargo as ever set sail for Greenland from either east or west. Leif, that "shrewd and vigorous" man, would not have frittered away his opportunities.

The ship doubtless carried other articles of local produce, including dried berries and grapes, for raisins were known to the Norse. It may be that the tale of filling one of the boats with such dried fruits was no exaggeration, for a boat would have made a good enough receptacle, chocked down on deck and covered with hide tarpaulins.

Grapevines would have been of great value too, for the

planks of Norse ships were not spiked to the timbers but were bound to them with withes—and wild grapevines make first-rate withes.

There is an impression implicit in the saga accounts that Leif's feelings for Vinland were peculiarly ambivalent. Although he must have valued the place as a source of wealth and also for the renown which came to him as a result of his voyage there, he never made any attempt to return to it; and it seems clear from his subsequent actions that he did not wish to see it settled. In taking this stand he may have been perpetuating Erik's assumed antipathy toward the development of new and distant lands which might have tended to drain away the Greenland settlers—for Leif was heir apparent to the chieftaincy of Greenland. Or perhaps, having discovered his personal Eldorado, he was jealously concerned to prevent anyone else from sharing its riches. He was a shrewd man, was Leif the son of Erik.

Whatever his motives may have been, Leif not only failed to return to Vinland himself but, so it appears, did nothing to help others reach it after him.

But if Leif wished to keep Vinland in limbo, it is unlikely that his men shared his feelings. As the knorr ran down the tidal river into the open waters of Trinity Bay on a morning in late spring or early summer, many of them would have looked back with hungry eyes at this place which of all the places they had ever known must have most nearly resembled a paradise on earth.

Through the years ahead their nostalgic descriptions of the land they could never possess for themselves did much to buttress the legend of that country which Leif called Vinland—but which eventually became known across the northern world as Vinland the Good.

12

LEIF'S NORWAY VOYAGE

The Saga Tale (c. 996–997)

Now they sailed to sea and got a fair wind until they saw the mountains under the glaciers of Greenland. Then one of the men asked Leif: "Why do you steer the ship so far off the wind?"

Leif replied: "I can take care of my course [lit: I take care of my rudder]; but there is something besides that [attracting my attention]. Don't you see anything remarkable?"

The men answered that they saw nothing unusual.

"I do not know," said Leif, "if I see a ship or a reef."

Now the men saw it and said it was a reef, but Leif had sharper vision than they did so that he distinguished men on the islet.

"We will beat to windward," said Leif, "so as to approach them, if they want to be found by us and need assistance, but if they are not peaceably inclined we will have the advantage [of position] and they will not."

Then they sailed up to the reef, let fall their sail, cast anchor, and put out another small boat which they had with them.

Tyrker [who went in the boat] asked who was the leader of the [shipwrecked] party; and the leader replied that he was called Thorer and was of Norse descent. "But what is your leader's name?" he asked.

Leif told him his name.

"Art thou the son of Erik the Red of Brattalid?"

Leif replied that he was. "And now," said Leif, "I invite you all to come aboard my ship; but bring as much of your goods as my ship will hold."

They accepted his terms. The ship was then sailed into Eriksfiord, to Brattalid. They unloaded the ship and Leif took Thorer, Gudrid his wife, and three of his men, to live with him; but he got other quarters for the rest of Thorer's crew as well as for his own.

Leif saved fifteen men from the islet. He was afterwards called Leif the Lucky. He was now well off both as to riches and honour.

[SOURCE: The Greenlanders Story]

When sixteen winters had passed since Erik the Red went out to take land in Greenland, Leif Eriksson went to Norway. When Leif sailed from Greenland that summer he was driven out of his course and came to the Hebrides. It was late in the season before they got fair winds again and so they remained there far into the summer.

Leif fell in love with a certain woman there whose name was Thorgunna. She was a woman of fine family and Leif believed she had supernatural wisdom.

When Leif was preparing to depart, Thorgunna begged to go with him. Leif asked her if she had the approval of her kinsmen and she replied that she did not care about that.

Leif told her he did not consider it a wise move to abduct so high-born a woman, in a foreign country, and "we so few in numbers."

"It is by no means certain that you will find yours is the best decision," warned Thorgunna.

"Nevertheless I intend to stick to it," Leif answered.

"Then," said Thorgunna, "I must tell you that I am not the only one concerned, for I am pregnant, and you are responsible. I foresee that I shall give birth to a male child, and though you are indifferent, I will rear this child and send him to you in Greenland when he is of an age to take his place with other men. And I foresee that you will get as much profit from this son as you deserve, considering the nature of our parting. Moreover, I mean to come to Greenland myself before I die."

Then Leif gave her a gold finger-ring, a Greenland wadmal cloak, and a belt of walrus ivory.

The boy later came to Greenland and his name was Thorgils. Leif acknowledged his paternity. Some men say this same Thorgils reached Iceland in the summer before the Froda-Wonders. When this Thorgils was in Greenland there seemed to be something not altogether natural about him, before the end came.

Leif and his companions now sailed away from the Hebrides and arrived at Drontheim [in Norway] in the autumn, at the time King Olaf Tryggvason came from Halgoland. Leif laid his ship up at Nidaros and went at once to visit King Olaf.

He was well received by the King, who believed he could see in Leif a man of great possibilities. The King expounded the [Christian] faith to him, as he did to all heathen men who came to visit him, and the King dealt gently with Leif. Leif and all his shipmates were then christened and they remained with the King all winter and were well treated.

[SOURCES: Erik the Red Saga, Karlsefni Saga and the Short Saga]

LEIF'S RETURN

THE ACCOUNT OF LEIF'S homeward passage and his rescue of Thorer not only throws light on Leif's character. It also provides further indications that he made his Vinland voyage direct from southern Greenland.

Thorer was evidently a Norwegian trader. From a later reference in the Greenlanders Story it appears that he had sailed from Norway for Greenland with a cargo which included timber. Since he still had his cargo aboard when he was wrecked we can assume that he had not yet reached the Eastern Settlements. In all probability he had rounded Cape Farewell and was beating his way up the coast when his ship was driven onto an off-lying islet or reef and wrecked.

The skerry where his ship went ashore most likely belonged to the large group of islets and reefs which runs for some fifteen miles on a line about ten miles offshore between Herjolfsness and Ketilsfiord. These, together with a smaller group off Hrafnsfiord, are the only offshore skerries near the Eastern Settlements, and the saga makes it clear that Thorer was wrecked well offshore. The Herjolfsness skerries are the ones which a ship inbound from the east would have been most likely to strike. Thorer may well have been making for the Herjolfsness haven when he came to grief.

If we combine this identification of the skerries with the saga description of Leif's approach to Greenland, "they sailed to sea and got a fair wind until they saw the mountains under the glaciers of Greenland," it seems clear that Leif made his landfall while steering northeasterly, a direct course from Vinland to south Greenland.

Considering that he was returning to his own land and to a country dominated by his own family, the caution Leif displayed in approaching the shipwreck seems curious. Either social conditions in Greenland were a good deal more disturbed than most historians have believed, or else Viking pirates had already become a threat on the Greenland coasts. Pirates from Norway and the Outer Islands are known to have been raiding Iceland about this time, and the Floamanna Saga records their presence off the Eastern Settlements of Greenland about the year 1004; so this may well be the explanation for Leif's display of prudence.

When Leif was satisfied that the wrecked mariners were bona-fide traders he offered to rescue them; but he instructed them to bring aboard as much of their goods as his already heavily laden ship could carry. He would not have been referring to Thorer's cargo of lumber, but to such things as ironware and manufactured goods. Thorer's people apparently understood this to mean that Leif would keep the goods, either as salvage or as recompense for saving their lives. This may have been one of the normal mores of the times; but on the other hand it may be an indication of how shrewd Leif was.

With the castaways on board, Leif bore up for Eriksfiord and ran down its familiar waters until he came to his moorings off the complex of buildings at Brattalid.

That would have been a proud homecoming and a memorable one. Not only had Leif reached Bjarni's fabled land but he had overwintered there successfully. He had obtained a lading of timber and other goods of great value there, and had then made a good passage home during which he had topped off his cargo with an assortment of Norwegian trade goods. It was little wonder that he received the nickname Lucky as a consequence. The voyage had been a singularly prosperous one, bringing him, in the words of the saga, "both riches and honour."

Leif was now well on his way to becoming a made man, and it is not likely that he would have been inclined to rest on his laurels. His ambitions would have been whetted by the successful Vinland voyage, but Greenland offered him little opportunity to increase his fame. The road to personal power was blocked by the unyielding figure of his father.

Erik was not yet an old man and was still exercising vigorous control over his family and over the Greenland settlements. The saga records demonstrate that Norse fathers were seldom prepared to relinquish their patriarchal powers to their sons before senility forced the issue; while their sons do not always appear to have allowed filial loyalties to stand in the way of their struggles to climb into their fathers' boots before the elder men were ready to take them off.

Erik may have been proud of Leif's exploits, but we can believe that he took a jaundiced view of Leif's ambition. The events of the next few years suggest that Leif, for his part, did what he could to unseat his father and to usurp his position.

THE RISE OF OLAF TRYGGVASON

While Leif had been making local history in the west, an illegitimate descendant of King Harold Fairhair had been making a different kind of history in the east. In 995 Olaf Tryggvason, a sea-Viking of dubious repute, deserted his brother-in-law, the King of Denmark, during an attack on England and made a sudden assault on the seaward coast of Norway, which was then under the Viceroyship of Jarl Haakon of Lade acting for the King of Denmark.

Olaf slaughtered Haakon and then busied himself with conquering the country for himself and for God. Olaf was a Christian convert, not because he had any regard for the Christian ethic but because he seems to have been one of the earliest of the north European rulers to have realized how useful Christianity could be to an autocratic monarch.

His methods of Christianizing Norway were ferocious but effective. Recalcitrant pagans of ordinary rank were summarily butchered or burned in their homes. If they were of sufficient importance to justify an effort being made to convert them, they were sometimes treated to the ordeal of the snake. The mouth-piece of a metal war-horn was forced well down the victim's gullet; a snake, usually an adder, was placed in the bell and a lid was clamped over it. The horn was then heated until the tortured snake tried to escape by crawling down the victim's throat.

Tales of the prowess of this imaginative king were quick to spread through the Scandinavian world. Skalds began singing his praises to such purpose that despite his brief reign, the Saga of Olaf Tryggvason is one of the most famous accounts of the achievements of a Norwegian king of the Viking age.

Word of King Olaf's brisk exploits doubtless reached Green-land in the summer of 996 with Thorer and his crew. The recounting of the mighty deeds of slaughter, burning and rapine which Olaf was performing would have stirred the hearts of young men of Viking character even in this far distant outpost of the Norse, and we can believe that Leif listened in jealous admiration.[45]

Having spent the winter as the guest of the Greenlanders, Thorer the Norwegian would have been anxious to return to Norway in the spring, but he had no ship of his own and he may not have had the wherewithal with which to purchase a vessel, even if the Greenlanders had had one to sell—which they probably did not.

But Leif was the owner of a sea-going ship. Consequently we can assume that Thorer would have used his best arguments to persuade Leif that the young man ought to make a voyage to Norway, perhaps offering to be the pilot and to supply the services of his own men as part of the crew, in exchange for a passage east. Thorer may have had an entree into King Olaf's court, but even if he did not he could doubtless have arranged for Leif to be received there. We can readily imagine him plying Leif with stories of the glory of the court; of Olaf himself; and of the honours a brave adventurer like Leif might expect to receive from such a king.

Leif would have been easy to persuade. Now that he had become a man of wealth and substance in his own right, he would have been able to appear at Olaf's court as someone of importance, not as a mere homespun rustic from the edge of nowhere. Moreover, he had a tale to tell of such strange adventures in the unknown Western Ocean as would have gained him a respectful hearing even among royalty.

There could also have been a hard practical purpose to goad Leif into undertaking such a voyage. He may have hoped to win acceptance as one of Olaf's liegemen, an honour which would have vastly increased both his prestige and his power in Greenland after his return.

The time was wholly propitious for such a venture since Leif not only had a well-found and well-tried ship but could count on Thorer's skill and experience as pilot and sailing master on the long and difficult voyage to Norway. Relations between Leif and his father may have already become sufficiently tense so that the idea of a Norway voyage for Leif might have seemed attractive to both of them.

So much for speculation. The fact is that Leif did make a voyage to Norway. Furthermore, almost all authorities are agreed in believing that he sailed a direct course from southern Greenland, bypassing Iceland. This in itself suggests that he was accompanied by a skilled pilot and navigator who was familiar with the route.

THORGUNNA'S STORY

The dating of this voyage has never been satisfactorily resolved, and since a knowledge of the correct date is important in establishing an intelligible chronology, I must reluctantly digress.

Happily, this digression also enables me to tell the story of Leif's mistress, Thorgunna.

Although most authorities state that the voyage was made in the year 1000, the last year of King Olaf's life, I can find no convincing grounds to support such an assumption. It seems more likely that it was made about 997.

The Short Saga, which seems to be the oldest and therefore the most reliable recension of the lost Old Erik Saga, tells us that Leif arrived in Norway when King Olaf had just come down from Halgoland. Halgoland—Land of the Northern Lights— was in the northern part of Norway, and Olaf seems to have visited this district early in his reign, when he was still actively engaged in unifying his new kingdom by fire and sword. Nevertheless, the actual date of his visit to Halgoland is disputed. The Saga of Olaf Tryggvason states that it was made in the spring of the year following the death of Eyvind Cheekrift, and some scholars believe that this man died in 999. If this was the case, Olaf would have had to go to Halgoland in the year 1000, which was the year of his death when he committed suicide by jumping overboard during a naval battle with the Danes and Swedes in the Baltic.

Perhaps the matter can be settled by another quotation from the same source. The Short Saga tells us that Leif undertook his Norway voyage sixteen years[46] after Erik the Red went out to "settle," "take land," "go land-seeking," in Greenland (the three variants are three translations of the original by three different scholars). If the disputed word is taken to mean that Leif sailed sixteen years after Erik led the colonists to Greenland, then the year of his voyage to Norway would have had to be 1001, by which time Olaf was dead. On the other hand, if the word is to be translated as meaning that Leif sailed sixteen years after Erik first *went out* to Greenland, there is no problem, for this would date his voyage at 997.

Another event which seems to show that the voyage was made about 997 is Leif's affair with the Hebridean woman Thorgunna. Having seduced her and made her pregnant, Leif got out while the going was good.

We hear no more about Thorgunna in the sagas dealing with the western voyages. We are told only that a son was born to her and that, true to her word, she saw to it that he went to Greenland to join his father there. We are also told that this child, whose name was Thorgils, reached Iceland the summer before the Froda-Wonders. The Froda-Wonders took place during the winter of 1000–1001, which would mean that Thorgils reached Iceland by the year 1000.

The Eyrbyggja Saga tells us that a Hebridean woman named Thorgunna arrived in Iceland in the summer of 1000 aboard a ship from Dublin and went to lodge temporarily at the farmstead of Froda on the western coast. This woman was wealthy, high-born, and a most extraordinary person. She was strangely gifted with supernatural abilities. The description of her is in such close accord with what we know of Leif's Thorgunna, and the dates involving the child Thorgils tally so exactly, that we conclude that the two Thorgunnas were one and the same woman.

Thorgunna died at Froda in the summer of 1000. She left specific instructions as to what was to be done with her possessions, including a gold ring and a scarlet cloak which sound like two of the gifts given her by Leif. The acquisitive mistress of Froda disobeyed these instructions, with macabre and catastrophic consequences.

Following the appearance of a "weird moon" the members of the household began to sicken. One by one they died; but their ghosts remained about the homestead to haunt the living.

All told, eighteen members of the household died, and the grim visitation was only brought to an end when Thorgunna's last wishes were belatedly carried out. The survivors not unnaturally believed that this terrifying siege was due to Thorgunna's supernatural powers; but we can deduce that the Froda household was afflicted by an epidemic disease which was doubtless introduced by Thorgunna from Ireland, and of which she was the first to die.

According to what the Karlsefni and the Erik the Red sagas have to tell us, Thorgils was eventually sent on to join his father in Greenland; but of his subsequent history we know nothing except that he also was believed to have had something unnatural about him, something presumably inherited from his mother.

The fact that the Erik the Red and the Karlsefni sagas deliberately link the arrival of Thorgils in Iceland with the Froda-Wonders, which were brought about by Thorgunna's death, instead of saying that he arrived there in the year that Christianity was adopted in Iceland, which was the usual saga method of pinpointing the year 1000, seems to be a final confirmation of the single identification of the two Thorgunnas.

Using the combined sources, we have enough information to be able to trace Thorgunna's actions with some assurance of accuracy. To start with we know that Thorgils was conceived in the summer of Leif's visit to the Hebrides, and consequently he would have been born the following spring. Even if Thorgunna had wished to take him to Greenland as soon as possible, she would hardly have risked the life of so young a baby by attempting to take him on a long ocean voyage in an open knorr in the summer of the year during the spring of which the child was born. Since there was no winter navigation to Iceland—and little if any between the Hebrides and Dublin—she would have had to wait until the following summer before setting out on her voyage.

This would indicate that Leif's visit to the Hebrides could not have taken place later than 998, with 997 being an even more likely date.

Thorgunna must have been an indomitable and greatly courageous person. Hers was an odyssey which few lone women would have dared under any circumstances, let alone encumbered by a small child. If death had not intervened she would undoubtedly have found passage from Iceland to Greenland. One wonders what her reception would have been at the hands of the man who had deserted her.

LEIF'S VOYAGE

If we assume that Leif heard about Olaf's usurpation of the Norwegian throne in the summer of 996 from Thorer, or even from some other trader, the rest follows logically enough. As soon as navigation became possible in 997 he set sail for Norway.

We have few details of the voyage except that the ship encountered bad weather. It must have been very bad to set her so far to the south of her intended course that she reached the Hebrides; but the summer of 997 was remarkable for its foul weather. Much of the fishery was a failure in Greenland that year because men could not put to sea. A number of fishermen who tried it were lost in the attempt. Thorbjorn Vifilsson, en route from Iceland to Greenland, very nearly lost his ship, which was blown helplessly about for several weeks. Another vessel, belonging to Thorgisl Orrabeinsfostri, and engaged on the same voyage, was blown ashore and wrecked far up the Greenland or Baffin Island coast.

After the interlude in the Hebrides, Leif managed to make Drontheim and from there went on to visit Olaf. The record of this meeting has many important overtones. The king, so the saga tells us, "was gentle with Leif"; by which we are to understand that he did not use a heated horn or a sword to bring the Christian message into Leif's pagan heart. It may also mean that Leif was an easy convert, having realized—as Olaf had done before him—the potentialities for the extension and consolidation of personal power which existed in an alliance with a strong and closely integrated religious organization.

All of the saga sources agree that Olaf treated Leif with great consideration, and the king's motives for this are not hard to deduce. Olaf knew that Leif was the son of the Greenland chieftain, and he doubtless guessed, if he was not told directly, that Leif's ambitions pointed impatiently at that chieftainship. He would have seen that in Leif he had at hand an instrument with which he might be able to forge a link between Norway and Greenland, a link which would eventually have had the effect of making that far-distant land subject to King Olaf Tryggvason.

So Leif wintered at the court, where he was held in high esteem, and where he gathered to himself still more of the appurtenances of power and honour with which, in due course, he could put his father's mettle to the test.

13

THE ODYSSEY OF
THORGISL ORRABEINSFOSTRI

THE EXCEPTIONALLY STORMY weather of 997, which had driven Leif so far off course, brought hard times to several other voyagers. One of these was a man named Thorgisl Orrabeinsfostri (Scarleg's Fosterson), who had received an invitation from his old friend Erik the Red to come out from Iceland to Greenland, either for a visit or to join the new colony there.

The storms which gave Leif so much difficulty dealt even more harshly with Thorgisl. After a long time his ship was driven ashore and wrecked on an unknown coast. The location of the shipwreck has been a matter for much dispute. Most authors have claimed it was on the northeast coast of Greenland; but if this was the case, we need an explanation as to why the survivors spent four or five years trying to work their way to the Eastern Settlement instead of returning to Iceland, which would have been the simplest way out of their difficulties.

We conclude that Thorgisl missed Greenland (as so many others did before and afterwards) and, as a climax to his efforts to reach the Eastern Settlement, was blown north through Davis Strait, to be ultimately wrecked somewhere on the Baffin Island coast to the northward of the Cumberland Peninsula. The evidence supporting this conclusion is to be found in the saga text, and I have commented on it in the various endnotes.

Apart from the fact that Thorgisl's saga deserves a place in any book dealing with the western voyages, it is also the most detailed and explicit account of the hazards of voyaging in the northwestern Atlantic during the Norse period.

What follows is a free translation of that portion of the Floamanna Saga which deals with the voyage. When the story opens Thorgisl had recently become a convert to Christianity and consequently was being plagued by his old god, Thor.

Time passes, and after the navigation season opened one spring, Erik the Red sent messages from Greenland to Iceland asking Thorgisl to join him there, and making him very good offers if he would come. At first Thorgisl was not much interested. However at that time his son Thorleif arrived home from a foreign-going voyage [perhaps a Viking raid] bringing considerable treasures with him and Thorgisl was delighted to see him. Shortly afterwards he made up his mind to make a Greenland voyage in his son's company.

Thorgisl asked his wife Thorey if she would go with him to Greenland. She replied that it was a risky business to change one's home. But Thorgisl said that Erik the Red had sent word to him to come. "You can stay home if you want to, and look after the homestead, but I intend to go," he told her. Thorey still insisted it was a mistake, but reluctantly agreed to go since he was going. This intention of Thorgisl's was widely spoken of throughout the land.

He planned to take his son Thorleif with him, together with a freeman called Col and Col's brother and sister, Starkad and Gudrun. He also took ten slaves including Snae-Col and Ozur. Thorgisl picked out big, powerful men, in case he decided to stay and settle in Greenland. He took cattle as well. There were seventeen people in Thorgisl's party. However, he also took with him another franklin, named Iostan, who was accompanied by his wife Thorgerd and his son Thorarin, and whose party totaled thirteen in all.

Thorgisl bought a ship at Leiravage and then he arranged for his estate to be looked after in his absence. He had intended to take his eight-year-old daughter Thorny with him but she became sick before they sailed and after waiting for three days for her to get better, Thorgisl decided he would sail without her.

They all got on board and waited for a fair wind. Thorgisl had a dream in which a big fellow with a red beard[47] warned him he was in for a hard time of it unless he changed back to his belief in Thor. But Thorgisl cried out in his dream: "Begone, foul fiend!" When he woke up he told his wife about it and said that if he had had such a bad dream earlier he would have given up the voyage, but now he was determined to go on. He warned her not to tell Iostan about it. Thorey took it as a bad portent but reassured Thorgisl that he was wise to have nothing to do with Thor.

Then a fair wind came and they sailed out of Faxafiord. Iostan and his party lived in that part of the ship forward of the mast, while Thorgisl's people lived abaft the mast. When they got out of sight of land the fair wind failed and they were tossed about at sea for a long time until both meat and drink ran short.

Thorgisl had more dreams in which Thor offered help on condition that he give up the Christian religion but Thorgisl spurned these offers. The state of the people grew even more miserable. It was getting on for harvest time and still they were at sea. Some of the people were all for placating Thor, but Thorgisl said: "If I get wind of anyone sacrificing to Thor and becoming an apostate, it will go hard on him."

Another night Thor came again in a dream and promised Thorgisl that he would reach a haven in seven days if he would only do homage to him. Thorgisl replied: "Though I never get to harbour, I won't do you a favour. What's more, if you bother me again I'll do you any evil I can."

"Then," said Thor, "at least give me back my own, and what you owe me."

Thorgisl woke up and thought about this dream a long time and then he remembered that he had once dedicated a calf to Thor. He told his wife Thorey about this and said that nothing belonging to Thor should remain aboard the ship. The calf was by now grown to be an old ox, but Thorgisl and Thorey agreed to throw it overboard.

When Iostan's wife heard about this she begged for the meat of the ox since they were running out of food. Thorgisl refused, for he was bent on getting completely rid of the ox. So they threw it overboard, but they were still at sea for a long time afterwards. They had now been three months afloat, blowing about, and with seldom a fair wind.

It is told that one evening they wrecked their ship under the ice mountains of Greenland on a sandbank in a certain fiord.[48] The ship broke up and the stern drifted ashore to the south of where they were. All the people and livestock were saved and the afterboat came safe to shore as well. It was then early in October, a week before winter began.

Glaciers ran around the sides of the bay and the most habitable spot lay in the western part of it. Here they all laboured together to build a hall which they divided with a cross-partition. Thorgisl's party had one end of the hall and Iostan's party had the other. They had saved some meal from the wreck and some flotsam, and the two parties shared these things in common. Most of their cattle died [for want of fodder].

Thorgisl's men were always better at hunting and fishing than Iostan's. He made his people be temperate, and kept them quiet in the evenings and forced them to stick to the [Christian] faith. Goodwife Thorey was far gone with child at this time, and not very strong.

Iostan and his people stayed up late in the nights and had a wild time of it, engaging in mummery and gaming and one thing and another.

One time Iostan spoke to Thorgisl, saying that there seemed to be a great difference in their catches. Thorgisl told him this was because they did not work in the same way: "You keep longer at it in the evening," he said, "but we get started at it earlier in the morning." After that there was a coolness between them. Thorgisl and his people stayed quiet, but Iostan and his kept up their gaming, with lewd uproars and ribald times.

Thorey had her baby about midwinter. It was a boy and they called him Thorfinn. Thorey could not thrive on the food they had.

After Yuletime a sickness came on Iostan's company and six people died. Then Iostan himself got sick and his wife watched over him, but the sickness wore him out and he died and he and the others were buried in new-fallen snow. Then his wife died, and one after another all of Iostan's party died [in all likelihood of scurvy].

Thorarin Iostansson died last and he was buried under the wreck of the ship. There were great hauntings after that. The spirits mainly haunted the part of the hall which had been the Iostaners' in life, but they came into the other part too, and the ghost of Iostan's wife was particularly troublesome. Finally Thorgisl had all their corpses piled up and burned in a balefire, and after that there was no more trouble.

During the rest of the winter Thorgisl and his men worked at the ship [building a new one out of the wreckage]. But they could not get away that summer because the fiord ice did not clear out of the bay. They hunted all summer and built up their stock of provisions. That next winter Gudrun, Col's sister, died. Col buried her under her berth in the house.

Thorey became unable to leave her bed and she prayed to the men to find a way to get them all out of those desolate regions; but Thorgisl replied that he could see no way for them to escape.

Finally one fine day in the spring Thorgisl decided he would climb up the glaciers to see if there was any sign of the fiord ice loosening. Thorey said she did not like him going any distance away from her, and when he replied that he would only go a short distance she answered that she supposed he would have his own way this time, as always. Thorleif [and the freemen] Col and Starkad asked to go along with Thorgisl. He told them that if they did so there would be none to keep an eye on things at home, and "We should be trusting the slaves too much if we did that." Nevertheless they all took their pole-axes and went along with him. The slaves were out fishing and the overseer, a man called Thorarin, was left at the house with Thorey.

They walked and climbed most of that day, and bad weather caught them so it was late before they got back. As they approached they could see no sign of the ship. They reached the hall and went in, and all their chests of goods were gone, their supplies rummaged, and the slaves had vanished. "This is a bad lookout," Thorgisl said. They went into the dark, back part of the hall and heard a gurgling sound from Thorey's bed.

Thorgisl found that she was dead, but that the boy was sucking at her even though she was a corpse. They examined her and found that under her arm the flesh was clotted with blood and there was a little wound as if a fine knife blade had pierced her. All the bedclothes were soaked in blood.

This was the most terrible sorrow Thorgisl had ever known. They buried Thorey beside Gudrun, and Thorleif did his best to cheer his father up. The slaves had stolen all the provisions; had taken the very doors off the hinges; and all the bed coverings and blankets were gone.

All that night Thorgisl watched over his infant son and he could see that the boy would not survive unless something drastic was done. He did not intend to let him die if he could help it. Then he showed his mettle, for he took a knife and cut his own nipple. It began to bleed, and he let the baby tug at it until blood mixed with fluid came out. He did not stop until milk came out; and the boy was nursed upon that.

When Snae-Col and the other slaves went off in the ship they took the big kettle and all the tools out of the tool chest. Thorgisland the others survived by hunting and fishing, and they tried to construct a boat, even though they had so few tools. Eventually they built a wooden-framed boat covered with hides.

So this summer passed, but they could never get enough food on hand to provision their boat for a voyage. They hauled her up in the autumn and covered her with a shed. They lived on such small game as ground squirrels and on whatever drifted ashore.[49]

One morning when Thorgisl came out he saw a big piece of flotsam drifting in an opening in the ice. It was some kind of sea mammal. Beside it were two giant women wearing skin clothing, and they were making up bundles of meat from the animal. Thorgisl ran up to them and slashed at one of them with his sword, which he called Earth-house-loom. He cut the woman's arm clean off at the shoulder. Her bundle dropped down and she ran away.[50]

The Norse took the flotsam for themselves and after that they were not short of provisions through the winter, but they ran short again before spring came.

Thorgisl declared that he was weary of this place and once the ice had loosened he gave the order to set out in their boat. They did not wait for the fiord ice to clear but dragged their boat along the ice-foot and, when necessary, over the floes between leads of open water.[51]

That summer they got south to the Seal Islands, but they had a hard time surviving on fishing alone. [This was evidently a locality well known to the Greenland Norse, and could have been a particularly good sealing place in the Vestri Obygdir; perhaps in the vicinity of Home Bay.] However, at the Seal Islands they got enough seals to last them through the succeeding winter.

At the beginning of the next summer they set out again. On one occasion they found some black-backed gull's eggs. They boiled them and the child Thorfinn ate one egg but would not eat any more. They asked him why he refused, and he replied: "You eat little enough of our food and so I will eat but little too." They spent their nights ashore and their days aboard the boat. They got only small catches of food.

One day they found the stump of an oar with these runes carved on it:

> The lazy fellow had his head washed while wearily I rowed.
> Often out of the cold sea, I swung the oar.

> The sea gave me sore palms to my hands
> While the lazy fellow had his head in the lather.[52]

On another occasion they dragged their boat ashore over the ice-foot and came to a cliffy place where they set up their tent.[53] They were almost out of food. In the morning Col walked out of the tent and found that the boat had vanished. He went back inside and lay down. He would not tell Thorgisl, thinking that he was depressed enough as things were. But after a time Thorgisl himself got up and went out and saw that the boat was gone. Then he came back and said: "Now I can't see how we can go on. Take the boy and kill him." [He meant that, since they would all soon be dead, it would be better for the boy to die quickly.]

Thorleif argued and said there was no reason to give up and kill the boy, but Thorgisl insisted that they obey orders. They took the child away and Thorleif ordered Col to kill him, because "such a deed does not befit me, as his brother, and I won't do it." Col would not do it either since, as he said, the effect of the deed on Thorgisl might have been to finish him off entirely.

They left the boy outside and went back into the tent and when Thorgisl asked if the boy was dead, they answered no. He thanked them and was greatly relieved. "I am badly upset," he told them. "But you have prevented me from committing a terrible crime." Now they all had many dreams and visions, for they were starving [details of these dreams have been omitted].

Then they heard a great deal of noise and when they went out they saw their boat was back, and there were two women near it holding onto it. These people went away at once.[54]

Some time after that the men discovered a bear struggling in an opening in the ice. It could not get out because its forepaw was broken. They ran toward it and Thorgisl hacked at it with his sword until it was dead. Then they drew it up on the ice and loaded it in their boat. The beast was frost-bitten on its forepaw, from which it can be judged how hard conditions were, when even the beasts were maimed by the cold.

Thorgisl gave a chunk of meat to every man, but they thought it was too little and grumbled among themselves, saying that he was niggardly. Thorleif spoke for the rest: "The men say you are stingy with the meat, father." Thorgisl replied: "It has to be done this way, my son, for we are starving and therefore we cannot eat too much for a while."

Next they rowed down out of a fiord [out of Home Bay?] and it took them a long time too. And then they turned toward the open sea and rowed along past many bays, taking the shortest way across the mouths of the bays [toward Cape Dyer?]. Then the ice began to open and the whole sound began to broaden out and they went straight on out [across open water—across Davis Strait]. Sometimes they dragged their boat over the ice between the leads.

They were terribly weary and even Thorgisl was half dead with thirst. There were only the five of them left now: the boy Thorfinn, Thorgisl himself, Thorleif his son and the brothers Col and Starkad. There was no drinking water near and they were almost finished for lack of a drink. Then Starkad spoke up: "I have heard tell that men have mixed together salt water and urine as a drink." So they took the bilge scoop and made water in it, and they agreed it was right to do this if men's lives depended on it. They asked Thorgisl's permission, and he replied that he would neither forbid it nor give them leave, but he himself would not drink the mixture. So they mixed it up.

Then Thorgisl asked for the scoop, saying he would give them a health. He took it, and he spoke like this: "You cowardly and evil beast [Thor] who are holding us up on our journey—you won't get your evil way and persuade me or any of the others to drink such filth!" And with that he threw the stuff overside out of the scoop.

Then he said to the rest of them, "This is a poor way for me to reward you after you saved me from committing a fearful crime when I would have had the boy killed, but the shame and abomination would always have stuck in your minds if I had let you drink. Now maybe our luck will mend."

Later that same day they were able to get drinking water from ice.[55]

At last they came to the mouth of a great fiord [on the other side of the sound? Possibly one of the great fiords near Holsteinsborg] and found a berth there. Later they came to a certain island and they were there three days before they discovered a linen tent. They recognized it as Thorey's tent. When they went in they found Thorarin, the slave-overseer, lying sick. They asked him how in the world he had got there. He told them that Snae-Col and the other slaves had given him the choice of going along with them or of being killed at the hall where Thorey died. He said they had spent the past winter not far from the Seal Islands.

They asked him many questions. He told them that he had been forced to take part in everything; that the slaves had taken all the goods aboard the ship; and that it was Snae-Col who had stabbed Thorey. Thorgisl told him he did not know whether he was one of the guilty or not, but in any case he would not abandon him. But before they could get Thorarin out of the tent he died, and they buried him there.

They kept on along the coast and when harvest time was drawing on again they came to a fiord where there was a boathouse. They pulled up their boat there and walked up to where they saw a small homestead.

A man was standing out of doors and he greeted them. They told him about their journey. He said his name was Herjolf, and he invited them to come and stay with him, and they gladly accepted.

The women of the house tended Thorfinn and gave him real milk to drink, whereat he said that his father's milk did not look like that.

Herjolf explained that he had been outlawed from the settlements of Greenland because he had committed manslaughter. He was very hospitable to Thorgisl and told him a ship had come that way in the summer [presumably this was the stolen ship, manned by the runaway slaves] but her people had not come ashore. He also said it was a long and a difficult journey to the Eastern Settlements, which was where Thorgisl wished to go, and so they stayed that winter with him.

In the spring Herjolf told them they could either stay on with him or take any of his boats if they wanted to continue to the settlements. Thorgisl accepted the offer of a boat and said he would do whatever he could to reward Herjolf. Herjolf replied that he expected Thorgisl would succeed in his journey, and he therefore requested that he try and get him in-lawed into the settlement. Thorgisl promised to do what he could and when they parted they blessed each other.[56]

Now they journeyed on southward along the coast, passing Hvarf [this may have been Cape Desolation, which was at one time known as Hvarf], and they were on their way until harvest time. Early in October, when winter began, they reached Eriksfiord, which they entered. They moored their ship and set up their tent ashore ...

Erik the Red asked Thorgisl and his men to his house at Brattalid and they accepted. Thorfinn was given a nurse but he would not drink milk before dark, and he was weaned soon after. Erik was not very gracious and the visit did not go well [perhaps because Thorgisl had become a Christian]. Thorgisl got news that his slaves were living in the country in great estate and telling very little that was true about the voyage.

That winter a [polar] bear came in among the sheep and did a lot of damage. Men from both settlements[57] got together and agreed to pay a bounty for the bear's death. One day when Thorgisl was in the storehouse the boy Thorfinn called out to his father, saying: "There is a beautiful white dog outside. I never saw one like it, he is so big." His father was busy and told him not to bother about it, and not to go out. However, the boy ran out anyway.

It was the bear. It had come down off the glacier. It caught the boy and he cried out. Thorgisl ran out with his sword, Earth-house-loom. The bear was toying with the boy. Thorgisl struck the bear so hard that he split its skull in two; then he took up his son, who was not badly hurt.

Thorgisl became famous for this deed and many brought him their share of the bear bounty. But Erik did not like the deed at all. Some say this was because he had an evil and heathen belief in bears.

One day when men were gathered around at Brattalid they began to talk about the relative merits of Erik and Thorgisl. One of Erik's servants claimed that Erik was a great chief, but that Thorgisl was an unimportant sort of a fellow; he wasn't even sure if he was a man or a woman. Whereupon Col snatched up a spear and ran the servant through. Erik ordered his men to seize Col, but a number of traders who were there took Col's side, and Thorgisl told Erik that it was his business to avenge his servant himself. It came close to a battle, but men made peace between them although it was hard going.

After that Thorgisl went to the Western [Ivitgut] Settlement to collect the bear money from that district. There he found Snae-Col and the other slaves. He was going to slaughter them, but he was persuaded it would make better sense to sell them for cash, and this is what he did.

Soon after that Thorgisl and his men put to sea [on the ship of Thorstan the White, a trader and a relation] and they had a hard voyage until they neared Iceland. Then they had a southerly gale and made toward the land, but for two days Thorgisl would not let them approach too close for fear of being driven ashore. They lay off for those two days, bailing to keep afloat in the heavy seas. Eight big seas swept over the ship and then a ninth came, and it was the biggest of them all. It drove Thorgisl from the bilge beam where he was bailing, and it picked Thorfinn off his knee and carried him overboard.

Then Thorgisl cried out that there was no use bailing any more since the sea which had gone over them had almost swamped the ship. But at that moment another great wave washed the boy back on deck again and he was still alive. Then they took heart and bailed for all they were worth, managing to empty the ship. But Thorfinn vomited blood, and after a while he died.

Thorgisl nearly went out of his mind with grief. He did not sleep or eat for forty-eight hours, and even after they had made land safely he would not part with the body of his son. He had to be tricked into leaving it, whereupon Col took the body to the graveyard and buried it. Thorgisl threatened to kill him for that, but later he came to his senses and they were reconciled.

Thorgisl said it was no wonder that women loved the children they had nursed at their own breasts better than they could love anyone else.

Thorgisl remarried when he was fifty-five and took over his old estate, and prospered. When he was seventy years old he challenged Helge Easterling to combat and killed him. When he was eighty-five he took ill and after a week he died, but there are many great men come from his seed and scattered far and wide over the land.

14
GUDRID

STILL ANOTHER VOYAGER who set to sea in that stormy year of 997 was a man named Thorbjorn Vifilsson. He was a well-known Icelandic franklin who had taken Erik's side during the troubles with Thorgest which had led to Erik's exile in the west. Probably at the same time that Erik issued his invitation to Thorgisl Orrabeinsfostri, he also sent a message to Thorbjorn Vifilsson asking him to come out and take land in Greenland. Pressed by financial troubles at home, Thorbjorn accepted. He may have set sail from Iceland in consort with Thorgisl. At any rate both ships sailed in the same year, probably from the same port, and encountered the same abominable weather.

The sections of the Erik the Red and Karlsefni sagas which tell of his experiences not only introduce us to his daughter Gudrid, who plays an important role in some of the later voyages, but also give us one of the few surviving vignettes of life in Greenland during the last decade of the tenth century. We have therefore reproduced the story in full as a free translation, interjecting such small explanations and additions from other sources as are necessary to clarify its meaning.

There was a man named Vifil, a high-born Westman who had been captured and brought to Iceland, where he gained his freedom from

Queen Aud. Vifil had three sons, one of whom was named Thorbjorn.

Thorbjorn married Hallveig Einarsdottir and got with her, as a dower, the farm of Laugarbrekka. They went there to live and Thorbjorn prospered and became an important man, for he was a good farmer and his estate grew to be a fine one.

During the time when Erik the Red and Thorgest were at odds, Thorbjorn gave Erik his support and assisted him to make his escape to Greenland when he was exiled from Iceland.

Thorbjorn had a daughter named Gudrid. She was the most beautiful of women, and in every way a remarkable person. When she was still a young girl she went off to live with Orm of Arnarstapi and his wife Halldis. Orm was a great friend of Thorbjorn's. According to the customs of the times he had asked to become Gudrid's foster father, and Thorbjorn had agreed to this.

There was a man called Einar who was a handsome and well-bred man, although his father had been a slave. Einar was very fond of showy clothes. He was a foreign-going trader and he had done very well at the business. He spent his winters alternately either in Norway or in Iceland.

Now it is to be told that one autumn when he had come from Norway, Einar travelled out along the Snaefells peninsula peddling his trade goods. When he reached Arnarstapi, Orm invited him to stay for a while, since these two were friends of long standing. Einar accepted and his goods were carried into a storehouse and unpacked. He displayed them to Orm and the people of the household and asked Orm to pick out what he liked as a gift. Orm did so, commenting that Einar was a good merchant and well favoured by fortune.

While they were busy looking at the goods a woman passed by the open door of the storehouse and Einar saw her.

"Who was that beautiful woman who just passed by the door?" he asked.

"That is Gudrid, my foster daughter, and the daughter of Thorbjorn Vifilsson of Laugarbrekka," Orm replied.

"She must be a good match then," Einar said. "Has she any suitors?"

"Many have courted her, my friend," Orm replied, "but she is not to be easily won, I can tell you. Both she and her father will be hard to please when it comes to the choice of a husband for her."

"No doubt that's true enough, but all the same she is the woman for me," said Einar. "And so I wish you to make an offer to her father on my behalf. Do everything you can to persuade him, and if you succeed you will have earned the full measure of my friendship. It looks to me as if Thorbjorn should regard such a match as being to our mutual benefit. Although he is a man with a great reputation and a good home and valuable possessions, I hear his fortunes are declining. Since neither my father nor I suffer from any lack of lands or money, Thorbjorn could benefit by our help if this match can be arranged."

"Much as I value your friendship," said Orm, "I am not very anxious to act for you in this matter. Thorbjorn has a haughty spirit and is jealous of his honour."

Einar replied that he expected nothing more of Orm than that he should present the suit, and so Orm reluctantly agreed.

That autumn Thorbjorn Vifilsson held a great feast, as was his custom, for he had a high position in the land. Many of Thorbjorn's friends attended, including Orm of Arnarstapi.

When Orm found an opportunity to speak to Thorbjorn alone, he told him that Einar Thorgeirsfell had paid him a visit not long since, and that he was becoming a very prosperous man. Then Orm broached the proposal of marriage between Einar and Gudrid, adding that some people might consider it an appropriate match for a variety of reasons. "This might prove to be of great benefit to you from the financial point of view," he said, "for there is a great deal of money at stake."

Thorbjorn reacted to the offer with indignation.

"I never expected to hear such talk from you suggesting that I should marry my daughter to the son of a slave in order to recoup my fortunes! If you think a match as mean as this one is suitable for her, she shall no longer remain in your keeping."

When the feast was over everyone returned home, and Orm among them. But Gudrid stayed with her father henceforward.

In the spring Thorbjorn gave another feast and a great many people attended. After the eating was over Thorbjorn called for silence and spoke to the assembled guests.

"I have lived a long time in this place," he said, "and I have had the good will of many men, and their affections too. All things considered, our relationships have been pleasant ones. But although my estate used to be thought a considerable one, I now find myself running into hard times.

"Rather than lose my honour and bring disgrace on my family I have decided to give over this farm and leave the country. I am going to put to the test the promise my friend Erik the Red made to me when we parted company in Breidafiord, he to go out to Greenland, and me to return to my own lands. It is my intention to go out to Greenland this summer and it may be that I will do better there than here."

Everyone was greatly astonished at this admission of Thorbjorn's fallen fortunes, as well as at his plans. There was much sympathy for him; for he had many friends. However, they also realized that Thorbjorn was so fixed in his purpose that nothing would dissuade him from carrying it out.

Thorbjorn gave gifts to all his guests, after which the feast came to an end and the visitors returned to their homes.

Thorbjorn then proceeded to sell his lands and such of his property as he could not take with him, after which he bought and outfitted a merchant ship which was laid up at the mouth of Hraunhofn.

Thirty persons joined him for the voyage, including Orm of Arnarstapi and his wife, for the friendship between the two men had been restored. With them went others of Thorbjorn's friends and relations who could not bear to be parted from him.

They put to sea in weather which seemed favourable for a Greenland voyage, but after they had gone beyond sight of land the fair wind failed and there came great gales and a huge sea got up. They lost their directions and drifted far off their course.[58]

Then illness broke out on board the ship and half their company died, including Orm and his wife.

The storms continued and they had a very long, wretched and wearisome time of it; but eventually, at the end of autumn, they made land at Herjolfsness.

Among those living near this place was a franklin named Thorkel who was a very able fellow and a good husbandman. He took in Thorbjorn and the survivors of his party and entertained them well during the winter, for which Thorbjorn and his shipmates were very grateful.

This was a year of great shortages in those parts, for the fisheries had largely failed due to the bad weather that summer, and some of the men who had gone fishing never returned.

Now there was a certain woman in the settlement whose name was Thorbiorg. She was a prophetess, and was known as the Little Seer. She had had nine sisters, all of whom were also prophetesses, but now she was the sole survivor.

During the wintertime it was Thorbiorg's custom to go about from house to house attending the winter entertainments. She was eagerly sought after by those who were curious to know their fates, or who wanted to find out what the next season would be like.

Since Thorkel was the chief franklin of the neighborhood it was considered to be his responsibility to find out when the evil times which were upon them would cease. Thorkel therefore invited the Little Seer to visit his house, and careful preparations were made to receive her, according to the customs which governed the reception of women of her kind. A High Seat had been prepared for her on which a cushion filled with poultry feathers had been placed.

Toward evening she arrived with the man who had been sent to fetch her. She was clad in a dark blue cloak, fastened with a strap and decorated with jewel-stones right down to the hem. She wore a string of glass beads around her neck, and upon her head she wore a black lambskin hood lined with white catskin. In her hands she carried a staff upon which there was a knob ornamented with brass and set with jewel-stones. Around her waist she wore a girdle of touch-wood and hanging from it was a great skin pouch in which she kept the charms she used in the practice of her profession. On her feet she wore shaggy calfskin shoes with long laces, the ends of which were ornamented with brass buttons. She had catskin gloves upon her hands.

When she entered the house all of the folk felt it was their duty to offer proper greetings, and she received the salutations of each individual according to how well pleased she was with them.

Franklin Thorkel took her by the hand and led her to the seat which had been prepared for her. Then he bade her look carefully at man, and beast, and house and all therein. But the prophetess had nothing much to say.

The tables were brought forth and now it must be told what manner of food was prepared for the prophetess.

A porridge of goat's beesting[59] was made for her; and for meat she was given the stuffed hearts of every kind of animal which could be obtained. She had a brass spoon and a broken-pointed knife with a handle made of walrus tusk which had a double haft of brass around it.

When the tables had been removed, franklin Thorkel approached the Little Seer and asked her how she was pleased by the home and by the character of the people; and then he wished to know how soon she would have the answers to the questions he had put to her, and which the people were anxious to hear.

She replied that she could say nothing until the morrow, when she had slept in the house for a night.

Late in the following day all the necessary preparations were made for her to accomplish her soothsaying. Then the Little Seer bade them bring unto her those women who knew the incantation song which is called Warlocks, and the singing of which helped her work her spell by attracting spirits to the vicinity. But it did not seem that there were any such women about the place.

A search was made all through the house to see if anyone was familiar with this incantation, and at last Gudrid Thorbjornsdottir spoke up.

"Although I am not skilled in the Black Arts, nor yet am I a seer," she said, "yet my foster mother Halldis once taught me a spell-song which she called Warlocks."

"Then," said Thorbiorg, "you are wiser than I supposed."

"But," Gudrid added, "this is a spell for a ceremony of such a kind that I will not assist with it; for I am a Christian woman."

Thorbiorg answered: "It might still be possible to give your help to the company here and be no worse a woman than you were before. However, I leave it to Thorkel; it is up to him to provide me with my needs."

Franklin Thorkel now urged Gudrid so strongly that she felt forced to comply with his wishes. The women then made a ring around her while Thorbiorg sat up on the spell-dais where the high seat had been made ready for her.

Then Gudrid sang the song; and she did it so sweetly and so well that no one could remember ever having heard the song sung in so fair a voice.

The prophetess thanked her for the song and said: "She has indeed lured many spirits here; for those spirits which had formerly forsaken us and which had refused to submit themselves to us found this song so pleasant that they could not resist it.

"Many things are now revealed which were formerly hidden, not only from me, but from all others too. And now I am able to tell you that this period of famine will not endure much longer. Conditions will improve as spring approaches; thus the visitation of evil which has rested so long upon you will disappear sooner than you had expected.

"As for you, Gudrid, I shall reward you for the assistance which you gave us. The fate which is in store for you is now clear to me. You shall make a most worthy marriage here in Greenland, but it shall not be of long duration, for your future path leads out to Iceland, where a lineage that shall be both prosperous and famous shall spring from you; and the light shall shine over your decendants so brightly that I have not the power to describe it. And now farewell, and good health to you, my daughter."

After this the other people present crowded around the Little Seer and each of them besought her for information about whatever it was they were most curious to know. She was willing and ready with her replies, and very little that she foretold failed to be fulfilled. After this she was sent for by the people of a neighboring farm and she departed thither.

Thorbjorn Vilfilsson was then sent for. He had been absent, for he was not willing to remain in the house while such heathen rites were being practiced.

With the coming of spring the weather improved rapidly, even as the Little Seer had predicted. Then Thorbjorn fitted out his ship and sailed to Brattalid, where Erik received him with open arms and said that he had done the right thing to come thither.

Thorbjorn and Gudrid and his household lived with Erik through the following winter, but quarters for the rest were found among the neighboring farmers. In the ensuing spring Erik gave Thorbjorn land at Stokaness across the fiord from Brattalid, where he established a prosperous farmstead and where he lived thenceforward.

15

THE CROSS COMES TO GREENLAND

The Saga Tale (c. 997-999)

Erik was married to a woman named Thiodhild [Thorhild][60] and had two [three] sons, one of whom was named Thorstein, the other Leif [and another Thorvald]. They were promising men. Thorstein stayed at home with his father and there was not another man in Greenland at the time who was thought to be as promising as he.

Leif had sailed to Norway where he was staying at the court of King Olaf Tryggvason . . . there came an occasion when the King talked to Leif and asked him: "Is it your purpose to sail to Greenland in the summer?"

"That is my intention," said Leif, "if you permit it."

"I believe this will work out well," answered the King. "You shall go there on an errand for me—to proclaim Christianity."

Leif replied that the decision was up to the King, but gave it as his opinion that it would be difficult to carry this mission to a successful conclusion in Greenland.

The King replied that he knew of no man who was better fitted for the undertaking, "and in your hands the cause will surely succeed."

"This can only happen," said Leif, "if I enjoy the support of your protection."

Leif put to sea when his ship was ready for the voyage. . . .

He landed at Eriksfiord and went home to Brattalid, where he was well received by everyone. He soon proclaimed Christianity throughout the land, and the Catholic Faith, and he relayed King Olaf Tryggvason's messages to the people, telling them how much excellence, and how great a glory accompanied this faith.

Erik was unwilling to forsake his old beliefs, but Thiodhild quickly embraced the new faith. She caused a church to be built at some considerable distance from the house. It was called Thiodhild's Church, and there she and those persons who had accepted Christianity—and they were many—offered up their prayers. Thiodhild would not have sexual intercourse with Erik after she received the faith, which made him extremely angry.

From this [situation] there arose the suggestion that he should explore that land which Leif had found. Thorstein Eriksson, who was a good and intelligent man and blessed with many friends, was [to be] the leader of this expedition. Erik was invited to join them, however, for everyone believed his luck and foresight would be of great assistance. Erik did not say nay when his friends besought him to go.

They thereupon outfitted the ship in which Thorbjorn Vifils-son had come out [to Greenland], and twenty men were selected for the expedition. They took little with them except weapons and provisions.

On the morning when Erik left his home he took along a little chest containing [his] gold and silver. He hid this treasure and then went his way [toward the ship]. But he had only gone a short distance when he fell off his horse and injured his arm at the shoulder joint, whereupon he cried: "Ai! Ai!"

Because of this accident he sent word to his wife that she might take up the treasure he had hidden, for he attributed his misfortune to his having concealed it.

[SOURCES: Erik the Red and Thorfinn Karlsefni sagas. The section deal-ing with Leif's voyage to Norway is not included since we have presented it in an earlier chapter. The brief notice in this portion of the saga which attributes the discovery of Vinland to an accident of Leif's homeward voyage from Norway has been deleted for reasons given in Appendix L.]

ΛΛΛ

THORBJORN VIFILSSON and his family were warmly wel-comed by Erik, who showed his gratitude for Thorbjorn's aid during the "troubles" in Iceland by giving him a choice land-grant at Stokaness, directly across the fiord from Brattalid. However, the Thorbjorners did not occupy the land immedi-ately. Instead they spent that summer and the following winter as Erik's house guests.

The difficulties Thorbjorn had experienced with the fearful weather of 997, coupled with the nonappearance of Thorgisl Orrabeinsfostri's ship, would have made a gloomy subject for discussion among the older people at Brattalid and would have led to worried conjectures about Leif's fate. But the younger people of Brattalid had more stimulating things to think about.

Women were scarce in Greenland in those early years, and marriageable young women who were blessed with good looks, good family connections and a good dowry would have been a rarity. We can believe that a number of young bucks were soon courting Gudrid; but Thorstein Eriksson seems to have taken an early lead and to have held it. He was a respected and per-sonable young man and he was living in the same household with Gudrid. Being Erik's son he had the advantages of prestige and position, if not of wealth; and both Erik and Thorbjorn would have looked on an alliance between the two families as being to their mutual benefit. Thorstein probably would have felt secure against any rival until a day late in the summer when someone ran shouting up toward the house with the news that

Leif's ship was standing up the fiord. This was news which may not have roused Thorstein to much enthusiasm. Heroes provide notoriously stiff competition when they compete with ordinary mortals for a woman's love.

There was no doubt that Leif had now become even more of a hero to many Greenlanders. He had returned home a much greater figure than he had been when he departed. Not only had he made the fabled voyage to the Fatherland, but during his stay there he had become the confidante and liegeman of a king who had treated him with such regard that he was recognized as a great man even in Norway.

All the same, it could not have been very long before the pleasure of having him safe home again began to sour—at least for some of the settlers.

Leif had brought back with him from Norway several of King Olaf's men. One of these was a priest, and others are referred to vaguely as "some holy men." They may or may not have been holy, but they were almost certainly agents of Olaf's, entrusted by him with the task of preparing the ground for the eventual inclusion of Greenland into Olaf's domains. Leif and his Norwegian companions soon began proclaiming the Christian faith on behalf of Olaf, and it can be assumed that, as was the case in Iceland, they did not hesitate to urge its adoption by the use of threats.

In the previous year, 997, Olaf had sent a delegation to Iceland nominally to convert the independent islanders. The leader was one of Olaf's nobles, a warrior named Thangbrand. His fellow "missionary" was Ari Marsson's son Gudleif, who had become a mercenary abroad and who had won a champion's reputation with the sword and battle-axe. These two roamed the island from end to end bringing Olaf's message to the Icelanders. When they encountered resistance they frequently used their swords to quiet the opposition. After they had committed several murders the island finally became too hot for them and they were forced to retire rather hastily to Norway.

Olaf was so enraged at this treatment of his emissaries that he seized every Icelander then in Norway and gave orders for them to be slaughtered. This massacre was narrowly averted when two of his prisoners undertook to persuade their countrymen at home to accept Christianity as the official religion of the nation. Olaf stayed the executioner's arm and the Icelanders bowed to the inevitable. In the summer of 1000 they passed a law at the Althing whereby theirs became officially at any rate, a Christian country,

There seems to be little doubt that having once forced the Icelanders to obey his wishes, Olaf intended to apply further pressure until he had gained political control of the island. The Icelanders were aware of his ultimate intentions and they apparently Christianized their country to buy time. Luck was with them, for Olaf died that very autumn and the immediate threat to their independence was lifted.

Olaf's plans for Greenland were doubtless identical with those for Iceland. Just as he had employed the renegade Icelander Gudleif Arisson, so he seems to have commissioned Leif Eriksson to carry out a similar treasonable task. The motives which prompted these two men to accept Olaf's orders may have differed. In Gudleif's case money may have been the incentive. But Leif was probably prepared to act as Olaf's liegeman in order to achieve power in his own country, perhaps as Jarl, ruling the land for Olaf.

Leif and his Norwegian companions wielded a double-edged weapon. On the one hand they had a message which the women were glad to listen to, for it promised a more hopeful life than they had known. On the other hand they did their proselytizing under the protection of Olaf's fierce reputation, which cast a long, black shadow. All men knew that where Norwegian trading ships could sail, Olaf's fighting ships could follow after.

Leif seems to have done well in the early stages of his campaign. Many women embraced this new faith, and not a few men must have followed suit, either to gain influence with Leif, who they may have thought was the coming man, or for the same reasons of expediency which had prompted the Icelandic Althing to its decision. Nevertheless, by no means all the Greenlanders, and apparently not even a majority of them, accepted Leif Eriksson's leadership and the new faith. The old lion was not yet dead. Erik the Red not only refused to be converted; he spoke publicly and contemptuously of the Norwegian priest as "that faker Leif brought to Greenland." Erik was not a man to give in to threats. He was well aware that Greenland was a good deal farther from Norway than Iceland was, and would have been a long reach, even for Olaf's arm.

Although the intensity of this internecine strife is only hinted at in the sagas, this should occasion no surprise. It must be remembered that when the oral sagas were first committed to vellum, the work was done by clerks (clerics) of the Holy Church and it was these clerks who recopied and preserved the sagas until well into the Middle Ages. It would be naïve of us to expect to find much forthright information espousing the heathen point of view, or reflecting adversely on the motives and actions of those who carried the Cross. However, the Icelandic records preserve a number of fragments testifying to violent and sometimes bloody resistance to the new faith in Iceland. Similar reactions indubitably took place in Greenland too.

Emotions must have burned at white heat through the winter of 998–999. While Leif and his followers visited various out-settlements seeking to persuade or browbeat the settlers into an acceptance of White Christ, Erik and his supporters would have been struggling equally hard to offset his efforts. The struggle may have stopped short of bloodshed. Considering the nature of the Norse, it would be surprising to learn that it did.

Erik's personal position was singularly unpleasant. His hold upon the little kingdom which he had founded was being undermined by his own son, and Leif's actions were not only denying Erik the patriarchal supremacy which he had amply earned, they had even been instrumental in ousting him from his own marriage bed. The consequent loss of face would have been almost intolerable.

There must have been many who were envious or resentful of Leif's meteoric rise to power and position. His two younger brothers, Thorleif and Thorvald, would have been less than human if they had not begun to feel an urgent need to win fame and fortune for themselves. Thorstein in particular would have had specific reason to envy his brother, for he was in love with Gudrid and wished to marry her, yet he had comparatively little wealth or power of his own and he had accomplished no great deeds. Leif was a towering figure in both of these regards. Moreover, he was now at least a professing Christian; and Gudrid was a Christian too. There is nothing to tell us that Leif actually did compete with Thorstein for Gudrid's hand, but remembering his seduction of Thorgunna, we can assume that Thorstein had reason to be wary of his brother. From every point of view it would seem that Thorstein had urgent need to make a mark for himself.

Knowledge that the origin of Leif's wealth lay within relatively easy reach would have ensured that someone would eventually have attempted to emulate Leif's exploit, even if there were no other factors involved. The sagas tell us that such an attempt *was* made; and the plans for it probably took shape during that first, tense winter after Leif's return from Norway.

We are told that Thorstein was the leader of the group which planned the voyage. He may indeed have instigated it, but Erik also played a major role. It was to Erik's name and personality that the venturers rallied, and he was no doubt responsible for providing the wherewithal to make the voyage possible.

A successful Vinland voyage would have refurbished Erik's reputation as a doer of great deeds, and would have demonstrated that his vigor and his courage—the two prime requisites of a Norse leader—were still unimpaired. Furthermore, it promised to enrich both Erik and Thorstein, so that the one would have the wealth to sustain his power while the other would have the means to cement an advantageous and desirable marriage.

It is significant that the sagas make no mention of Leif as having had any part in the plans. Far from being involved as a supporter of the venture, it is more likely that he opposed it. It is significant that the expedition used Thorbjorn Vifilsson's ship, the implication being that Leif would not permit his father and his brother to use his own.

A further indication of how things stood in the divided Eriker family is revealed by the description of how Erik removed a chest containing his gold and silver from his own home at Brattalid and buried it for safekeeping during his absence. Safekeeping from whom? The only reasonable conclusion open to us is that he did not trust his wife and his eldest son. His motive in burying the money would have had to have been a strong one, since the Norse considered it extremely unlucky to bury treasure before setting out on a voyage.[61]

The picture of Erik riding down from Brattalid to where the expedition's vessel was berthed somewhere on the outer fiord is a moving one. He was about fifty years of age, which in those times of short, hard lives would have meant that he was past his prime. Behind him lay an estranged wife, an elder son who was doing his best to usurp his father's power, and a home which he could not even trust to call his own.

As he rode along he may have looked out over the fiord to where a score of sod buildings stood dark against green home-fields with herds of sheep dotting the lower hills behind them, and he would have reflected that this had been his life's work. Now it was no longer his; or, at any rate, his control over it was threatened, and by the eldest of his own children.

Erik's determination to make this voyage was an iron one. When he fell, or was thrown from his horse, and hurt his shoulder as a result, this accident and evil omen were not enough to deter him from his purpose. With a resolution as hard as the Greenland rocks, he went aboard the ship to sail westward once again, hoping to find there the solution to many a looming problem.

16

THORSTEIN THE UNLUCKY

The Saga Tale (c. 999–1002)

Thereafter they sailed confidently out of Eriksfiord, for they had high hopes of their venture.

Then they were storm-tossed on the ocean for a long time and could not lay their desired course. They came in sight of Iceland and likewise saw birds from Irish waters. In truth their ship drove hither and thither all over the sea.

In the autumn they turned back worn out by hardship and exposure and exhausted by their labours. They arrived at Eriksfiord at the very beginning of winter.

Then Erik said: "We were more cheerful when we put out of the fiord in the summer, but at least we are still alive, and it might have been worse."

[SOURCES: Erik the Red Saga and Thorfinn Karlsefni Saga]

DRIFT

THE SAGA TELLS US that the failure of this voyage was due to stormy weather which prevented Erik and Thorstein from steering their correct course. This is no doubt true enough as far as it goes; but it does not go far enough. An equally important reason for their failure was probably a lack of adequate sailing instructions and, specifically, a lack of knowledge of the relative latitude of Vinland.

When we examine the current and wind patterns which prevail in and over the Labrador Sea, we discover a hidden factor about which the early Norse could have known nothing. Having passed out of sight of the Greenland landmarks, a Norse ship bound for Newfoundland would have come under the influence of a current which first would set her westward, then southward and finally to the southeastward. Moreover, this current would have increased in strength as the voyage progressed and would have had its maximum effect at about the time the vessel entered the Grand Banks region. The effect would have been intensified by the eastward drift caused by the prevailing westerly and northwesterly winds of the region.

Assuming that her master steered and maintained a reasonably true course between south Greenland and Newfoundland, his actual track over the bottom would have tended to curve imperceptibly but steadily toward the south, an effect which would increase in direct proportion to the time expended in making the voyage. If he encountered any sizable delay due to unfavourable winds by the time he had run off his proper distance and was expecting to make his landfall, his real position might have been as much as 150 miles to the southeast of his calculated position. There would then have been no land anywhere in sight, nor would there have been any closer than 500 miles to the west of his position.

This is no mere theoretical calculation. Before the strong south-setting effect of the Labrador Current was recognized, scores of sailing ships bound to Newfoundland from Europe by the northern route were swept past Cape Race, missing Newfoundland entirely.

NO DIRECTIONS

The only way that an early navigator could have discovered what was happening to him, and so be able to make good his error, was by a comparison between his actual latitude and the known latitude of his hoped-for landfall. In other words, if he knew the relative latitude of the landfall, and if he was able to take sights at sea en route, he would have discovered that he had gone too far south. In order to correct the error he would then only have had to sail north until he reached the right latitude, then turn west and sail in that direction until he made the landfall he was seeking.

Knowledge of the latitude of Vinland was vital. Had Erik and Thorstein possessed it, there would have been small likelihood that Erik, a master of the arts of seafaring, would have failed so miserably where Leif, the merest tyro by comparison, had succeeded so easily.

There can be no doubt that Leif knew the Vinland latitude. Having obtained it in the first place from Bjarni Herjolfsson, he would have had ample opportunity to confirm it during his stay in the new land. Erik and Thorstein ought to have been able to obtain it either from Bjarni or from Leif. However, it looks as if Bjarni was not available at the time that Erik and Thorstein sailed. When the Christian immigrant Thorbjorn Vifilsson arrived at Herjolfsness in the autumn of 997 he was given shelter and hospitality by Thorkel, who is reported to have been the leading man in the community at that time. There is not a mention of the original land-takers and founders—the Herjolfers—in all of the long and detailed saga account of Thorbjorn's sojourn at Herjolfsness. If either Herjolf or Bjarni had still been living there, they would surely have extended their hospitality to a man of Thorbjorn's fame not only because they were the most prominent men in the area by right of settlement and so had the duty of providing hospitality for wayfarers, but also because they appear to have been Christians too.[62]

It is possible that Herjolf, who was born about 930, may have died around the time Bjarni sold Leif his ship in 997, in which case Bjarni might have disposed of his trading establishment and retired to Iceland to live out his days in relative luxury. On the other hand it is conceivable that the exile whom Thorgisl Orrabeinsfostri encountered while making his way down the coast to south Greenland could have been Herjolf Bardsson. Herjolf is an uncommon name in the Icelandic annals, occurring only twice in the records of the Greenland colony. If this exile *was* Herjolf Bardsson, Bjarni would probably have been living in exile with him. In any event, he would have been in no frame of mind to volunteer information to the leader of the Greenland community which had exiled his father to the obygdir.

If Bjarni was not available, Leif certainly was. And having made the voyage both ways between Vinland and Greenland, he would have been even better able to provide Thorstein and Erik with detailed and accurate sailing directions, together with the vitally important latitude observations. The question is: Did he do so? We conclude that even if Erik and Thorstein had asked for Leif's assistance he would not have given it; and pride probably kept them from asking.

Thus these new venturers to the west would have been limited to what was common knowledge about the Vinland voyage—information which was known by, and obtainable from, men who had served as crew members on the previous voyages. These men would have known the general airt course, the approximate sailing distance, and the appearance of the landfall. They almost certainly would not have been privy to Leif's latitude observations.

FAILURE

Erik and Thorstein must have departed from Greenland on the direct course for Vinland, since this is the only course which is consistent with what happened to them later. Doubtless they steered south-southwest, expecting to sight Vinland in about five days. But the prevalent northwesterly weather of the Labrador Sea, combined with the effect of the currents, evidently set them considerably off course to the southward. By the end of the sixth or seventh day they may have turned westward in the hopes of picking up the coast, but by this time they would have become subject to the strongly eastward-setting Gulf Stream currents. It would have been a vain effort unless they were prepared to beat to the westward for at least five hundred miles until they reached the shores of Nova Scotia, since although no Greenlander knew it, the Vinland coast did not run on to the south but turned sharply west at Cape Race.

A few days on such a westerly course would doubtless have been enough to convince Erik and Thorstein that they were lost—or rather that Vinland was lost; and bad weather at this juncture would have made the hopelessness of the situation even more apparent. Without a latitude to guide them they would have had no means of correcting their course to Vinland short of returning to Greenland and starting over again. Storm or no storm, they had no real alternative but to accept failure and head for home.

Home would not have been so easily regained.

Although Pole Star sights would have told them how far south they were from Greenland, they would have had no way of determining how far east or west of it they were except by dead reckoning; and dead reckoning which did not take into account the effect of the Atlantic Drift would have seriously misled them. The effect of the east-setting Gulf Stream and its subsidiary currents would have carried the knorr from ten to forty miles eastward every day that she was in their grip—and this may have amounted to several weeks in time and several hundred miles in distance. Added to this would have been the continuing effects of the prevailing westerlies. The total effect of the Atlantic Drift could have caused such a huge error in longitude dead reckoning that, in all likelihood, the voyagers were still steering northeast for Greenland when they should have been steering north*west*. It is not surprising that they eventually arrived in European waters.

This does not mean—and the saga does not say it does—that they came close to the coast of Ireland. They did see certain species of seabirds which were considered to be reliable indications that a mariner was approaching Irish waters. However, the ranges of most specifically European seabirds in the North Atlantic extend offshore to between 20 and 30 degrees west longitude. Consequently the Norse could have seen "Irish" seabirds when they were still several hundreds of miles to the west of Ireland.

Still holding to a generally northeast course, the weary mariners eventually raised the coast of Iceland and for the first time in many weeks knew where they were.

From Iceland they were at last able to lay a true course for home, and, as the saga tells us, early in the winter the ship finally came beating up into Eriksfiord at the conclusion of what was one of the longest and most harrowing voyages in recorded Norse maritime history. The spectre of death from starvation must have been a passenger on that ship for weeks; and death from thirst could have been averted only by collecting rain water. The ship herself would have been badly strained by the long weeks at sea. Doubtless she was leaking like a basket, and had to be bailed constantly to keep her afloat. It is remarkable that either ship or men survived at all.

One autumn day, just before winter began, the ship limped back to her moorings. It must have been a dreary homecoming. Thorstein's and Erik's arrival home, empty-handed and worn to shadows of themselves, would have been a great feather in Leif's cap, for it would have suggested that he was able to do what not even his father and his brother combined could equal. His sanctimonious followers doubtless shook their heads in mock piety and announced that this was White Christ's punishment upon those who still clung to Erik and the heathen gods.

Although the failure of the expedition must have weighed heavily on both Erik and Thorstein, they do not seem to have lost as much by it as might have been expected.

Christianity—and Leif's influence—presumably continued to gain ground; but it was still far from dominant. The pagans seem to have been able to hold their own and the Christians evidently failed to muster a majority in the local Thing, which was held each spring at Gardar, and consequently Greenland did not pass a Christianizing law, as Iceland had done.

As for Thorstein, his failure to find Vinland seems to have had no adverse effects on his courtship of Gudrid. Perhaps this is more revealing of Gudrid's character than of anything else; for it may be that she was the kind of woman who valued a man more for what he was than for the deeds he had done. In any event she married Thorstein in the autumn of the year after he returned, disheartened, to Eriksfiord.

Thorstein seems to have had a second string to his bow. Some time before sailing on the ill-fated Vinland voyage, he had made a partnership arrangement with a man named Thorstein the Swarthy to participate in the founding of a new settlement in the distant Godthaab fiord district. Thorstein the Swarthy sailed north first and hallowed land on Lysufiord, one of the main Godthaab fiords. We have no way of knowing if he was the inaugural land-taker in this region, but he may well have been. In any event he must have been one of the first.

In the autumn after his wedding, possibly in 1000, Thorstein Eriksson and his bride set out to help pioneer this new settlement, which was to extend the boundaries of the original Western Settlement nearly two hundred miles to the north and west.

The events of the first winter at Lysufiord are so fully dealt with in the sagas that I give the story in free translation, following the Erik the Red and the Karlsefni Saga versions. However, at the point where the corpse of Thorstein speaks, I have deleted a long passage consisting of religious propaganda and have substituted the version given in the Greenlanders Story.

THORSTEIN AND GUDRID

Now it is to be told how Thorstein Eriksson sought Gudrid Thorbjornsdottir in marriage. His offer was well received both by Gudrid and her father, and it was agreed that the marriage should take place at Brattalid that autumn.

The festivities went off very well and were attended by a great number of people.

Thorstein owned half of a stead in Lysufiord in the Western Settlement, the other half being owned by a man who was also named Thorstein, but was nicknamed the Swarthy. His wife was named Sigrid. Thorstein and Gudrid sailed up to Lysufiord in the autumn to stay with Thorstein the Swarthy. They were well received there and remained at the stead for the winter. Thorstein found lodgings for all the crew of his ship.

Now it happened that sickness appeared in their home early in the winter. Gard, who was the overseer of the farm and a man whom few liked, was the first to sicken, and he soon died.

Then one after another of the people took sick and died, including many members of Thorstein's crew. Thorstein Eriksson himself took sick, as did Thorstein the Swarthy's wife, Sigrid.

One evening Sigrid wished to go to the privy, which stood beyond the outer-door, and Gudrid accompanied her. They were seated in it facing the outer-door of the house when Sigrid uttered a loud shriek.

"We have acted foolishly in coming out," said Gudrid, "for you are in no condition to stand this cold. Let us go in again as fast as we can."

But Sigrid answered: "That we cannot do, for the corpses of all those who have died are standing between us and the door ... and look! Among them I can see your husband Thorstein! And I see myself too! It is too dreadful to look at."

Sigrid thought she also saw the overseer, Gard, holding a whip in his hand and about to scourge the other dead people. Then the vision passed and she cried: "Let us go in quickly, Gudrid, for I no longer see the thronging dead."

So they went in; but before the morning dawned Sigrid herself was dead, and a coffin was made ready for her corpse.

Later that morning some of the men of the household went out in rowboats to fish, and Thorstein the Swarthy accompanied them to the landing place. When they came back at twilight he went down again to see their catch.

While he was there word was sent to him that he should hurry back to the house, for dreadful things were taking place there. Sigrid had tried to rise to her feet and then crawl into the bed where Thorstein Eriksson lay sick.

When Thorstein the Swarthy arrived in the room he saw that the dead woman had caught hold of the edge of Thorstein Eriksson's bed. Her husband dragged her off, and then he drove a pole-axe into her breast.

Later that night Thorstein Eriksson died. Thorstein the Swarthy bade Gudrid lie down and try to sleep, saying that he would keep watch over the bodies, and this she did.

Not long after that the corpse of Thorstein Eriksson sat up and spoke, saying he wished Gudrid to be called, for he had something to say to her.

Thorstein the Swarthy went and woke Gudrid and bade her cross herself and pray to God for help. "Your husband says that he wishes to see you," he told her, "but you must decide for yourself whether to go or not, for I cannot advise you in this."

"It may be that this is one of those strange events which shall afterwards be long remembered," Gudrid said. "I must take courage and go to my husband and hear what he has to say, for even if there is danger in this, I cannot escape my fate. Besides if I do not go to him he may well come to me."

Then Gudrid went to where Thorstein lay, and she came near to him and it seemed to her that the corpse was weeping. She bent down and he whispered a few words in her ear, but in so low a tone that no one else could hear. Then he spoke again in a louder voice so that everyone could hear what he said, and these were his words:

"Now I wish to tell Gudrid her fate so that she can better bear my death—for I am come to my final resting place. I tell you, Gudrid, that you will marry an Icelander and long shall you live with him, and many children will you bear to him, and they will be handsome, illustrious and excellent in every way. You shall go from Greenland to Iceland with him and there you shall abide for a long time, and you shall outlive your husband. After he is dead you shall make a pilgrimage to the southern lands; and when you come back you shall build a church in Iceland and live there, and you shall become a nun, and there you shall die at the end of your days.

"As for me, I wish to be buried at Eriksfiord together with all those of my people who have died here, save only Gard the overseer. Him you must burn, for he is the cause of the visitations which have afflicted us so sorely."

Then Thorstein Eriksson fell back, and they laid out his corpse.

The bodies of the dead were placed in Thorstein's ship and in the spring of the year Thorstein the Swarthy took them to Eriksfiord, where they were buried.

Thorstein the Swarthy took Gudrid and all her possessions to the home of her father, Thorbjorn. But Thorbjorn died soon after this, and all his property passed into Gudrid's possession. After that Erik took her to live at Brattalid, where he treated her as a daughter and carefully saw to all her affairs.

THE WALKING CORPSES

Some authors have concluded that the macabre descriptions of the deaths of Thorstein and Sigrid are the results of the vivid and superstition-ridden imaginations of the saga writers; but this is probably not the case. There are a number of diseases which could have produced the effects recorded in the saga. Epidemic cerebro-spinal meningitis and typhus fever are two of them. Victims of both these diseases have been known to sink into a penultimate coma which, to any observer except a trained physician, seems like death. Under the conditions of near-panic terror which the epidemic must have engendered in the people of the Lysufiord settlement, the possibility of a temporary coma being mistaken for death would have been much intensified.

The description of Sigrid's vision of the walking corpses who barred the door to the house is doubtless elaboration on the delirious babbling of a woman in the grip of a raging fever. Her grotesque attempt to crawl into the dying Thorstein's bed after she herself had been presumed to be dead, and after her corpse had been laid out, could have been the result of a final, semi-conscious rally from the edge of death. The horror and revulsion which this pitiful last struggle aroused among the living is grimly testified to by the actions of her husband, who, believing she was in fact a corpse, ran her through with a pole-axe.

Nor does Thorstein's brief rally from his coma smack of the supernatural, if we except only the prophecy about Gudrid's future, which was doubtless inserted into the story at some later date after Gudrid's life had run its course.

While there is not enough evidence to permit any certainty in attempting to identify the disease, the likelihood that it may have been typhus is strong. Body lice were so common as to be endemic in those times, and typhus, which is transmitted through lice, might have been brought to Greenland by a trading vessel from Norway or Iceland. Ship fever, as typhus was often called, appears to have been widespread throughout Europe during this era.

Whatever the disease may have been, that long dark winter at Lysufiord when people sickened and died in the cold, crowded and filthy sod-walled houses must have represented an eternity in hell to Gudrid and to the rest who survived it.

3

LAND-SEEKING IN THE WEST

17

THORFINN KARLSEFNI

The Saga Tale (c. 1003–1004)

There was a man named Thorfinn Karlsefni who lived in the north of Iceland at Reyniness by Skagafirth. He was a man of fine family and was very wealthy. His mother was called Thorunn and his father was Thord Horsehead, son of Thord Bellower's daughter Thorhild Ptarmigan and Snorri, son of Thord of Hofdi and Frigerd who was the daughter of Thori the Loiterer, the son of Frigerd, daughter to Kiarval, King of the Irish. Thord of Hofdi was the son of Bjorn Chestbutter, the son of Thorvald Backbone, son of Bjorn Ironsides, son of Ragnor Shaggypants.

Thorfinn Karlsefni was a successful sea-going trader. One summer Thorfinn outfitted his ship with the intention of making a voyage to Greenland. Snorri Thorbrandsson of Alptafiord accompanied him, and there were forty other people aboard the ship with them.

At the same time Bjarni Grimolfsson from Breidafiord and Thorhall Gamlisson from the East Fiords also outfitted a ship carrying forty people, with the intention of making a voyage to Greenland.

When they were ready, Karlsefni and the others put to sea with these two ships in consort. It has not been recorded how long their voyage took them, but it is said that both ships arrived at Eriksfiord in the autumn.

Erik and other inhabitants rode down to the ships and a good trade was soon established. Erik was asked by the skippers to take such of their wares as he wished as gifts, and he responded with great generosity by inviting both crews to take up winter quarters with him at Brattalid. The merchants accepted the invitation with thanks. Their goods were then carried up to Brattalid, where there were plenty of fine large storehouses in which to keep them. There was very little shortage of anything they needed, and the merchants were well pleased with their entertainment at Erik's home during that winter.

However, as time drew on toward Yule, Erik seemed to become morose and less amiable than was his habit. One day Karlsefni spoke to him about it: "Is something bothering you, Erik? The people are saying that you are less cheerful than usual. Since you have entertained us with the greatest liberality it is only right for us to do whatever we can for you in return, so you must tell us why you are so low in spirits."

Erik replied: "You have been thoughtful and honourable guests and I am unhappy at the prospect that you may suffer as a result of our relationship. I am troubled by the thought that men in other places may say you never experienced a more wretched midwinter feast than the one at which Erik the Red was your host at Brattalid in Greenland."

"There is no need for anything like that to happen," said Karlsefni. "We have ample malt and meal and corn in our cargo, and you are welcome to take as much as you need to provide the wherewithal for as liberal an entertainment as you think fitting."

Erik accepted this offer and preparations were made for the midwinter feast, which turned out to be so magnificent that the people who attended it believed they had never before enjoyed such a superb entertainment.

Some time later Karlsefni approached Erik on the subject of his marrying Gudrid, for he assumed that Erik would have the right to bestow her hand in marriage, and Gudrid seemed to him a beautiful and accomplished woman.

Erik gave him a favourable reply, saying that by marrying Karlsefni, Gudrid would be following her fate, and he added that she was worthy of a good match and that he had heard only good reports of Karlsefni.

To cut the story short, the result was that Gudrid was betrothed to Karlsefni, a banquet was arranged, and the wedding was duly celebrated. And all of this happened at Brattalid during the course of that winter.

There was great good cheer at Brattalid that winter and there was much gaming and story telling and similar things which contributed to the entertainment of the household.

About this time there began to be much talk about the prospects of exploring Vinland the Good, for it was said that the country possessed many fine qualities. The result of the matter was that Karlsefni and Snorri outfitted their ship, intending to go in search of that country in the summer.

Bjarni Grimolfsson and Thorhall Gamlisson also joined the expedition with their ship and the people who had accompanied them.

There was a man named Thorvard who was married to Freydis, a bastard daughter of Erik the Red. He also joined the expedition, together with Thorvald Eriksson and Thorhall the Hunter.

Thorhall the Hunter had been a long time with Erik as his hunter and fisherman during the summers, and as his overseer during the winters. He was a strong and swarthy man of giant stature although getting on in years. In his manner he was overbearing. He was taciturn and usually spoke little, but when he did speak he frequently used abusive language and was always ready to stir up trouble. He paid little attention to the True Faith after it was introduced into

Greenland. Thorhall was not very popular, but Erik had long been accustomed to seeking his advice. Thorhall went on the same ship with Thorvald [Eriksson] and his companions, because he had an extensive knowledge of the obygdir. They had the same ship that Thorbjorn Vifilsson had brought out [from Iceland].

All told there were one hundred and sixty people [on the expedition].

[sources: Erik the Red Saga and the Thorfinn Karlsefni Saga]

That same summer when Karlsefni came from [Iceland[63]] there came a ship to Greenland from Norway. It was skippered by two brothers, Helge and Finnboggi, who were Icelanders from the East Firths. They stayed this winter in Greenland.

Now it is to be told that Freydis Eriksdottir made a trip from her home in Gardar to see the brothers Helge and Finnboggi. She asked them to go to Vinland with their ship and to go halves with her of all the profit they might get there. They agreed to this.

Then Freydis went to visit her brother Leif and asked him to give her the houses which he had built at Vinland. But he answered her saying he might let her use the houses, but would not give them [to her].

It was agreed between Karlsefni and Freydis that each ship [in the expedition] should carry thirty men of fighting age, and women also. But Freydis immediately broke this agreement and took five additional men and hid them.

Now they sailed out to sea having agreed beforehand that they should keep together if possible. . . .

[source: The Greenlanders Story]

THE GREENLAND SETTLEMENTS

AFTER THORSTEIN'S DEATH and Gudrid's return to the Eastern Settlement, there seems to have been a period during which the struggle between Christianity and paganism in Greenland became more or less stabilized, with Erik retaining control of the pagan part of the community while Leif was presumably the dominant man in the Christian group.

The growth of Leif's influence may have been curtailed by the news, which would have reached Greenland via Norwegian traders in the summer of 1001, that Olaf Tryggvason, the Sword of White Christ, had committed suicide in the summer or early autumn of the previous year when his ship was brought to bay by the fleet of the Danes. His inglorious death, the failure of White Christ to preserve him, and the removal of the threat which he had posed to Greenland would have heartened Erik's faction and discouraged Leif's.

Erik retained firm control of the Eriksfiord region—the most heavily populated part of Greenland—until at least as late as 1005, which is the last year in which his name is mentioned in the sagas. It is significant that during these important years there is hardly a mention of Leif in either the Erik the Red or the Karlsefni sagas.

The pagan element in Greenland may have been strengthened physically during this period. Although the Icelanders adopted Christianity as their official religion in 1000, it is clear from the saga records that many people were not prepared to abandon the old gods. Since Erik's country remained a stronghold of paganism, numbers of disgruntled heathens from Iceland may well have chosen this time to emigrate to Greenland.

The Greenland settlements were now fifteen years old, and life in them must have begun to follow established ways. Herds of sheep and cattle had multiplied. Distant pastures had been called into use. The growth of population through steady immigration had evidently spread into most of the new lands in the

Godthaab Bight district. Trade with Iceland and Norway had settled into a routine exchange, and prosperity, if of a rude and tenuous nature, had apparently become fairly general.

Summertime journeys to the hunting areas absorbed the energies of the younger men. Production of walrus ivory and leather was steadily increasing, and there was a sustained demand in Europe for these two items, which became the basic foreign exchange of Greenland.

The lure of walrus ivory and hides, and of even rarer and more valuable commodities such as narwhal tusks and Greenland falcons brought traders to Greenland in considerable numbers. These traders doubtless continued to supply Greenland with badly needed timber; but the price would have remained high and the supply limited. The virgin forests of Vinland must have steadily increased in allure; but the failure of Thorstein's voyage seems to have discouraged the Greenlanders from making any fresh attempts in that direction until about 1003—the date is arbitrary—when the arrival of two big Icelandic merchant ships, and of a man whose singular ability and energy made him the peer of Erik the Red, revived men's interest in prospects for a new Vinland voyage.

KARLSEFNI'S PURPOSE

Thorfinn Karlsefni had a most resounding genealogy and the claim that his was a famous family was no idle one. He was descended on one side from a fabled Irish king, and on the other from an almost legendary ancestor, Ragnor Shaggypants, who was claimed as a forebear by innumerable high-ranking Norwegians and Icelanders.

When Karlsefni took his place on the saga scene he would have been about twenty-five years of age. By the time he sailed for Greenland he was already a successful and wealthy sea-trader of considerable renown. What we know of his immediate background suggests a close resemblance to Bjarni Herjolfsson. The two men seem to have been very similar in outlook. They were both courageous in the best sense of the word; daring when there was a need for daring, but not reckless. Like Bjarni, Karlsefni was a seaman first and foremost, a man with a healthy regard for the safety of his ship and for the lives of his people.

The saga sources tell us almost nothing about the train of events which brought Karlsefni west from Iceland, but a good deal can be conjectured.

Following the usual trader's pattern, Karlsefni would have spent each alternate winter at home in Iceland. One winter he was presumably approached by a man named Snorri Thorbrandsson with the request that he consider making a charter voyage to Greenland during the ensuing summer.

Snorri, who was then in his fifties, was one of three sons of Thorbrand of Alptafiord (the other brothers being Thorleif-Kimbe and Helge) who had taken an active part in supporting Erik in his feud with Thorgest. When Erik sailed to Greenland to establish his colony he was accompanied by Helge Thorbrandsson, who took up land in the Eastern Settlement.

About 1002 the remaining brothers, Snorri and Thorleif-Kimbe, accompanied by several other men and their families, evidently decided to emigrate to Greenland. This may have been due to a distaste for the new religion of Iceland, but it was more likely a result of their involvement in a particularly gory feud in Alptafiord, of which another saga tells the tale. The Thorbrandssons would have required a large and well-found vessel to carry all the passengers, livestock and household goods belonging to the party; and Karlsefni's big trading knorr met their requirements.

Snorri's proposition would have been attractive to Karlsefni since it enabled him to visit Greenland on charter and at the same time to engage in private trading there. He was young and, as later events proved, adventurous. He had no doubt heard many yarns about the lands discovered by Bjarni Herjolfsson and later visited by Leif, and like any seaman he must have been curious about those new lands, new ports and new sea routes in the western reaches.

So much is conjecture, but one thing is certain: Karlsefni's voyage to Greenland was not undertaken solely as a trading venture. Even the crew of a ship engaged on the long voyage to Norway seldom numbered more than fifteen men; whereas Karlsefni's ship carried forty-two people when she sailed for Greenland. The conclusion that this was essentially an emigrant voyage is strengthened by the fact that a second vessel, carrying forty people, sailed in company with Karlsefni's knorr.

Thorhall Gamlisson from the East Fiords of Iceland was the owner-master of this second ship, and he too was a trader. Bjarni Grimolfsson appears to have been the leader of the group of emigrants aboard Thorhall's ship, even as Snorri Thorbrandsson was the leader of those travelling aboard Karlsefni's knorr. The passengers on both ships may have comprised a single party of emigrants all from the Alptafiord region.

The passage out to Greenland seems to have taken a long time, considering that the ships sailed in the summer and are not reported to have reached Eriksfiord until the autumn. However, they may not have sailed direct to Eriksfiord. Visits may have been made to the intervening fiords, either to allow Karlsefni and Thorhall to do some trading or to give the immigrants an opportunity to look for suitable lands.

By the time the ships reached Eriksfiord, the would-be settlers may already have become aware of a distressing fact.

The Eastern Settlement lands were already fully occupied and the rush to the Godthaab Bight had probably left little to be looked for in the way of new lands, even in that direction.

Where then were the settlers to find satisfactory land? Although Greenland eventually supported a much larger population than that which occupied it in Karlsefni's time, this came about not through the pioneering of new homesteads so much as through the gradual splitting up of existing farms into ever smaller and less productive units in order to provide land for the new generations. The relatively few people who held most of the usable land in 1003 were probably not anxious to sell significant portions of their holdings, since money was of little value in Greenland. True value lay in land capable of supporting large enough herds to keep people in food throughout the year.

THE WESTERN PROSPECT

Eventually someone seems to have made the electrifying proposal that the would-be settlers should seek land in the new country to the west. It would not be surprising to learn that it was Erik himself who first made the proposal. Once such a fascinating project had been broached, it would have fired the imaginations not only of the Icelandic land-seekers but of a good many Greenlanders as well. Everyone would have heard stories of the unparalleled richness and goodness of Leif's Vinland, and such stories would have lost nothing over the years.

Initially the prospect of a Vinland Settlement voyage may not have been of much personal interest to Karlsefni or Thorhall Gamlisson. The two trader-skippers had successfully completed their charter voyage to Greenland, had doubtless disposed of most of their trade goods, and would have expected to complete their trading in the spring and then sail back to Iceland or perhaps on to Norway with a cargo of Greenland specialties.

But as enthusiasm for a land-taking voyage began to mount, Karlsefni and Thorhall would have been involved, since their two ships were vital to the scheme. The only locally owned sea-going vessels which might have been pressed into service seem to have been Leif's and Thorbjorn Vifilsson's. Leif did not make his ship available, and Thorbjorn's vessel had quickly been bespoken by a group of Greenlanders, headed by the last and youngest of Erik's sons, who intended to employ it themselves on the Vinland venture.

There was a third foreign-owned ship in Greenland that winter, but she was not available to the Icelandic settlers either. This ship belonged to the brothers Helge and Finnboggi, who, like Thorhall Gamlisson, were merchant-traders from the East Fiords of Iceland. They had sailed her direct to Greenland from Norway with a load of trade goods.[64]

The Greenlanders Story tells us that Freydis Eriksdottir made a journey from her home in Gardar to visit Helge and Finnboggi, who were wintering with local settlers on some nearby fiord. Freydis persuaded the brothers to join the general expedition and to carry her and her party to Vinland, offering them a half share of whatever profits might accrue from the voyage.

Karlsefni and Thorhall Gamlisson must have been under heavy pressure to make their vessels available to transport the Icelanders to the new lands. Likely they did not need much persuading. They too would have heard all about the fabulous cargo of lumber and other products which Leif had brought back from Vinland. The opportunity of fetching back such a cargo for themselves would have been hard to resist. In addition, Karlsefni had become emotionally involved, for he had fallen in love with Gudrid. Whether or not Gudrid was influenced by the prophecy that she would marry an Icelander, she seems to have had no objection to Karlsefni's proposal, and the marriage was celebrated with no loss of time.

THE COLONISTS

The more that people talked about the projected voyage, the more irresistible it must have seemed. Indeed a much larger number of the Greenland settlers might have taken part if there had been enough ships to carry them. However, four vessels seem to have been all that were available, and these four could have carried, at the most, about one hundred and sixty adults together with their cattle, personal belongings, settlers' goods and essential supplies.

The expedition consisted of two divisions and apparently had two sets of leaders. One party consisted of the immigrant Icelanders under the overall leadership of Thorfinn Karlsefni, Snorri Thorbrandsson and Bjarni Grimolfsson; and the second included the Greenland emigrants led by Thorvald Eriksson. Freydis's party seems to have operated on its own to some extent, but perhaps it gave lip service to Thorvald's leadership.

The presence of some incipient distrust between the Greenland and Icelandic contingents even at this early stage is suggested by a statement in the Greenlanders Story to the effect that Karlsefni and Freydis (and presumably the other leaders also) agreed between them that each ship should carry only thirty men of fighting age, together with an additional and unspecified number of women. This was obviously an attempt to keep both sides as nearly equal in strength as possible; but the unscrupulous Freydis broke the agreement by smuggling an additional five Greenland men aboard the Helge and Finnboggi vessel.[65]

Because the word "exploring" occurs in reference to this voyage, it has sometimes been assumed that the expedition was primarily an exploring venture. This is clearly an error in interpretation. One hundred and sixty men and women, with their cattle and all the gear which they needed to set up a permanent settlement, all embarked on four overcrowded ships, do not comprise the elements of an exploring expedition. This was undoubtedly a colonizing venture, as indeed the Greenlanders Story specifically confirms. It was, in fact, the first recorded attempt by Europeans to establish a settlement on the North American continent.

18

THE OUTWARD VOYAGE

The Saga Tale (c. 1004)

They sailed away from land to the Vestri [O] Bygd and from thence to Bear Island.

Then they sailed south beyond Bear Island for two doegr, when they discovered land and rowed to it in boats and explored that country. They found there many hellur [great stones], some of which were so large that two men could lie at full length on them, sole to sole. There were many arctic foxes there. They gave a name to this country and called it Helluland.

From thence they sailed for two doegr and bore away from the south toward the southeast until they reached a wooded country containing many animals. An island lay off to the southeast of this country and there they killed a bear so they called this Bjarney, while they called the wooded land Markland [Forest Land].

Then they sailed southward along this land and after two doegr they came to a cape [beyond which] they beat into the wind having the land to starboard. Here was a havenless coast with a long sandy beach and dunes. They rowed to the shore in boats and found upon a headland there [a hill which resembled?] the keel of a ship from which they named that headland Kialarness [Keel Point]. They called the strands there Furdustrandir [Marvelous Shore, in the sense of amazing] because they took so long to sail past them.

[SOURCES: Erik the Red Saga and Thorfinn Karlsefni Saga]

PLOTTING A COURSE

DURING THE WEEKS FOLLOWING the decision to make the Vinland voyage, the leaders of the expedition doubtless spent long hours in Erik's hall discussing the problems they would have to face. Chief among these would have been the question of which route to follow. The choice would have been governed by the fact that this time the ships were not to be manned solely by tough male adventurers who could withstand a great deal of hardship, but were to transport women and children whose physical endurance was limited, together with numbers of livestock which could not have survived a too prolonged deep-sea passage.

The direct route followed by Leif offered certain advantages. Not only was it the shortest way to the western lands, but a southwesterly course was in some ways the best in relation to the prevailing winds over the Labrador Sea, which in summer generally blow between north and west. Nevertheless it was unacceptable if it involved a risk of missing the landfall at the other end; and that this risk existed had been all too well established by the voyage of Thorstein and Erik. However, their unhappy experience need not have eliminated the direct route as a possibility for the new expedition, providing that Karlsefni and his fellow skippers possessed the relative latitude of Vinland.

Armed with this information, the new expedition could have departed from Greenland on a more westerly course than Thorstein and Erik had steered. When they had been out for a distance of five or six doegr they could then have altered to the southward, if they had not already sighted land, until they reached the desired latitude. After that they would only have had to beat to the west for a short distance before raising Vinland.

But the Karlsefni expedition did *not* know the latitude of Vinland. We are certain of this since although the expedition reached the Newfoundland coast, it never found Leif's Vinland because the search for it was not carried far enough to the south.

Leif appears to have withheld the secret of Vinland's position from the members of this new expedition, even as he evidently withheld it from Thorstein and Erik. The suspicion that he was distinctly uncooperative is strengthened by the fact that his name is not even mentioned in the Erik the Red and the Karlsefni saga accounts of the new voyage, except for a single casual reference. This concerns two Scots slaves originally given to Leif by King Olaf. The saga tells us that Erik and Leif loaned these slaves to Karlsefni, but it was evidently Erik, and not Leif, who made them available to the expedition.

Deprived of the benefit of Leif's information, the careful merchant skippers would have been forced to rule out the short, direct route to Vinland for fear that their voyage might become a repetition of the Thorstein voyage. They would also have had doubts about the wisdom of attempting to backtrack Bjarni's course from Greenland to Vinland. Even helped by a following wind it had taken Bjarni four days to cross the stretch of open water lying due west of the Eastern Settlements. If easterly weather was as rare in Norse times as it is now over the Labrador Sea, Karlsefni and his fellow skippers would have realized that an attempt to reverse this passage might result in their being kept at sea for many days.

There remained one other route to the new land. It was perhaps suggested by Erik, who was the first Norseman to use it. "If you sail north up the Greenland coast," he may have told the Icelandic skippers, "you will come to a great mountain on the edge of the sea, which we call Hrafnsgnipa. Take your departure from there in clear weather, and after one doegr sail westward you will raise another big mountain lying near the coast of the

Vestri Obygd—the Western Wilderness. It is a short crossing and there is little danger of losing touch with the land even in stormy weather.

"Once you gain the coast of the Vestri Obygd, turn south along it. Our hunters do this when they go to Bear Island. Bear Island cannot lie far to the north of the last land Bjarni Herjolfsson found. You may even be able to coast all the way to it. In any case your course will be southward, so you will have good use of the northwesterly winds and run little risk of being swept out into the open sea as happened to Thorstein and myself. If this plan strikes you as being good, I can give you a pilot as far as Bear Island, for my factor, Thorhall the Hunter, knows the Vestri Obygd well."

Although this was a roundabout route, it offered many advantages. It was, in effect, a coasting route, and ships following it need never have been far from a supply of fresh water for the livestock, or from shelter for the ships in case of storms. Since drift ice was apparently no threat in those times, it was the safest as well as by far the shortest route across the great Labrador Sea-Baffin Bay inlet. Nor can we eliminate the possibility that, during almost two decades of Norse occupancy of Greenland, hunters in the Vestri Obygd might have penetrated some distance to the south of Bear Island—perhaps even as far as Hudson Strait.[66] If they had done this they would have been quick to realize, from their relative latitude vis-à-vis the Eastern Settlement, that Bjarni Herjolfsson's departure point from the last of his three western lands was on the south side of a comparatively narrow strait or sound (Hudson Strait) separating Bjarni's third land from the Vestri Obygd.

For whatever reasons, this was the route chosen by the Karlsefni expedition. Presumably led by Thorvald Eriksson's ship, carrying Thorhall the Hunter as pilot, the convoy put out from Eriksfiord one day in early summer and headed north under the towering ramparts of the west Greenland coast.[67]

NORTH, WEST AND SOUTH

Taking advantage of the long hours of daylight the four ships made their way up the coast to their departure landmark—the 7300-foot coastal peak near Sondre Stromfiord. They were then practically on the Arctic Circle and would have had almost twenty-four-hour daylight as they turned westward and began their crossing of Davis Strait on a day when the winds were northerly and the arctic sky was white and clear.

The lookouts would have raised the loom of the peak behind Cape Dyer only a few hours after they sank the tip of Hrafns-gnipa into the sea astern of them. Once the Cape Dyer coast was clearly in view, Thorhall the Hunter may have ordered a course alteration to the southwest, for as an experienced navigator on this coast, he would have felt no need to close with the land before turning south for Bear Island.

A landing was probably made at Bear Island to refill the water casks and do a little hunting and fishing in order to replenish the supplies of fresh food. The expedition may now have reached the limits of the Greenlanders' local knowledge. If so, they were facing a leap into the unknown. In any event the careful skippers would have taken advantage of this pause to make everything shipshape and secure.

The location of Bear Island—a vital element in reconstructing the rest of the journey—can be fixed with some exactness. The Greenlandiae Vetus Chorographia (a detailed analysis of which appears in Appendix D, Part II) states that Bear Island lay three days' rowing distance from Karlsbuda, which is identifiable with Cape Dyer. Karlsefni's expedition would hardly have visited Bear Island if it had lain north of Karlsbuda, so we conclude it must have lain south of that locality. Three days' rowing distance (between 90 and 105 nautical miles) southward along the coast of Cumberland Sound takes us to Leopold Island, which is at the southernmost tip of the peninsula.

Leopold Island is 2000 feet high. During the nineteenth century it was a valued landmark for whaling ships making an arrival after crossing Davis Strait or making a departure bound south for Newfoundland. Furthermore, it acts as a collecting point for polar bears which have been carried south with the polar pack during the winter. To this day it is famous among the local Inuit as a place to hunt polar bears.

From Leopold Island the coast of the Cumberland Peninsula —the Vestri Obygd—runs sharply off to the northwest into Cumberland Sound, and to anyone unfamiliar with the inner reaches of this great inlet, Leopold Island seems to be the southern tip of a large independent landmass. Even if the Greenland hunters had explored the sound and discovered its true nature and the existence of a continuing coast to the southward, Leopold Island would still have been the obvious point of departure for Karlsefni's ships when leaving the Vestri Obygd.

The saga says that they took a departure from Bear Island and sailed "for two doegr to the south, when they discovered land." A due south course from Leopold Island runs down longitude 63 degrees 15 minutes. If it is followed without much deviation, it will bring a vessel's lookout within sight of the northern tip of Labrador after a passage out of sight of land from Leopold Island of about 250 nautical miles, or as close as need be to two doegr.

Furthermore, a ship holding to such a course will pass out-·side the visibility range of most of the intervening stretches of the Baffin Island coast and of Resolution Island. She might just possibly raise the loom of Cape Murchison, twenty miles to the westward of her course line, and she would probably pick up Lady Franklin Island. But Lady Franklin Island is only a few miles long and lies more than twenty miles offshore, so it might well have been ignored by the Karlsefni expedition as being unimportant. Cape Murchison could have been missed because of poor visibility in daylight, or it might have been passed during the twilight period.

It is also likely that the prevailing winds during this lap of the voyage would have been westerly to northwesterly, tending to set the ships a little to the eastward of the chosen course and farther offshore, with the consequence that the vessels would have made landfall on the Labrador slightly to the south of the Button Islands—possibly in the Cape Chidley region. Any increase in distance would have been offset, in terms of the time required for the voyage, by the influence of the southward-setting Canadian Current, which here runs at a rate of one-half to one knot.

It is significant that if Karlsefni did make his landfall on the northern tip of Labrador, he would not have seen the spectacular snow-capped mountains described by Bjarni as a feature of his third landfall. The northern tip of the peninsula has a maximum elevation of only 1700 feet. The land form rises gradually from there southward to its maximum elevation in the vicinity of Rama Bay, one hundred nautical miles south-southeast of Cape Chidley. In the saga account of Karlsefni's Helluland landfall, mountains—snow-capped or otherwise—are not mentioned for the good reason that there were none to see.

If they had made good a southerly course with a slight set to the eastward, Karlsefni's ships would have come within sight of the Labrador coast about opposite the Cape Chidley Islands in latitude 60 degrees 26 minutes. The lookouts could have raised the land off the starboard bow at a distance of up to forty miles, for these islands rise almost sheer from the sea to a height of more than a thousand feet. Directing their course to starboard, the ships would then have closed with a country which Karlsefni could have tentatively identified as being Bjarni's point of departure from his third and most northerly land.

THE LABRADOR COAST (HELLULAND AND MARKLAND)

There are probably few bleaker, more barren places in the arctic regions than the granite snout of northern Labrador. Seen from seaward it appears to be completely devoid of any vegetation. The cold gray northern seas pound it unmercifully and the naked granite cliffs snarl back at the dark ocean in a grimace of perpetual ferocity. At the foot of the immense sea cliffs, and in the steep-walled gashes which pass for coves and harbors, immense slices of frost-riven rock have slipped free of the cliffs and have come to rest in the landwash. These huge, flat slabs are as impressive now as they were to Karlsefni's people, who called them hellur (flat, or great, stones) and who named the land Helluland because of them.

Great flocks of seabirds haunt the cliffs, but there are very few land animals of any size except for arctic foxes, which prey on lemmings and such small fry or descend to the landwash to search for dead fish and other flotsam.

It can be imagined that the Norse ships did not linger long at this inhospitable landfall, but continued coasting southward as rapidly as wind and weather would allow. The two-doegr voyage southeast—a direction which the saga is careful to specify—along the mountainous coast of north Labrador would have been an exciting and a chancy one. The winds which whip down through the great valleys from the Torngat Mountains, to burst out through the narrow fiord mouths, often reach hurricane velocity even in summer, and ships under sail along that coast go warily.

Still, the Greenlanders on the expedition would have been used to such conditions, even if the Icelanders were not; and they had no doubt warned their fellow voyagers of the dangers inherent in sailing close under mountain walls.

Soon after they left the Chidley region and began to see higher and higher mountains, which eventually grew so lofty that they bore snow on their peaks and glaciers in their higher valleys, they would have been confirmed in their belief that they were coasting Bjarni Herjolfsson's northern land. They would doubtless have been keeping a sharp lookout for the spectacular landmark which marked the southern end of this land, as Bjarni had defined it. When they raised the gargantuan bulk of the Kaumajet Peninsula standing off to the southeast from the land like a Gibraltar of the north, they could not have failed to recognize it.

Very likely they coasted close to this gigantic rock and were as awed as modern observers are at the sheer slopes of the Bishop's Mitre plunging four thousand feet into the sea. They may have sailed through Mugford Tickle, thereby establishing the fact that the tip of the peninsula is a 3000-foot-high island, now known as Cod Island. It seems possible that the Norse named it—in honour of its first discoverer—Bjarni Island. Later saga scribes who copied the original versions of the Erik the Red and the Karlsefni sagas, but who seem to have possessed no knowledge of Bjarni Herjolfsson's voyage, would have been responsible for interpolating the explanation that the island was called Bjarney in honour of a polar bear which Karlsefni's men found there. It is noteworthy that at an unknown point in the history of the sagas, some scribe apparently set himself the task of explaining the meaning of certain otherwise obscure names given to geographical features by the original explorers; and in at least two other cases his explanations have been shown to be interpolations.

Immediately south of Cod Island, and at a distance of two doegr from the north tip of Labrador, the voyagers would have opened Okak Bay and would have seen a dark frieze of trees stretching around its shores and covering many of its islands.[68] It can be taken for granted that a landing was made here. The water butts would have needed replenishing; people would have been anxious to get ashore where they could again build fires and have hot, cooked meals; and an effort would have been made to collect grass or rough forage in order to give the live-stock some fresh food.

It is also probable that caribou were encountered here for the first time on the voyage. The forests at Okak were restricted to the lower and more sheltered areas, while the tundra upland plateau, which comes close to the coast in this area, must have been (it still is) excellent caribou country. The Moravians found that caribou were numerous even on the outer islands as late as the eighteenth century.

The rugged Torngat range comes to an abrupt end at the Kiglapait Peninsula, and except for a few outlying heights, which are of relatively gentle contour and which are well wooded almost to their crests, no more real mountains are to be encountered on the coast of Labrador. South of Okak Bay the land is transformed into a rolling coastal plain rising slowly toward the interior. In Norse times it would have been so com-pletely forested as to display the underlying rock rarely except on the most nakedly exposed islands off the coast.

This was the start of Markland—Land of Forests.

Departing from Okak Bay, the colonists probably made no attempt to follow Bjarni's course along the next leg of the jour-ney south. They would have had nothing to gain by putting to sea, out of sight of land. Furthermore, they now knew, since they could see it for themselves, what Bjarni did not know—that

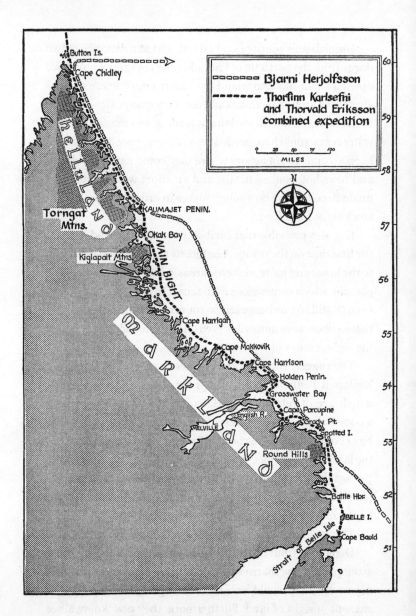

The discovery and exploration of Helluland and Markland

the coast was continuous southward from the vicinity of the Kiglapait Peninsula. They undoubtedly chose to follow the coast since such a course would have enabled them to stay within reach of fresh water and cattle forage.

Not that proximity to this coast would have been an unmixed blessing. The great Nain Bight, which they would have entered soon after passing the Kiglapait, doubtless gave the skippers some bad attacks of nerves. It is filled with an almost unbelievable number of islands, islets, half-awash rocks and unseen reefs. In clear weather, and with a good lookout at the masthead, navigation along the seaward fringe of the bight is not too difficult. However, in thick weather, or with an onshore wind and heavy seas, it gives the most experienced seaman palpitations.

There may have been occasions (although easterly weather on this coast is uncommon in summer) when the ships had to stand off the land until the weather improved. They may also have done this at night as a routine precaution, since as they gained more southing the period of twilight would have been deepening to real darkness.

As the four ships made their cautious way to the south, the skippers would have noted that the coast—or what they could make of it beyond the chaotic mass of islands in the foreground—seemed to bend westward, then southward, and finally to swing sharply eastward once again as they passed Nain and Hopedale bights and picked up the relatively unobscured mainland coast beyond Cape Harrison.

This great, if gentle, swing to the eastward would have demonstrated to them that Bjarni's second and third lands were in fact one continuous country; but this conclusion must have become briefly suspect when they reached the extremity of the long, eastward-pointing Holton Peninsula, which lies just north of Grosswater Bay. They probably threaded their way between some of the outer Indian Islands—possibly through Cut Throat Tickle—at which point they would have discovered that they had apparently reached the end of Markland.

Looking south, they would have been able to see no more land. It is doubtful if they would even have been able to raise land to the southwest from the limited vantage point of their mastheads, particularly if the weather was at all unfavourable; and the sagas give us reason to think that they were then experiencing southeasterly weather, which would have meant poor visibility.

Under these circumstances they would doubtless have decided to stick with the land until they were sure of its trend, and to run to the westward under the northern coast of Grosswater Bay. Four or five hours on such a course would have brought them into the narrowing neck of the bay, and sooner or later they would have picked up the land lying to the south of them and would have realized with relief that they had been coasting into a deep fiord.

At this juncture they would have changed course to the southward on a long reach (if the wind was southeasterly) and crossed the bay, perhaps in the vicinity of Saddle Island. Sailing eastward now, they would have been able to reach on the other tack until they came to the massive headland abeam of George Island, whereupon they would have had to beat directly into the wind in order to round it.

The distance given in the saga for the passage from the first landing in Markland to the cape where they altered course is two doegr, which is close to the direct-line distance from Okak Bay to George Island. The distance actually sailed by the knorrir, if they coasted the fringe of islands in the Nain Bight, would have been greater; but since the ships were being helped on their way by the Labrador Current, which here flows at speeds of up to one and one-half knots, the loss from one factor would have been roughly offset by the gain from the other.

Depending on how far they ventured in Grosswater Bay, they would have had a more or less revealing glimpse of its inner reaches, which were very heavily wooded. As they sailed out of the bay they would have realized that they were sailing through a sound which ran east and west between a cape "running to the north from the land" and an "island lying to the north of the land." Someone would have been certain to comment on how closely these facts paralleled the description of the approaches to Leif's Vinland. It may even be that the suggestion was made that they should explore this fiord more fully on the chance that Vinland lay near at hand.

THE MARVELOUS SHORES

If such a suggestion *was* made, it was not acted upon. The ships continued around Pottles Cove Head and began to beat to the southward, and almost immediately they came in view of the most singular feature the voyagers had seen on the coast of Markland. Running away out of sight to starboard of them was the forty-five-mile stretch of almost perfectly straight coast, unbroken by the smallest cove or indentation and composed for the most part of a fifty-yard-wide strip of dark yellow sand backed by rippling dunes, which is now called Porcupine Strands.

The only break in this mighty beachline is a most peculiar spoon-shaped headland thrusting out from the sand beach at a point about two thirds of the way along the strands. This headland has a long, smooth spine rising from ground level near the beach, extending seaward for three miles and then falling off to sea level at the eastern extremity of the cape. Seen from some distance away it resembles nothing so much as the hull of an upturned ship lying with her keel against the sky. This headland is now called Cape Porcupine, and it is a famous landmark on that coast. Although the highest point of its spine is only 300 feet above sea level, the surrounding country is so low that it offers a superb vantage point from which the entire sweep of Porcupine Strands can be seen.

There are short stretches of sand scattered here and there on the coasts of Iceland and Greenland, but they mostly lie at the feet of bays, and none of them remotely approaches the magnitude of the Porcupine Strands of Labrador. The strands have, in fact, no rivals on the Atlantic seaboard of North America north of the New England states, and even there they are not overmatched.

The Norse were properly impressed, as is shown by the name they gave to this strange sight. They called it Furdustrandir, which means the Marvelous, or Amazing, Shores. They were also intrigued by Cape Porcupine (which is known locally as Sandy Beach Hill) and they seem to have yielded to its invitation, to have anchored their ships in its lee, and to have rowed ashore in order to scale its heights. They called this headland Kialarness which means Keel Point, and the Erik the Red and Karlsefni sagas say they did so because they found a ship's keel here. On the other hand the Greenlanders Story says that the name was bestowed on it when Thorvald Eriksson was driven on this cape during a storm, with the result that his ship's keel was damaged and had to be replaced.

Neither story is convincing. Since the local current drift is from north to south, and the general Atlantic drift is from west to east, the likelihood of Karlsefni's people having found a ship's keel here is extremely slim. As for the Thorvald Eriksson story, the account is patently apocrophal, as will appear later. There are three other Kialarnesses in Iceland and Norway, and since all of these are believed to have received their names because of their resemblances to capsized ships, we conclude that *this* Kialarness obtained its name in the same way.

19

STRAUMFIORD

The Saga Tale (c. 1004)

Then the country became indented with bays [vagskorit] and they steered their ships into a bay.

Now when Leif was with King Olaf Tryggvason, and the King bade him proclaim Christianity in Greenland, he gave him two Scots [slaves]. The man's name was Haki and the woman's Hekia. The King advised Leif to make use of these people if he should ever stand in need of fleet runners, for they were swifter than deer. Erik and Leif had given Karlsefni the use of this couple.

When they sailed past Furdustrandir [into the bay] they put the Scots ashore and directed them to run to the southward and investigate the nature of the country. They were to return before the end of the third day. They were each clad in a garment which they called "kiafal," and which was so fashioned that it had a hood on top, was open at the sides, was sleeveless and was fastened between the legs by buttons and loops. Apart from this they were naked.

Karlsefni and his followers cast anchor during their absence, and when the Scots came back one of them carried a bunch of vine-berries and the other an ear of wild wheat. They came on board the ship, whereupon Karlsefni said they seemed to have found goodly things, and then he and his followers held on their way along a coast which was indented with fiords [fiardskorit].

They stood into a fiord with their ship. There was an island out in the mouth of this fiord about which strong currents flowed, therefore they called it Straumey [Island of Strong Currents]. There were so many eider ducks on the island that it was scarcely possible to walk between their eggs.

They sailed into the fiord and called it Straumfiord [Fiord of the Strong Currents]. They carried their cargoes ashore from their ships and established themselves there.

[SOURCES: Erik the Red Saga and Thorfinn Karlsefni Saga]

SANDWICH BAY

WHEN THE NORSE LANDED on Kialarness and climbed its spine they would have been able to look inland for many miles. In the foreground, just behind the beach, they would have seen a border of tall grasses, including strand-wheat, which not only makes excellent cattle fodder but which can be used as a substitute for domestic grain in the making of meal. Beyond the dunes and the verge of grasses, the country would have appeared to be one vast expanse of low-lying forest that gradually lifted to become an undulating, forest-clad highland in the far distance.

Attractive as the land was, this was no place for ships to linger. The wide-open coast offered no shelter and the sand bottom gave poor holding for the big killock anchors. Despite the anxiety of the settlers to get ashore, the skippers would have been anxious to leave this exposed place, and so the anchors were brought home and the vessels got under way.

After leaving Cape Porcupine the ships entered Trunmore Bight and probably coasted the gently curving beach at no great distance off until they rounded Sandy Point. They would then have opened a huge bay stretching away to the southwestward. The saga says, "the country became indented with bays and they steered their ships into a bay," and it is noteworthy that the specific word for bay, as opposed to fiord, is used. The reference is evidently to the two great bays, Grosswater and Sandwich, both of which are plotted in their correct latitudes on the ancient Stefansson Map (see Appendix G) so that we can be in no doubt about their correct identification.

The ships were now entering Sandwich Bay, which is one of the most attractive inlets on the Atlantic seaboard. The shores are low, and on the northwestern side they are fronted for considerable distances by sand beaches or by patches of open grassland lying between tidewater and the encroaching forests. Four large and placid rivers enter the bay through broad and shallow estuaries. They are full of salmon, have grass and marsh verges, and can be navigated for many miles by small craft.

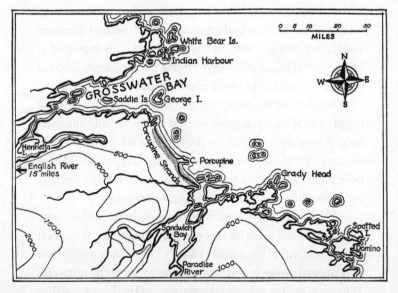

Grosswater Bay

Liveyers, as the local residents call themselves, say that the climate is always much better in the bay than elsewhere on the Labrador, and some early visitor was sufficiently impressed with the place to name one of the major rivers Paradise.

As they worked their way past Earl Island, which almost plugs the throat of the bay, and opened the quiet reaches beyond, the Norse may again have wondered if this might not be the place they were seeking. They would have seen a large island, Huntingdon, lying off from the mouth of the bay "to the north of the land" and separated from the mainland by a sound which ran east and west. This would have fitted very well into the specific description of the approach to Vinland as it has been preserved in the saga accounts.

By the time they reached the bottom of the bay they were "a long way from the sea," and if they tried to enter the northeast arm on a falling tide they would probably have grounded on sand flats a mile or two from land. The only salient feature of Leif's Vinland which was lacking in Sandwich Bay was, and is, a barachois harbour.

That the Norse were intensely interested in the place is established by the fact that they anchored here for three days and sent the two Scots runners ashore to explore to the south "to discover the nature of the country" and probably also to look for Leif's booths. The saga does not say so, but it can be assumed that the party also launched some of their boats and sent them to explore the shoreline. When the runners came back they are said to have brought samples of vine-berries and wild wheat. The wild wheat would have been strand-wheat, and the vine-berries may have been high-bush cranberries. That they were not wild grapes seems to be established by Thorhall the Hunter's acid comment later on about the absence of grape wine, or by implication the wherewithal to make it, in that portion of the new lands which he saw.

Karlsefni seems to have been impressed by the good qualities of the country, but nevertheless to have decided to sail on. This decision may not have been a unanimous one. From what happened later it seems that at least some of the Greenlandic contingent felt that Vinland *did* lie in this neighborhood, if not even farther to the north. Thorhall the Hunter, for one, seems to have believed this, and Thorvald Eriksson may have agreed with him.

By this time there may also have been a growing feeling among the settlers that, Vinland or no Vinland, it was time to pick a site and go ashore. The summer was drawing on, and apart from being heartily sick of the crowded shipboard life, the colonists had doubtless begun to worry about their livestock, and about the vital necessity of establishing a camp and harvesting sufficient forage to see them through the coming winter. Sandwich Bay would have seemed more than satisfactory to some of the colonists, and there may have been hot-tempered disagreement when the order was given to hoist sail once more.

BELLE ISLE (STRAUMEY)

Disagreement or no, the expedition sailed on, presumably leaving Sandwich Bay through the sound to the south of Huntingdon Island, with the mainland running off ahead of them to the eastward until they cleared Grady Head and found the coast again trending southeast as far as Spotted Island.

From Spotted Island the coastline runs off almost due south and undergoes another abrupt change in character, becoming, in the words of the *Labrador Pilot*, "indented by many irregular inlets"—which is almost a paraphrase of the saga description. The hundred-mile-long stretch of coast between Spotted Island

and Battle Harbour is indented by a dozen major fiords and innumerable smaller ones. However, although it is a good coast for fishermen, it has little to offer prospective farmers, for it is generally rather bleak, steep-to and rugged, although it possesses good forests. By comparison with Sandwich Bay it would have looked uninviting to the Norse, and it can be imagined that discontent and grumbling grew worse as the ships sailed on past what must have seemed like an interminable stretch of inhospitable coast. The colonists seemed to be getting no nearer to Vinland. In fact they were drawing away from the only country they had so far seen which bore any marked resemblance to Leif's fabled land.

Karlsefni and some of the other skippers must by now have become seriously concerned about their whereabouts. After leaving Cod Island, they would hardly have been able to identify any place which would have fitted what they knew of Bjarni's voyage, for they had been coasting while he had made direct sea-passages between widely isolated points along the coast. Their chances of identifying Spotted Island and the country immediately south of it as Bjarni's second land would have been small, for there are few easily recognizable features on this section of the coast. But they had committed themselves to the coast, and could go only where it led, hoping that it would eventually take them to Vinland.

When they reached Battle Harbour and rounded Cape Charles they would have been in for a severe shock. The land, which had been generally trending to the southeastward ever since they reached Helluland, now began to fall off sharply toward the southwest. South of them they would have seen what looked like open ocean (the mouth of the Strait of Belle Isle) with, far away to the southeast, the loom of an island or a distant and isolated headland.

In such a situation we can suppose that the skippers followed standard Norse practice and sent someone ashore to climb the 700-foot peak on Cape Charles in order to see what lay beyond. From this peak, or from any similar point they may have chosen in the general vicinity, an observer with ideal viewing conditions would have been able to see about thirty nautical miles. He would have had a good view of the distant land to the east and would have realized that it was in reality a big island (Belle Isle). He would have seen no sign of land beyond it, nor to the southward. He would also have been able to confirm that the coast of Markland continued to trend southwest until it ran out of sight.

The problem of what to do next must have been a difficult one to resolve. Doubtless some of the people clamoured for a return to the known advantages of Sandwich or Grosswater bays. Some may have been willing to venture a little further into the unknown, but would have preferred taking the safer course and following the coast to the southwestward, although from what could be seen of its abrupt and looming contours it could hardly have looked very prepossessing.

On the other hand the more daring and resolute men may have argued for an investigation of the distant island. They might have reminded the pessimists that on a previous occasion— at Holton Peninsula—it had looked as if Markland had come to an end, but that they had again picked up the southeast-trending coast beyond it. They may also have pointed out that the off-lying island was obviously very high and that a view from its crest would enable them to decide conclusively whether the open water was only another great inlet or was in fact open sea defining the end of Markland. Those who did not feel that the expedition had as yet reached the Vinland country probably argued strongly for one final sally to the south and in the event they won the day.

Leaving the Labrador coast at some point near Battle Harbour, the ships sailed out across the intervening eighteen or twenty miles of open water to Belle Isle. Belle Isle is a most striking plateau island, ten miles long and rising almost sheer from the sea on all sides to a tableland whose maximum altitude is just over 800 feet. It has no harbors, but there are a number of coves. The knorrir could have anchored temporarily in one of these on the leeward side of the great rock, while a few men rowed ashore and scaled the cliffs to the high tableland above.

They would probably not, as the saga says, have found "so many eider ducks on the island that it was scarcely possible to walk between their eggs." Eiders do not commonly nest on this type of large, high island; they prefer small, low-lying islands close to a mainland shore. Also, the eider egg season (as well as the egg season for all other seabirds) in the Strait of Belle Isle area would likely have been over by the time the Norse arrived. What has happened here (and it has misled many commentators) is that this first island—Straumey—and some other much smaller island or islands lying near the Straumfiord Camp of the Norse have lost their separate identities and have become one island. Later references to the spring gathering of eggs seem to make this clear.[69]

Straumey literally means Stream Island; but in the usage of the Norse period it meant an island surrounded by especially strong currents. There are numerous applications of the word "straum" to islands, fiords, headlands and even coasts in Norway, Iceland and Greenland; and in every case the word is used to distinguish a place where the currents are particularly noteworthy.

Belle Isle stands in such a position that it receives the full force of the inshore branch of the southbound Labrador Current. It also lies full in the path of the extraordinarily powerful tidal currents flowing in and out of the Strait of Belle Isle. When the tide is ebbing through the strait, bolstered by the flow of the St. Lawrence River, it runs at an average of three knots and has been known to run as high as six knots at certain places. With a flood tide, assisted by the westbound offshoot of the Labrador Current, the stream has been known to average three and one-half knots, with a maximum of seven knots.

Fishermen who use Belle Isle as a summer base report that the current flowing eastward past the island frequently reaches four knots, and when it meets the southbound Labrador Current, maelstroms or bores occur of sufficient violence to make it impossible to keep fishing gear in the water, no matter how firmly it may be anchored.

There is no other place on the Atlantic seaboard between Cape Chidley and the Bay of Fundy where there are such strong currents covering such a broad sweep of water. It seems impossible to doubt that Straumfiord is the Strait of Belle Isle, and that Straumey is Belle Isle itself.

The argument is sometimes raised that since the Norse used the word Straum*fiord* they could not have meant the Strait of Belle Isle because it is actually a sound. However, it was not until the 1533–1536 voyage of Jacques Cartier that Europeans appear to have realized that Newfoundland was an island not connected to the mainland of Labrador at some point far to the westward of Belle Isle. For at least fifty years before Cartier's discovery, Basque, French and English fishermen had been catching cod and whales in the northeastern arm of the Gulf of St. Lawrence, which they called the Grande Bay, under the impression that it was no more than a deep inlet opening on the sea through the Strait of Belle Isle. It is unreasonable to insist that the Norse voyagers of circa A.D. 1000 should have recognized a truth which eluded later-day voyagers for half a century.[70]

If it was a clear day when the men from Karlsefni's flotilla scaled Belle Isle, they would have been rewarded by a stupendous view. From the high plateau they would have been able to look down the throat of the strait as far as L'Anse Amour on the bald northern shore—a distance of nearly sixty miles. They would have seen far less of the southern shore, for it is generally low and is partly hidden behind the Cape Norman headland. Nevertheless, the impression of the strait which one gets from the crest of Belle Isle is of a very deep fiord narrowing away into the blue distance, and anyone who did not know otherwise would be convinced that the land swung eastward again from the bottom of this inlet. Consequently the Norse would logically have mistaken the tip of the Great Northern Peninsula of Newfoundland for a continuation of the Markland coast.

The most prominent feature in the foreground of this coast would have been Quirpon Head and Cape Bauld, with an elevation of five hundred feet, lying fourteen miles due south of Belle Isle. To the west of it the Norse would have seen other land, but it would have been hard to determine whether they were looking at islands or headlands, since apart from Quirpon the coastal section of the tip of the peninsula is mostly low lying and rather featureless.

They must have felt a great surge of hope as they looked south from Belle Isle. The description of the approaches to Leif's Vinland, as preserved into our time in the saga accounts, comes very close to being a description of the Belle Isle-Quirpon-Cape Norman area. It seems likely that the voyagers were convinced that they had at long last reached the portals of Vinland, and that nothing remained but to search the nearby coasts until they found Leif's harbour and his booths.

The saga tells us only that after leaving Straumey they sailed into Straumfiord, went ashore, and established a wintering camp.

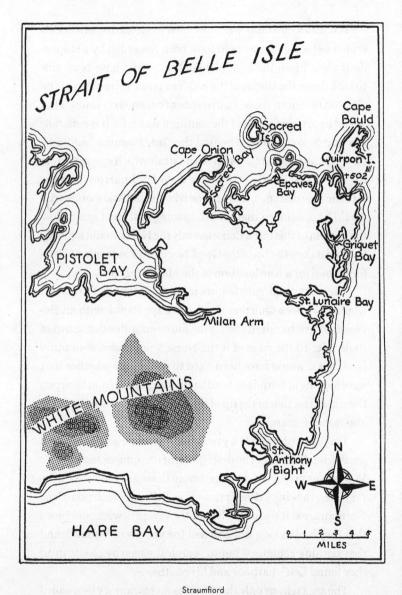

STRAIT OF BELLE ISLE

Cape Bauld

Sacred Isl.

Cape Onion

Quirpon I.

+502

Sacred Bay

Epaves Bay

Griquet Bay

PISTOLET BAY

St. Lunaire Bay

Milan Arm

WHITE MOUNTAINS

St. Anthony Bight

N

W   E

S

HARE BAY

0 1 2 3 4 5
MILES

Straumfiord

This passage is so brief that we must assume the loss of a portion of the original account which not only explained why they went ashore, but described in some detail where they landed. As things stand we are not even told whether the camp was on the north or the south coast of the strait, nor is there any indication of what sort of harbour was chosen—an omission which could hardly have existed in the original oral saga.

THE CAMPSITE AT EPAVES BAY

We must locate the Straumfiord campsite for ourselves. We can eliminate the north shore of the strait since the voyagers would hardly have turned back from Belle Isle toward the forbidding line of thousand-foot bluffs which guard the coast from Chateau Bay to L'Anse Amour. Even if they had done so, they would have found no settlement site suitable to their needs.

The southwest coast from Cape Norman to Savage Cove can also be eliminated. It is a low limestone shore offering no reasonable shelter even for vessels of the knorr type, and it is backed by a useless morass of black spruce bogs and barrens which present almost as inhospitable a face to the sea as do the brooding highlands of the northwestern shore.

There remains only one small stretch of coast which could have been sufficiently attractive to the Norse to encourage them to establish even a temporary camp. This section encompasses the extreme northern tip of the Great Northern Peninsula of Newfoundland between Cape Bauld and Cape Norman, and includes Pistolet and Sacred bays.

From Belle Isle the flotilla would have sailed for Quirpon and Cape Bauld since this is not only the most prominent feature on the coast, it is the part of Newfoundland lying closest to Belle Isle. As they closed with Cape Bauld, the low coast to the westward of it would have begun to take form, and lookouts at every masthead would have been anxiously scanning these new shores for clues to Vinland's whereabouts. If the voyagers identified Straumey with Leif's "island lying to the north of the land," they would then have identified Quirpon with the "cape stretching to the north of the land." The fact that Quirpon is actually an island would not have been apparent to them, since it is separated from the mainland only by a very narrow and twisted gut. If, on the other hand, they felt that Straumey lay too far offshore to be Leif's island, they would have been searching for another island lying closer to the coast. In this case Great Sacred Island, lying four miles westward of Quirpon, would certainly have caught their eye.

Great Sacred Island, Cape Onion to the southwestward of it, and the sound which separates the two fit the Greenlanders Story description of the approaches to Vinland with remarkable fidelity. Consequently they bear a marked resemblance to the Baccalieu Island-Bay de Verde Peninsula-Baccalieu Tickle complex. Only the scale is wrong; for these latter features are much larger and more prominent than their Sacred Bay counterparts.

Karlsefni's problems in trying to resolve what he knew about Vinland with what he could now see of the country ahead of him may not have been so very different from those of those later-day commentators who have been attracted to the Pistolet-Sacred Bay area in the belief that it must have harbored Leif's Vinland. Apart from the Tickle Cove Pond location, there is no other place on the Atlantic seaboard of North America which so nearly (but not quite) answers to the description in the Greenlanders Story. And therein lie a set of frustrations and paradoxes which have driven a number of authors to the verge of desperation, and which have forced others to undertake heroic changes in local topography, in the sea level, or in other intractable features of the country in order to force a perfect fit.

Karlsefni and his companions were not interested in any such academic solution to the problem. They were looking for the physical reality of Vinland, and they urgently needed to find it since the time left to them for exploration must have been growing perilously short.

The probability is that they cruised west from Quirpon to Sacred Island, tentatively identifying it with Leif's island, and so rounded Cape Onion in the hope that Pistolet Bay would prove to be the fiord at whose foot lay the lagoon lake and the Vinland booths. The hope would have been tentative, because if Great Sacred Island was to be accepted as Leif's "island off the land," what were they to make of Belle Isle and Quirpon, one of which Leif would have been bound to see before raising Sacred Island? On the other hand, if Belle Isle was the indicator island, how were they to account for the excessive width of the sound—fourteen nautical miles—which separates it from the mainland cape?

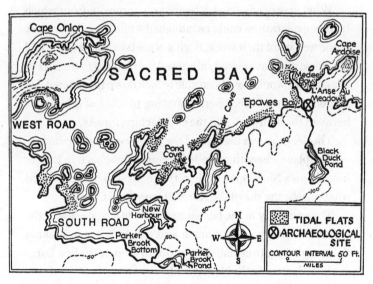

Things must have looked *almost* right, but not *quite* right. And when ships, or afterboats put off for the purpose, had descended into and explored the shallow, reef-strewn reaches of Pistolet Bay, the explorers would have found nothing to answer to the saga description of of the lagoon lake, of the grassy forelands, or of the magnificaent mixed forests which had made Leif rich.

Constantly fluctuating hopes and a general feeling of frustration must have plagued the leaders of the expedition almost beyond endurance. Some of them evidently continued to believe that Vinland lay somewhere close at hand, and they would have been in favour of persevering in the search. On the other hand, the colonists must have become increasingly concerned about the condition of their livestock, and of their women and children, and must have been clamouring to be put ashore, if only temporarily. Karlsefni himself may have been willing to agree to their demands for personal reasons, since Gudrid was by then at least six months pregnant.

What was needed was a temporary campsite from which further explorations could be launched while the colonists saw to the welfare of their stock. Such a place lay close at hand, and the Norse may have already glimpsed it. In sailing to the Sacred Islands they would have been able to look down into Sacred Bay and observe that there were tempting patches of grasslands between the landwash and the encroaching forests.

The decision was made, and the ships turned in to shore.

The place where they landed seems to have been in Epaves Bay, where a Norwegian author, Helge Ingstad, has excavated what may be the site of the Norse Straumfiord Camp.[71]

Thus on a day in the late summer of the first decade of the eleventh century, men, women and children began making their way ashore to establish what was to become the first European settlement in the New World.

20

THE SEARCH FOR VINLAND

The Saga Tale (c. 1004–1005)

They had brought with them all kinds of livestock.

Now they explored the country thereabouts. There were mountains in the vicinity and the land was fair to look upon. They did nothing but explore the country. There was tall grass thereabouts.

They spent the winter there but they had a hard winter and one for which they had not prepared. The fishing fell off and they grew short of food. They went out to the islands in the hope that they might find something in the way of fishing or some flotsam. Although their livestock fared well, there was little food left [for the people]. They called on God to send them food, but did not get a response as quickly as they needed it.

Then Thorhall the Hunter disappeared. They searched for him for three days and on the fourth day Karlsefni and Bjarni [Grimolfsson] found him on a clifftop.

He was lying there with eyes, mouth and nostrils gaping, and was scratching himself and muttering something. They asked him why he had come to this place and he told them not to be concerned by what he did, for he was old enough to look after himself.

Then they asked him to go home with them, and this he did.

Soon afterward a whale appeared and they got it and flensed it, but no one could tell what kind of whale it was. Karlsefni had much knowledge of whales, but he did not recognize this one.

When the cooks had prepared it the people ate of it and they were all sickened by it.

Then Thorhall the Hunter approached them and said: "Did not Red Beard [Thor] prove more helpful than your Christ? This [whale] is my reward for the verses I dedicated to Thor the Trustworthy. Seldom has he failed me."

When the people heard this none of them would eat, and they threw [the meat] into the sea and invoked God's mercy,

The weather then improved so they could row out to go fishing and they no longer lacked the necessities of life. In the spring they went out into Straumfiord and obtained provisions from both regions, hunting on the mainland, and gathering eggs and going deep-sea fishing [on the Fiord].

[SOURCES: Erik the Red Saga and Thorfinn Karlsefni Saga]

THE CHOICE OF EPAVES BAY

BY THE TIME THE SETTLERS went ashore the summer must have been almost spent, and if they had intended to remain all hands ought to have buckled down to the task of making ready for the winter. The Greenlanders, at least, were seasoned colonists who had good reason to know the vital importance of making every possible preparation. Yet, in the words of the saga, they did nothing but explore the country. This apparent fecklessness could have been due only to the fact that the colonists did not expect to have to remain at Epaves Bay.

Certainly it was not an ideal location. The Norse preferred the inner reaches of protected fiords or bays as settlement sites and seldom tried to establish pastoral settlements on exposed outer coasts unless there was no alternative. And there were a number of alternatives in the Sacred Bay region, all of them preferable to Epaves Bay.[72] In South Road, for example, less than six miles away, there were excellent sites at Parker Brook

Bottom and at New Harbour. These offered many advantages which Epaves Bay could not boast. The grasslands at New Harbour are, and apparently always were, much more extensive than those at Epaves Bay, and in addition there was a huge adjacent stretch of bog pasture. Parker Brook is, and probably was in Norse times, an excellent salmon river; but Black Duck Brook at Epaves Bay was far too small ever to have had a significant salmon run. New Harbour and Parker Brook Bottom are well protected from the prevailing winter winds of the strait, which are northwesterlies. Epaves Bay lies wide open to these winds.

In the nineteenth century there was a settlement of twenty to thirty families at New Harbour, and these people existed primarily on what they could grow for themselves, depending on fishing only to provide money for the purchase of those few items that they could not produce. At one time there were as many as fifty head of cattle and innumerable sheep at New Harbour. In the twentieth century the New Harbour folk gradually moved out to sites on the open coast, nearer the fishing grounds, as a result of a shift from a self-sustaining economy to one dependent on the sale of dry cod. There is no record of there ever having been a pastoral—or even a fishing—community at Epaves Bay during colonial times. The bay was used, as we have noted in Appendix N, only by transient Europeans as a summer whaling base. Even the settlement at nearby L'Anse aux Meadows was always a fishing community, although some sheep and cattle were kept by the residents.

Perhaps most important is the fact that New Harbour and Parker Brook Bottom both offered good, secure winter harbors for the knorrir. The safety of their vessels to people who were venturing into an alien world would have been of paramount importance. It is hard to believe that the Norse would have deliberately chosen to risk their ships on the open strand at

Epaves Bay, where no harbour of any sort existed, through the crucial winter months. The ships could have been secured at Epaves Bay only by hauling them ashore for a distance of several hundred feet beyond high-water mark, and the amount of time and effort which would have been required to accomplish such a feat would be tremendous.

I believe that Epaves Bay was originally intended to serve only as a transient camp. It was a convenient halting place where the animals could be fed back to health and where the colonists could refresh themselves after the long, crowded and uncomfortable voyage. Meanwhile the balance of the men were organized into exploring parties and sent out to search the coasts of the northern section of the Great Northern Peninsula for Leif's Vinland booths.

Karlsefni and his fellow chiefs perhaps hoped that Leif's haven might lie hidden at the foot of some fiord or bay which they had not seen from the ships, or which they had been unable to fully explore. What was needed was a detailed search of the coast both east and west, and this was a task for the ships' boats.

The afterboats belonging to the knorrir were about thirty feet long and could carry twenty people in an emergency, or eight or nine on a prolonged voyage. They were equipped with oars and sails. Being lightly built and finely fashioned, they were fast and easy to handle. Because of their shallow draft they could enter almost any body of water. The foreboat which each large knorr also carried was similar but smaller. All told the expedition probably possessed six or eight boats, and we assume that most of these were dispatched to search for Leif's booths.

"They did nothing but explore the country." This can hardly refer to overland exploration, since attempts to penetrate the dense black spruce forests which at that time covered almost all of the tip of the peninsula would have been pointless. The phrase can refer only to boat explorations. In a matter of several weeks a flotilla of six boats could have thoroughly explored the coast for some distance beyond Cape Norman to the south and west, and to Hare Bay, or beyond, to the south and east.

As the boats sailed or rowed back into Epaves Bay, and as one by one their skippers reported finding no signs of Leif's haven, the hope of locating Vinland that season would finally have failed. By then it would probably have been too late to think of seeking another site at which to spend the winter, and so Epaves Bay, where temporary booths had doubtless already been erected, would have become the location of the wintering camp, by default rather than by choice.

THE NATURE OF THE PLACE

Despite the fact that Vinland had so far eluded them, the colonists—though probably not the traders—may have been moderately well satisfied with Epaves Bay.

Apart from the shore meadow, which would have provided sufficient pasture for the limited number of cattle that the Norse could have transported in their ships, this was fine berry country; there was no shortage of firewood lying in windrows above the high-tide mark and already dry and ready for use; the shore-fishery would have been excellent, and harbour seals and whales would have been relatively abundant. Late summer ducks probably abounded, and the condition of the adjacent islands would have demonstrated that these were favoured breeding grounds for ducks and other seabirds.

However, although the sea was rich in food resources, the land would have proved disappointing. The black spruce forests, exposed as they were to the prevailing gales and nurtured on scanty soil, would not have been very promising as a source of export timber. There were no hardwoods of any size to be found nor, as the saga later testifies, were there any grapes.[73]

Land animal life would have been scarce. The spruce forests do not provide caribou range[74], nor are they a good habitat for arctic hares or ptarmigan. Snowshoe rabbits (varying hares), which ought to have been abundant in such a forest, did not then exist in Newfoundland but were introduced during colonial times.

It is unlikely that the people were much concerned about the food supply at first. The immediate problem was to build winter houses and to put the ships into winter quarters. With one hundred and sixty people to house and four big ships to haul out and secure, there would have been little free time left for worrying about what the winter might bring.

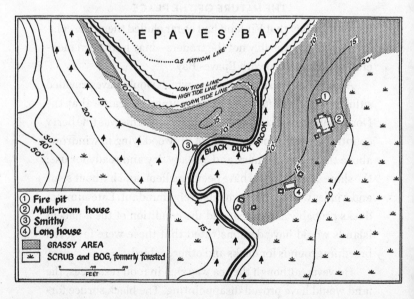

① Fire pit
② Multi-room house
③ Smithy
④ Long house
▨ GRASSY AREA
⅃ SCRUB and BOG, formerly forested

0   100   200
FEET

THE HARD WINTER

When winter came, the Norse found that life was not going to go as easily as they had hoped. The one factor which they had not considered—because they could not—was the weather. Winter weather in the Epaves Bay area today is not only cold, it is about as wild as it can be. The low coast is exposed to every wind from east through north to west, and the winds which blow over the Strait of Belle Isle in wintertime can and do blow at hurricane strength for days on end. The strength of the winter winds is alone sufficient to keep small boats from venturing out into the strait except on rare occasions; and in addition the pack ice coming south on the Labrador Current so plugs the strait and jams its shores that even big steel steamers cannot force a passage through. Consequently the strait is normally closed to all navigation, except by specially reinforced ships, from the end of October until the end of June.

Although the climate in Karlsefni's time was milder than it is now, the winds were probably just as strong; and although arctic pack ice did not close the strait for as long a period as it does at present, it would still have been a major problem during the midwinter months. From December to April it may well have blocked the strait, or at least denied its use to vessels as lightly built as the Norse boats were. Thus there would have been long periods when the settlers could not have launched their boats in order to go fishing. Furthermore, the ice would have raftered on the open coast, thus keeping small boats ashore for weeks or months on end.

As the storm winds blew and food grew scarce in the crude sod shanties, many people must have wished that they had given up the search for Vinland long before, and had used the extra time to make dry fish or to go whaling. They were probably not actually starving or they would have turned to the almost-last resort and begun butchering their cattle, which were doing well enough by foraging for themselves on the shore pastures, which would have been kept largely snow-free by the strong winds.

Nevertheless the people were hungry enough to call on their gods for help; and at this juncture some of the flesh of the original saga has remained more or less intact so that we have more than a skeletal account of the events which took place.

Presumably the Christians in the party (who were probably not numerous) began praying to White Christ for help; whereupon that intractable pagan, Thorhall the Hunter, decided to call on Thor. But one did not pray to Thor. The way to gain his aid was to go to some lonely place[75] and alternately argue, bribe, threaten, and cajole him into providing assistance—and the most efficacious cajolement was to compose a poem of praise in his honour and recite it to the wind and sky.

The clerics who were responsible for transcribing and preserving the written sagas during the Middle Ages must have been distressed by the original version of what happened, for it is quite clear that Thorhall was answered and that the Christians were not. Shortly after Thorhall followed Karlsefni and Bjarni back to camp, a whale blundered into the bay or was found dead among the ice.

Great fires were promptly lit and everyone gathered around while the cooks filled the pots with meat and hung strips of meat and blubber beside the fires to roast. The gorging which followed doubtless resulted in some stomach aches, but it is questionable whether the meat actually poisoned those who ate it. This could be an interjection by some righteous priest at a much later date.

It is also extremely unlikely that when Thorhall made his claim to having been responsible for procuring the whale, with

Thor's help, the starving people rose up en masse and heaved the whale meat back into the sea. What they almost certainly did was go right on eating whale until the carcass was stripped and spring was approaching. That this was in fact the case is strongly indicated in the second verse of Thorhall's song, presented later in this chapter, which, with a few other fragments of verse preserved in the saga, is believed by scholars to be an unaltered fragment of the original oral saga.

With the approach of spring, the shortage of food ceased to be a problem. As the weather improved and the pack ice disappeared, the boats were able to get out into the open waters of the strait, where they engaged in "deep-sea" fishing, a term which doubtless includes whaling and perhaps sealing as well, since both whales and seals were considered to be fish in those times and were so referred to.

It had been a long, hard winter, but one event took place which makes this winter remarkable, from our point of view at least. At some time in the autumn or early winter Gudrid gave birth to a son. He was named Snorri, possibly in honour of Snorri Thorbrandsson, who seems not only to have been Karlsefni's closest comrade but to have also been the elder wise man of the expedition.

Snorri Thorfinnsson, who lived to become a famous man in his own right in Iceland, was presumably the first child of white parents to be born in North America, and in this sense he becomes the first North American of full European descent ... whatever that may be worth.

Although the settlers were no longer suffering from hunger, they seem to have remained rather discontented and there was evidently a good deal of bickering and contention among them, bickering which perhaps originated from differences of opinion as to what they should do when summer released them.

A degree of dissatisfaction with the Straumfiord Camp was probably general. It had certainly not lived up to the expectations, based on the descriptions of Vinland, which the colonists and the traders must have had when they set out from Greenland. Apart from the absence of wild grapes—which seem to have had the same magical significance to these early voyagers as spices had for later ones—suitable hardwood forests and fur-bearing animals, the weather at Straumfiord must have proved to be much worse than the settlers would have been led to anticipate.

This not only affected the fishing; it seriously endangered the invaluable boats and ships. As we have noted, there was no harbour at Epaves Bay into which the ships could have been brought for safekeeping, or where the boats could have sheltered during stormy weather. In particular the open gravel beach offered no protection from the ice, which sometimes rafters forty yards inland from high-tide mark.

The shortcomings of the area may have caused the various contingents to react in different degrees. The Greenland colonists, who were particularly inured to hardship and a tough existence, would have been the least discontented, since compared with Greenland the Straumfiord area was a land of milk and honey. The Icelandic settlers would have been less inclined to accept this substitute for Vinland, not only because they were not as rough and ready as their Greenland counterparts, but also because they were subject to the influence of Karlsefni and Thorhall Gamlisson. The two shipowners were not settlers. They were traders, whose prime interest in the western lands lay in their expectations of gathering a valuable lading of local products to carry back to Greenland, Iceland or even to Norway. For them Straumfiord would have been a major disappointment, and Karlsefni seems to have been personally convinced that Vinland *could* be found and that the expedition ought to carry on a major search for it.

Some of the leaders of the Greenland contingent, and particularly Thorvald Eriksson, evidently shared this view. The trouble was that there was no agreement as to the direction in which the search should be made. In fact there appear to have been three quite divergent opinions about the matter.

WHERE IS VINLAND?

One group apparently believed the expedition had already passed Vinland during the voyage down the Markland coast—a belief which may have arisen as a result of the flotilla's brief incursion into Grosswater and Sandwich bays.

The opinions held by the other two groups were related in that both evidently rested on the belief that one of the islands near the mouth of Straumfiord was the indicator island for the mouth of Leif's fiord, and despite the failure of the local exploring parties to locate his booths, the expedition was still on the right path. This belief may have been strengthened by the discovery, during the explorations late in the preceding summer, that Quirpon was an island; for Quirpon answers moderately well not only to the saga description of the approaches to Vinland but also to a verbal description of the Baccalieu-Bay de Verde landfall.

Those who believed in the likelihood that Vinland lay somewhere at the foot of Straumfiord would therefore have been united in the conviction that they should steer to the west; but beyond this their views differed.

Perhaps because one of the westward boat expeditions of the previous year had found the south coast of the fiord beyond Cape Norman to be barren, devoid of harbors, and generally unprepossessing as far as anyone could see, some of the people may have reasoned that the search should be prosecuted along the northerly coast of the fiord. The remainder apparently felt that the southerly coast *beyond* the barren stretch offered the best prospects.

The division of opinions seems to have generally followed national lines. The Icelandic colonists together with Karlsefni and Thorhall Gamlisson, were evidently united in the belief that Vinland ought to be sought for to the southwest of Straumfiord Camp. This view was doubtless shared by Freydis and by Helge and Finnboggi. On the other hand the Greenlanders, excepting only Freydis and her band, seem to have been convinced that Vinland lay either to the north in the Grosswater Bay area, or to the west somewhere along the south coast of Labrador.

Furthermore the Icelanders apparently felt that the entire expedition should abandon Straumfiord Camp and undertake a ship-borne expedition to the southwest, while the Greenlanders appear to have felt that it would be wiser for the majority of the people, together with the cattle and the precious ships, to remain at Straumfiord Camp while long-distance boat expeditions were sent out to search for Vinland to the north and west.

In the event this divergence of opinions led to the dispatch of three separate exploring expeditions during the first summer season in the New World. In the balance of this chapter we deal with those which the Greenlanders led.[76]

The Saga Tale (c. 1005)

Now they took counsel together concerning their expedition, and came to an agreement. Thorhall the Hunter wished to go northward around Furdustrandir and Kialarness and so seek Vinland, while Karlsefni wished to proceed southward off the coast, believing that the farther to the southward, the better the country would be.

Thorhall prepared for his voyage out by the islands. He had only nine men in his party. All the rest stayed with Karlsefni.

One day while Thorhall was watering his ship he took a drink and then recited this poem:

> Famous Leaders told me I would have
> The best of drink when I came hither,
> Therefore I cannot blame the land.
> But see, you Helmeted Champions,
> How instead of drinking wine
> I must raise this pail [of water]
> Which I had to stoop to fill at the spring.

Then they [Thorhall and his men] put to sea and Karlsefni accompanied them out beyond the island. Before they hoisted sail Thorhall recited another poem:

> Let us go to that quarter
> Discovered by our countrymen.[77]
> We will explore well
> Beyond the keel place and the sweeping sands,
> Travelling on the sea
> While these Great Warrior Chiefs
> Who think so highly of this land
> Remain behind and gorge upon
> Whale meat on this so marvelous strand.

Then they sailed away to the northward past Furdustrandir and Kialarness, intending to cruise to the westward around the cape. But they encountered westerly gales and were [eventually] driven ashore in Ireland, where they were savagely treated and thrown into slavery. And there Thorhall was killed, according to what traders [from Ireland] have related.

[SOURCES: Erik the Red Saga and Thorfinn Karlsefni Saga]

Thorvald Eriksson gave orders to have an afterboat made ready for a voyage to the western part of the country, [intending] to make use of the summer exploring in that direction.

To [those who went on this voyage] the land seemed good. It was well wooded and it was not far from the woods to the sea, and there were white sands. There were many islands and shoals.

They found no dwellings of men or beasts but in one of the western islands they found a storage shed of wood, but no other work of man. They came back to the [Straumfiord] booths at harvest time.

[SOURCE: The Greenlanders Story]

THORHALL'S SEARCH

Thorhall put out to sea in an afterboat. Nine men would not have been a sufficient crew for a knorr, and in any case it is established that none of the knorrir were missing when the expedition finally turned back for Greenland.

Thorhall intended to head for Grosswater Bay, just north of Porcupine Strands. On the southbound voyage the convoy had crossed this bay, and as we have noted there were enough similarities between this area and the described approaches to Leif's Vinland to suggest that Vinland might lie at the western end of the bay.

The saga is quite definite about this, for it states that Thorhall set out in search of Vinland and that once having passed Furdustrandir and Kialarness and reached the cape beyond these places, he intended to cruise to the westward. This could have taken him only into Grosswater Bay and thence, if he had persevered, into Lake Melville itself. My belief that this was what he planned is confirmed by the course followed by Thorvald Eriksson in the following summer, when he went looking for the missing party.

Luck was against Thorhall. Somewhere along his route, perhaps when the little vessel was rounding Spotted Island, he and his men were caught by a hard westerly gale and blown offshore. Probably their small craft was dismasted, for had she kept her sailing capabilities she ought to have been able to run before the gale and still make a steady northing which would eventually have brought her to Iceland, if not to Greenland. But without her sail, or with only a makeshift jury rig, she would have been largely at the mercy of the North Atlantic.

Thorhall's afterboat may have been the first small vessel manned by Europeans to be blown from Canadian waters to Europe, but she was by no means the last. During the past century alone there have been sixteen authentic records of dories which, having been swept away from Newfoundland waters, either reached the shores of Europe at points as widely separated as Vigo in Spain and the Hebrides off Scotland, or were picked up in European waters by passing ships. Unhappily in many of these cases the two-man crew of these seventeen- to nineteen-foot boats did not survive. Thorhall and his men fared better—their boat was much larger and presumably better provisioned—but their luck ran out completely when they reached Ireland. The Irish, having managed to cast off the Viking yoke, were not inclined to look kindly on Norsemen who fell into their hands; and it can be assumed that the stiff-necked and prickly-natured Thorhall would soon have given them an excuse to murder him.

Norse merchants, who, as we have noted earlier, were tolerated in Ireland as elsewhere on the continent because they were of value, heard something of the story and may even have spoken with some of Thorhall's enslaved crew, and so were able to carry word of the disaster back to Iceland.

Some time soon after Thorhall's departure, Thorvald Eriksson launched the second part of the Greenlanders' twofold exploration plan. Another afterboat was made ready, manned by about the same number of men as had accompanied Thorhall; and this second venture may have been led by Thorvald himself. The account of the expedition states that they sailed to the western part of the country. Starting from Straumfiord, this would logically mean that they cruised westward along the north shore of the Gulf of St. Lawrence.

The genesis for this voyage was probably one of the local explorations made late in the previous summer, when a boat party reached Cape Norman and, from the elevation behind it, looked out over the strait to the far shore, a distance of about fifteen nautical miles, and saw enough of the towering south Labrador coast to suggest to them that it might contain fiords which would answer to the Vinland descriptions.

Thorvald and his men doubtless crossed Straumfiord near Cape Norman and then coasted southwestward under the bluff and forbidding coast to Blanc Sablon, at which point the nature of the coastline changes abruptly.

From this point they would have swung nearly due west, along a far more amiable shore, and would have begun to see the deposits of shining white sand which lie at the bottoms of most of the succeeding bays and which give Blanc Sablon its name. These white sands do not form seaward beaches, as do the yellow sands at Porcupine Strand, but are found only deep inside the inlets or behind the protection of off-lying islands.

After passing Riviere St. Paul the expedition would have encountered stretches of coast which are shrouded by thousands of islands of all sizes, and which culminate in the Grand Rigolet and Mecatina regions, where for a distance of sixty

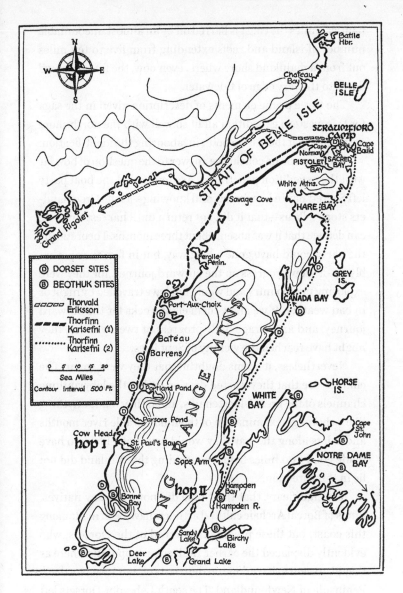

The search for Vinland

nautical miles the coast is barred off by an almost uncountable number of island and reefs extending from five to ten miles out from a mainland shore where, even now, the forests crowd down to the very edge of tidewater.

The three prime elements of description given in the saga for this western expedition all fit so well with the north shore of the gulf that there is no point in labouring the identification.

There can be no conclusive answer to the question of how far west the expedition penetrated. Assuming that the boat party left Sacred Bay in late spring, and knowing—as the Greenlanders story tells us—that it did not return until harvest time, we can deduce that it was absent about three months. Theoretically the party could have gone a long way, but in fact they probably made slow progress on the outward journey, for they were exploring new country and would not have travelled by night or in bad weather. If we allow them eight weeks for the outward journey, and an average daily progress of twenty miles, they might have reached the vicinity of Sept Isles.

Nevertheless, it seems doubtful that they went so far. The chances are that they wasted days on end in the labyrinthine channels of the great island chains, and if they made anything like a thorough examination of the innumerable river mouths and inlets along the way they would have been lucky to have made good 200 miles before concluding that Vinland did not lie in this direction.

It is significant that the Norse did not meet any natives. Finds of Boreal Archaic cultural artifacts have been made along this coast, but these predate the arrival of the Dorsets, who evidently displaced the earlier Indigenous population here as they also seem to have done on the coasts of the Great Northern Peninsula of Newfoundland. The south Labrador Dorsets left evidence of their presence as far west as Anticosti Island, but by about the year 1000 they seem to have abandoned this region together with the shores of the Strait of Belle Isle and the east coast of the peninsula—and for the same reason[78]—leaving it temporarily uninhabited.

The structure which the Norse took to be a grain storage shed may have been the remnant of a Dorset house or, if they found it far enough to the west, it might have been a bark-covered meat storage shed of the type built by the Montagnais people, who reoccupied the south Labrador coast some time after the Dorsets disappeared.

When Thorvald's party arrived back at Straumfiord they would have had marvelous tales to tell of the western lands, but nothing to report about the whereabouts of Vinland. Their accounts of the western country would have been glowing ones, for the coast beyond Blanc Sablon offered any number of attractive settlement sites. The possibility of moving west may have been discussed, but nothing could have been done until Thorhall returned from searching for Vinland to the north—and Thorhall never did return.

So the second winter closed in on the Straumfiord Camp, which must by then have begun to take on the appearance of a permanent settlement. It would have been a somewhat lonely camp that winter, and one filled with dire forebodings. Not only was there no word of Thorhall and his men, but there was no word of what had happened to the ships which had sailed south that summer under the leadership of Thorfinn Karlsefni.

21

THE LAND OF HOPE

The Saga Tale (c. 1005)

Now it is to be told that Karlsefni cruised southward off the coast with Snorri and Bjarni and their people.

They journeyed a long time until they came at last to a river which flowed down from the land into a lake and thence into the sea. There were such great sandbars at the mouth of the estuary that it could only be entered at the height of flood tide. Karlsefni and his people sailed into the estuary and called it there, Hop.

They found wild wheat-fields on the low-lying land, and wherever there was woodland they found [grape] vines. Every brook was full of fish. They dug trenches on the tidal flats and when the tide fell there were flatfish in the trenches. There were a great number of wild animals of all kinds in the woods.

They remained there two weeks enjoying themselves and not keeping any watch. They had their livestock with them.

Now one morning when they looked about they saw nine skin boats, and staves were being brandished from these boats and they were being whirled in the same direction that the sun moves, and they made a noise like flails.

Then Karlsefni asked: "What can this mean?"

Snorri Thorbrandsson answered him: "It may be that this is a peace signal, so let us display a white shield."

This they did, whereupon the strangers rowed toward them

and came ashore and [the Norse] marveled at them. They were swarthy people and queer looking, and the hair of their heads was ugly. They had remarkable eyes and broad cheeks. They stayed for some time, staring curiously at the people they saw before them, then they rowed away to the southward around the point.

Karlsefni and his men had pitched their booths above the [shore of] the lake, some of their houses being at the lake [the estuary], and some farther away near the main part of the land. They remained there all that winter. No snow came and their live-stock found their own food by grazing.

[SOURCES: Erik the Red Saga and the Karlsefni Saga]

The cattle went up on the land there, but it soon happened that the males became unruly and caused much trouble. They had a bull with them.

They profited by all the products of the land thereabouts; both grapes, deer, and fish and all good things.

[SOURCE: The Greenlanders Story]

WHILE THE BALANCE of the Greenlanders remained at Straum-fiord waiting for the boat expeditions to return from their search for Vinland to the west and north, the Icelandic contingent packed themselves aboard their ships and departed southward.

This southbound squadron evidently included the Helge-Finnboggi ship, since the saga account tells us that Frey-dis accompanied it, and she and the Icelandic brothers would have been interested in the same things which drew Karlsefni south: grapes, furs and hardwoods.

THE SOUTHERN VOYAGE

Rounding Cape Onion, after clearing from Sacred Bay, the three ships stood across the mouth of Pistolet Bay. Cape Norman came abeam, and course was altered to follow the bleak unbroken shore which stretched away to the south-southwest. [79]

During the second day the shore would have begun to look more interesting, even though it was obviously not Vinland country. The ships may have entered St. Margaret Bay and perhaps explored it, but it was wooded to the shores and could not have had much of an appeal to colonists.

For one reason or another they may not have sailed close to the seaward face of the projecting Port au Choix Peninsula. Had they done so they might have had their first warning that they were not alone in this new land.

One of the most important Dorset sites so far discovered lies on the seaward face of the Port au Choix headland. It has been studied by Dr. Elmer Harp, of Dartmouth College, over a five-year period, and the results of his work indicate that it was occupied for many centuries. The ground in and around the house ruins is so heavily carpeted with seal bones that in places they form a layer almost a foot thick. There is little evidence that much other game was taken, and most of the seal bones are from young seals.

When the harp seals are whelping on the pack ice in the Gulf of St. Lawrence, the prevailing westerly winds often set the pack tight against this section of the coast, and from an outthrust peninsula like Port au Choix it is no trick for men to go off on foot and make a great slaughter of the young seals as they lie helpless on the pans. It looks as if the Dorsets came to Port au Choix around March of each year, made a big kill of young seals, and then subsisted on stored meat and blubber until early summer, when they abandoned the sealing camp and withdrew to various rivers along the coast, where they could engage in salmon fishing.

If the Dorsets were at Port au Choix when Karlsefni's flotilla sailed past, they would have marveled at the ships; but even with good visibility it is unlikely that the Norse would have observed the low, skin-covered Dorset houses against the background of somber scrub and broken rocks of the peninsula.

From Port au Choix southward the ships sailed past a flat coastal plain which has only recently (in geological time) emerged from the sea, and which extends inland fifteen miles to end abruptly at the foot of the Long Range Mountains, which lift almost perpendicularly to heights of 2000 feet and more. This plain is a morass of spruce bogs and muskeg, with here and there a black stand of larger conifers clinging to the low back of a drowning ridge. It is a singularly depressing place, and even if there had been any cove along its coast to provide shelter for the knorrir, it is unlikely that the Norse would have bothered to go ashore.

As they sailed past this dreary coast the people on the three ships would have observed that the mountain wall was drawing closer and closer to the sea, and by the time they were abeam of Portland Creek the coastal plain had shrunk to a mere five miles in breadth.

Now they would have begun to see a change in the nature of the land. At Portland Creek they may well have been tempted to go ashore, for although there is no harbour there and the creek is too shoal and rapid to admit anything bigger than a dory, there is a cove of sorts, fringed with sandy beaches and backed by good-sized spruce standing on dry, hard ground.

Two hours' sail past Portland Creek, the Icelanders would have seen the limestone shingle of the long coast giving way to more and more stretches of yellow sands, and shortly afterward they would have entered a shallow bight across whose mouth stretched a broad gravel bar. Behind the bar lay a lagoon which could have harbored a hundred knorrir. This was Parsons Pond.

Here was a hop to delight the heart of any Norse mariner, and the broad reaches of grassy foreshore around its borders would have been equally attractive to a Norse pastoralist. But it was a hop which the Icelanders could not use. The bar across its mouth was not pierced by a deep tidal channel. The fresh waters of the lagoon drained into the sea through a shallow, winding creek to the north of the bar—a creek which would have been impassable to the ships of Karlsefni's flotilla. [80]

Parsons Pond must have proved a cruel disappointment to the settlers, who would have been desperately anxious to land their livestock so that the beasts could refresh themselves ashore. Nevertheless, Parsons Pond was a good omen. Although frustrated by the bar, they would have sailed on with high hopes that at long last they might be nearing—if not Vinland—at least a land of equal promise.

Only a few miles farther south they came to the twin crescentic indentations of Shallow Bay and Cow Head Harbour. These are not true harbors, being fully open to the west, but their broad sandy beaches might have been pressed into service as a place where the knorrir could have been hauled out if nothing better offered. Perhaps the ships were anchored in Cow Head Harbour while a party rowed ashore to climb the nearest elevation. This was Cow Head itself. Although it stands only 200 feet high, the surrounding country is so low and flat that from its top one can see fifteen or twenty miles up or down the coast, and inland to the foot of the mountains.

The Norse would have looked out over an apparently limitless strip of rough bog pastureland running out of sight to the north and to the south, and bounded inland by the canyoned lower slopes of the Long Range. They would have seen how those slopes and canyons were washed dark green with heavy forest growth. But it would have been to the southward that they stared with the greatest eagerness.

HOP (ST. PAUL'S BAY)

Barely three miles from them was the sheen of a great body of water running far back into the mountains from the sea. And where it entered the sea there was a hop—bigger than the one at Parsons Pond, and even more broadly fringed with grassy meadows. Most exciting of all, the bar was cut by a broad opening.

Shortly thereafter the knorrir would have been approaching the opening into St. Paul's Bay. If the tide was rising at the time they would have been able to feel their way in across the outlying sand shoals even if they were unable to mark the narrow, winding underwater channel. Perhaps led by men in boats sounding the way, the ships would have passed through the gap and entered the estuary which lay within.

St. Paul's Bay was shoal, but there was sufficient water, even at half-tide, to have carried the knorrir along the channel which runs through the estuary and which drains the waters of St. Paul's Inlet into the bay, and thence into the sea.

The estuary or bay extends inland about a mile and a half until it is barred by a limestone ridge. This ridge is pierced by a narrow watercut channel, a few hundred feet in length, which drains the waters of the inlet and which is known locally as "the river" because of its rapid and steady flow.

Not far inside the outer bar of the bay there is a small point with a fathom of water at its southern tip. Beyond it to the south lies a great flat which is water covered only during spring tides, and which supports a luxuriant growth of salt-water grass. The point itself and the broad foreshore to the south are covered with a rank growth of cattle grass.

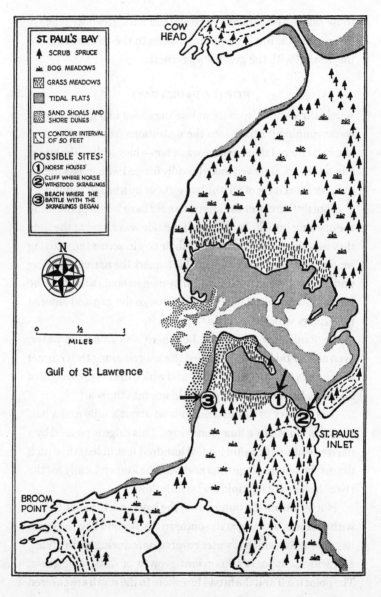

St. Paul's Bay

As the three ships felt their way cautiously into the bay, the penned cattle on the decks would have smelled the fresh grass and raised their voices in a lugubrious chorus of desire. Nor would they have been alone in their impatience to get ashore.

Within a very few days the colonists would have concluded that, Vinland or no Vinland, they had found an excellent place to plant a settlement. The amount of rough pasture immediately available around the shores of the estuary would have supported twenty times the number of animals they could have brought with them. There was sufficient hay on the flat, sandy meadows to fill any number of barns. The estuary and the lake behind it teemed with birds and with a big resident population of harbour seals. Shellfish of half a dozen species abounded, and lobsters could be had for the taking. The short river which breached the rocky dyke separating the estuary from the lake proper was full of salmon, as were the several rivers which emptied into the lake. In the shallow waters of the estuary numbers of flatfish of the sole family drifted over the gravel, and it was no trick to spear them. Later, using what was an ancient trick (it is still in use in parts of Newfoundland), the men dug trenches near the half-tide mark into which they dumped offal. When the tide rose over the pits, flatfish came in to feed, and when the tide fell again they stupidly remained in what seemed to them to be a safe depth of water; but the Norse would have been able to fork them out of the trenches with ease.

Some of the people would have rowed through the breach in the limestone ridge into the main lake (St. Paul's Inlet) to find a magnificent sheet of water running eastward for six miles and deeply penetrating the mountain ramparts. Within a mile of the south side of the lake the Long Range peaks rise from sea level to 2400 feet, and their lower slopes still support a dense forest. From the eastward extension of the lake two great canyons run into the heart of the mountain range, and each of them holds a big salmon river. While they were exploring the shores of the big lake the Norse would have noticed the crisscross pattern of innumerable caribou trails deeply impressed into the surface of the many open bogs and muskegs, and they probably saw numbers of the animals themselves, even though at this season of the year the major part of the herds would have been out in the open barrens to the north or else high up on the mountain plateau country.

From the viewpoint of the colonists there could hardly have been a better site for a settlement. St. Paul's would have provided everything Vinland offered, except for stands of good mixed timber. The forests at the western foot of the Long Range seem to have always been composed for the most part of coniferous softwoods. Even the larger stands growing far back in the mountain valleys did not include much hardwood, and what there was of it would have been difficult to get out to the coast.

But if valuable export timber was scarce, wild grapes were apparently abundant. No wild grapes grow now on the west coast of Newfoundland, but as we have noted, they are reported to have been common in those parts of Newfoundland inhabited by the French as late as the seventeenth century. The St. Paul's area was part of the French coast.

St. Paul's fits every point in the saga description of Karlsefni's Hop to perfection—with one possible exception. The saga states that no snow fell, and that all winter long the livestock found their own food by grazing.

When I visited St. Paul's I mentioned this description to a local farmer. He could see nothing surprising in it. He told me that as recently as the winter of 1958 there was so little snow that the ground never did become covered. The occasional light snows, which were all that fell that winter, vanished within a few days. He also told me that, except during very unusual winters, most of the livestock was left out to forage. Several other farmers confirmed this. One of them, a man of eighty, could recall seven separate winters during which the snow had not lingered on the ground for more than a few days.

Considering that the climate was much better in Karlsefni's time, the likelihood of his having encountered what would have been in effect a snowless winter would have been much greater. Nevertheless, the saga may have been incorrectly translated on this point. What the phrase was perhaps intended to mean was that there was so little snow that the cattle could forage for themselves all winter.

The number of animals kept at St. Paul's has greatly diminished in recent years, not through any lack of forage but through disintegration of the human community. However, in the summer of 1963 I counted 260 sheep, 87 horses and 9 cattle all grazing on the natural meadows around the shore of the estuary. I was told that twenty years earlier I would have seen double that number of sheep and horses, and as many as fifty cattle.

An investigation into the origin of the grass meadows—as opposed to the bog pasture, which is obviously natural—could uncover no evidence that any significant portion of it had been cleared by human efforts. As is the case at Epaves Bay and Tickle Cove Pond, the meadow soil consists of a very thin coating of humus on top of deep sand which would not have encouraged forest growth. Furthermore, most of the true meadows at St. Paul's are close to the sea and exposed to strong prevailing westerlies which still inhibit any growth of forest on the coastal plain. [81]

I examined the whole coast of the inlet and estuary, and found the most likely site for a Norse camp on the south shore, midway between the grassy point and the river leading through the limestone dyke. This site fulfills all the requirements of the saga. It lies on a level shelf about twenty feet above high-tide mark, with a tidal grass flat on three sides of it. Fifty yards to the southeast is the beginning of an immense bog meadow. The shelf itself is part of an ancient beach and is composed of a mixture of gravels and sand, overlain by an inch or two of light soil. Unfortunately the subsoil makes excellent road fill, and in 1955 much of the site was bulldozed. Two large gravel pits now occupy about half its area.

In the cutbank along the side of one of these excavations I found a firepit which had been laid open by a bulldozer blade. An overhang of matted roots and low scrub had preserved it from serious weathering. The bottom of the pit was about 18 inches below present ground level, and in the bottom was a three-inch layer of compacted charcoal overlying a bed of well-leached gray ash. This was the only evidence of ancient occupancy which came to light during a superficial examination of the site.

An interrogation of the inhabitants of St. Paul's failed to turn up any artifacts except an iron instrument, much eroded, which appears to have been the head of a pole-axe or pike-stave and which may date to the early French colonial period. I was later told about a rock inscription at the foot of the inlet. Unfortunately I did not hear of it until I was leaving, and so I could not examine it personally. The carving consists of several letters, or letterlike marks, contained in a square or rectangle about six inches on a side and with a diagonal tail some four inches long extending out from one of the corners. This figure is incised into a large, black rock about three feet long which lies half buried in the beach near the mouth of the St. Paul's River.

One find was made on the tidal flats not far from the possible Norse site. This consisted of four roughly worked rectangular pillars of stone lying haphazardly on their broadsides just below high-water mark. The exposed faces, which were considerably water-worn, did not appear to have borne any inscriptions. I did not disturb the pillars, and it is possible that their protected undersides may be more revealing. They are approximately four feet long, 12 to 14 inches wide, and 5 to 7 inches thick. Two of them are slightly tapered. At the present time no vessel could get within half a mile of them and it would be almost impossible to ferry them in by boat, except on an unusually high tide. They do not appear to be of local rock.

Their presence was unknown to the local residents, none of whom could offer any suggestion as to their origin. They do not lie near a place which has ever been inhabited so far as the residents have any knowledge.

It is possible that they may belong to the colonial French period, but the only identification so far attempted of them (from photographs) suggests that they are prepared ballast stones. It is known that the knorrir carried ballast, and because there was very little room for it under the floors, it was usually stone slab ballast which had been roughly shaped to fit into a confined space.

THE DORSET BOATS[82]

The two weeks which the Norse spent "enjoying themselves" would have gone by quickly, for there was a great deal to see and do. Having anchored the ships securely under the lee of the land, the people may have pitched their temporary booths either on the point or perhaps at the site which was later to become their winter home. The cattle were turned loose on the grassy meadows with someone to keep an eye on them in case they strayed away across the great bog pasture.

No watch was kept, and no doubt it seemed unnecessary.

One of the great attractions of the estuary site was that it offered almost unlimited visibility to seaward, to the south, and to the north. The view inland was obstructed by the limestone ridge, which rises to a height of about one hundred and fifty feet and was then well wooded; but a surprise attack from that direction would have seemed a remote possibility, since behind the ridge lay the open stretch of the big lake.

One morning during the third week at Hop some early riser went to the door of his booth and glanced casually out over the estuary. He must have been violently startled to see a flotilla of small boats approaching slowly across the shoal waters. His shout of alarm would have wakened the camp and brought the men pouring out all-standing, hastily buckling on their gear as they came. Since this was the first contact between North American natives and the Norse, it would have been a moment pregnant with tension—and with grim possibilities. It is doubtful whether the Norse would have felt any assurance that these unexpected visitors were even of human kind; for those were superstitious times, and mountain trolls and other weird beings still lurked in the wilderness country of Iceland and Greenland.

How the approaching Dorsets (for this is who the visitors were) must have stared at the Norse ships lying at anchor and the alien mob upon the shore. They must have felt considerable trepidation, and no doubt the Norse shared that feeling with them. Certain it is that the Norse had never before seen human beings who looked like these people, nor had they seen skin canoes similar to the ones which seemed to hover on the surface of the estuary, reflecting their owners' indecision.

At this juncture the Dorsets began doing something which seemed inexplicable to the Norse. As the saga teller describes it, the Skraelings began whirling wooden "objects" (the word is variously rendered as staves, poles, sticks, etc.) in the direction in which the sun revolves; and these objects made a noise like the sound of flails whistling through the air.

The saga description of these antics has puzzled many readers. Some have written the matter off as being an example of an imaginative adornment of the ancient saga. However, in recent years a number of authorities have leaned to the belief that what the Norse saw was Eskimoan double-bladed kayak paddles in action. In some ways this seems like a plausible explanation, but there are objections to it. It does not explain the noise; and the Norse were a sea-going people, so it is hard to believe that they would not have recognized paddles when they saw them, even if they were double-bladed. When the Skraelings landed, the Norse must have seen the paddles close at hand and could hardly have been in any doubt about their identity. Finally, most archeologists who have studied this culture do not believe the Dorsets had kayaks, or used double-bladed paddles. The kayak, which is technically one of the most sophisticated developments in the history of small craft, apparently originated with the Thule who displaced the Dorsets. Furthermore, it appears from later saga references that the skin boats of the Skraelings were not one-man craft, as kayaks are, but carried several people. They may have been similar to small umiaks of a type still used by some modern Inuit which are propelled by single-bladed paddles.

The mysterious whirling objects which made such a remarkable noise, and which so greatly impressed the Norse, were probably bullroarers. These objects (also known as whizzers) are wooden instruments common to many native tribes, whose genesis goes back to Neolithic times. Modern Inuit seldom use them now, but they were once found throughout the Inuit cultural zone. I personally encountered them in 1947 among a primitive tribe of inland-dwelling Inuit in Keewatin. At dusk one evening I became aware of a strange and disturbing noise. It sounded as if unseen giants were muttering in a wind-filled tunnel, and it seemed to come from all sides of me. The noise rose and fell in pitch and volume with an unearthly effect. The shaman of the band later gave me the instrument which he had used to make this noise. It consists of an elliptical spruce blade about three feet long and four inches broad at its widest part. It is less than a quarter of an inch thick and tapered to a knife edge all around. The edges are serrated with small notches. In operation the blade is whirled about one's head, either on a horizontal or a vertical plane, on the end of a sinew tether. Since one surface is slightly flatter than the other, the blade spins on its own axis at the same time that it describes rapid circles on the end of the sinew. This dual motion produces a baffling, ventriloquial sound. The visual impression is similar to an aircraft propeller turning at such speed that one sees only a glittering disc of flashing light.

Later I saw even larger bullroarers being used by the Inuit, and these were whirled on the end of a pole which increased the centrifugal effect and consequently made a greater volume of sound.

These inland Inuit used bullroarers primarily as a defence against supernatural beings. They believed that the weird sound would drive away, or at least hold at bay, a variety of unpleasant spirits. They may also have had other uses for the instrument, of which I remained in ignorance. Since the sound made by a bullroarer has great carrying qualities, it may have been used as a signal or as a warning device.

By analogy with known Inuit reactions to early European contacts, we can suppose that when the Dorset band stumbled on the Norse camp they thought they had encountered a group of supernatural beings and might have begun brandishing bullroarers as a matter of prudence. On the other hand the sagas say that the flail-like objects were used on both succeeding visits of the Skraelings to Hop, which suggests that they may have had some ritual significance when two parties of strangers met.

It is doubtful whether Karlsefni's reaction to the sight and sound of his visitors was quite so phlegmatic as the saga suggests. However he and Snorri concluded that the display was meant as a sign of peace and so they responded by showing a white shield.

The Inuit are a friendly people, inclined to expect the best from strangers. Once their initial surprise had eased, the Dorsets edged their boats toward shore, and when they felt secure enough, they made a landing.

The Icelanders seem to have been acute enough to treat these uncouth, fur-clad, dark-skinned and almond-eyed strangers with some degree of friendliness. After all, the visitors were obviously the occupants of this country and the Norse would have had no way of knowing how great their numbers were or how much of a threat they posed. Regardless of their individual prowess as fighting men, the settlers were a very long way from home and friends, and it behove them to walk softly.

Good relations between the two peoples seem to have been established at this first meeting, and when they parted it was in friendly style. The Norse evidently laid the basis for what they hoped would lead to lucrative trading, perhaps by giving small gifts to the Dorsets and indicating that they would appreciate furs in return. This visit of the Skraelings, as the Norse named them,[83] would have been fraught with many possibilities, both good and bad, and we can be sure that these would have been major topics of conversation in the Norse camp during the months which followed.

Apart from its overtones of racial superiority, the account given of the visitors is a very fair description of an Eskimoan people. It is particularly valuable because it is the only surviving eyewitness description of the now vanished Dorsets.

When the Skraelings left Hop they paddled away to the south around a headland which was evidently visible from the Norse camp. This could have been Broom Point, which can be clearly seen from the slight elevation near the gravel pits.

The question of how the Dorsets happened to visit the Norse merits examination. Possibly the Norse flotilla had been seen by Dorsets as it made its way south down the coast. Awed by the sight, but intensely curious, a party of Dorsets may have followed after in hopes of getting another, and closer, look at the great sailing craft. On the other hand it is perhaps more likely that the encounter was wholly accidental and came about when a party of Dorsets who had completed the seal-hunting phase of their summer activities rowed south en route to one of the main coastal rivers to begin salmon fishing. St. Paul's may have been their actual objective; but the discovery of aliens already in possession may have led them to conclude that it would be more discrete to go elsewhere. Eventually they would have spread the news of the arrival of the Norse at least as far south as the several major encampments whose sites have been discovered on and near Bonne Bay.

The meeting with the Skraelings does not seem to have deterred the Icelanders from deciding that St. Paul's would make a fitting place to establish their settlement. They began erecting permanent houses. Some of these were built close to the shore of the estuary, while others were sited "farther away, near the main part of the land." By this we are probably to understand that some houses were built in St. Paul's Inlet, doubtless close to the mountains.

The events of the balance of that summer and of the ensuing winter have vanished from the saga record. We can assume that the settlers were kept busy in the vicinity of the estuary with their colonizing chores. Meanwhile Karlsefni, Thorhall Gamlisson and the Helge-Finnboggi-Freydis group doubtless went into winter quarters at the foot of the inlet, where they would have engaged in cutting and preparing a cargo of spruce and pine timber in lieu of hardwoods.

All that we are told of this period is that the winter was mild and open; which must have been a matter for self-congratulation among the Icelanders, considering the miserable winter they had endured at Straumfiord.

22

THE FATAL ERROR

The Saga Tale (c. 1006)

When spring arrived they discovered, early one morning, a great number of skin boats rowing from the south around the headlands. They were so numerous it looked as if charcoal had been scattered on the surface of the water in front of the estuary.

From every boat, staves were being waved. Thereupon Karlsefni and his people displayed their [white] shields and when the two parties came together they began to barter with each other. The Skraelings particularly desired weapons in exchange for pelts and gray skins, but Karlsefni forbade the sale of weapons.

Karlsefni considered the matter and then he ordered the women to carry milk[84] outdoors to the Skraelings. As soon as they saw the milk they wanted it alone. So this was the way their trading went, that they carried off their bargains in their stomachs.

Some of the cattle were near at hand, and the bull ran out of the woods and began to roar and bellow. This terrified the Skraelings and they ran. [Some of them] turned toward Karlsefni's house and tried to enter it, but Karlsefni defended the door against them. Then the Skraelings raced to their boats and rowed away, leaving behind them their packs and their goods.

Now it is to be told that Karlsefni had a strong stockade of posts erected around the house and put everything in readiness.

"We had better take counsel," said Karlsefni. "For I think they may call on us a third time, with many men, and not in peace. We shall follow this plan. Ten men will go out on the point and show themselves there, but another part of our company shall go into the woods and cut a path [along which] our cattle can [be driven]. When the company [attacks] from out of the woods we shall have our bull go ahead of us."

It was planned that the battle would take place with the wood on one side and the water on the other side. Everything was done which Karlsefni had proposed.

For three whole weeks nothing more was seen of them, but at the end of this time a great multitude of Skraelings was discovered coming from the south like a river of boats. This time all of the staves were being waved counter-sunwise and the Skraelings were all uttering loud cries.

Thereupon Karlsefni and his men took red shields and displayed them. The Skraelings sprang from their boats, and they met and fought together.

There was a fierce shower of missiles for the Skraelings had slings. Karlsefni and Snorri observed the Skraelings lifting up on poles large ball-shaped objects nearly the size of a sheep's belly and blueish-black in colour. They hurled these inland over Karlsefni's followers, and they made a frightening noise when they fell.

This so terrified Karlsefni and all his men that they could only think of flight and of making an escape up along the edge of the river, for it seemed to them that the crowd of Skraelings was rushing upon them from every side. They did not pause until they reached some cliffs where they [halted and] offered a stout resistance.

Freydis came out of doors and seeing that Karlsefni and the men were fleeing, she cried: "Why are you running from wretches like these? I would have thought such gallant men as you would slaughter them like cattle. If I only had a weapon I think I would put up a better fight than any of you!"

But they paid no attention to what she said and so Freydis tried to join them [in their flight] but she could not keep up, for she was pregnant. Nevertheless she followed them to the woods with the Skraelings close behind her. Now she saw a dead man in front of her. This was Thorbrand, Snorri's son, and his skull had been pierced by a flat stone [point].

His naked sword lay beside him and Freydis snatched it up and prepared to defend herself with it. The Skraelings came closer, whereupon she let fall her shift and slapped her breasts with the naked sword.

Seeing this, the Skraelings were frightened and ran down to their boats and rowed away.

Karlsefni and his companions then joined her and praised her courage. Two of Karlsefni's men and four Skraelings had been killed. Karlsefni's party had been defeated due to the superior numbers [of the enemy].

They now returned to their houses, bound up their wounds, and puzzled over who the crowd of men could have been who had seemed to attack them from the landward side. Finally they concluded that there could have been only the one party—that which came from the boats—and that the idea that there had been another crowd must have been an illusion.

[SOURCES: Composite version, assembled from Erik the Red Saga and the Thorfinn Karlsefni Saga, and from the Greenlanders Story. An explanation of why this section of the saga story has been treated in this way, and how it has been done, is given in Appendix O.]

THE SECOND VISIT of the Skraelings to Hop took place early in the new year, doubtless at about the time the harp seals began to whelp on the pack ice of the gulf. The saga says they appeared at Hop "When spring arrived" which can be interpreted as sometime near the end of March. This would not have been too early for journeys by skin boats, since even if the westerly winds had begun to set the pack ice in against the land, the Dorsets had only to run ashore, lift their light boats up on the beach and camp until a lane of water between ice and land opened up again.

The flotilla of boats which entered St. Paul's Bay that spring morning so many years ago probably carried an advance group of the northward-bound seal hunters, and some of the people in it had no doubt been members of the party which had visited Hop the previous summer.

The saga says there were so many boats in the flotilla that it looked as if the whole surface of the estuary had been strewn with lumps of charcoal—a graphic but probably exaggerated image. The entire Dorset population on the west coast of New-foundland probably numbered no more than a few score fam-ilies at this late stage in their history, when the Dorset culture was rapidly declining. However, the saga speaker doubtless attempted to convey the impression of vast numbers to provide an alibi for the subsequent defeat of the Norse.

A hint of this tendency to exaggerate the enemy strength can be seen in the Thorfinn Karlsefni Saga report of the arrival of the first lot of Skraelings in the previous year. "A great number of skin boats appeared in the estuary," says this saga. But the Erik the Red Saga, which often tends to be more specific, reported that there were just nine skin boats.

Once more the mysterious staves are in evidence, but that they were not connected with the propulsion of the boats seems to be firmly established by the concurrent statement that the boats were *rowed* around the point.

Trading seems to have begun as soon as the Dorset party landed, and the saga description of how Karlsefni's people handled it demonstrates that there has been little if any change in business ethics since the days of the Norse. The vignette of the shrewd Norsemen maneuvering the Dorsets into exchanging their furs and skins for dollops of whey-cheese or skyr bridges the abyss of the centuries. It is noteworthy that Karlsefni astutely forbade the selling of weapons to the Skraelings. Obviously the Norse did not wish to see the natives armed with Scandinavian weapons, which the settlers probably believed were invincible. It could never have occurred to them that the Skraelings were not only their equals but their superiors in weaponry.

While the Norse farmers and traders were busily engaged in driving their bargains with the Dorset men, some of the Skraelings seem to have been tentatively investigating their surroundings. We can imagine them staring apprehensively, but with fascination at the buildings, the ships, and all the strange things which had appeared so mysteriously upon the shores of St. Paul's Bay.

Now something took place which was of paramount importance both to the immediate fortunes of the Norse expedition and to the entire history of the Norse attempts to establish colonies in North America.

It will be remembered that the settlers had brought a bull with them to Hop, and this bull was apparently a singularly intractable and evil-natured beast, for there are two separate references in the sagas testifying to his unruliness. Nevertheless he was allowed to run free at Hop, and he apparently chose this moment to appear out of the scrub woods which bordered the bog pasture. Apparently he did not approve of the fur-clad Dorsets whom he saw before him. He bellowed, pawed the ground, and perhaps charged the nearest group.

The effect upon the Dorsets would have been shattering. They must have been tense anyway in the presence of the awe-inspiring Norsemen with their great swords and axes, their long beards, their strange clothing, and their many quite inexplicable implements and possessions. The sight and sound of the bull would doubtless have struck terror into their hearts and triggered a panic flight. Those nearest the boats probably fled to them. Some who had ventured farther away from the shore in among the Norse buildings bolted for the shelter of the houses in a frantic attempt to escape the bellowing behemoth which had emerged out of nowhere.

At this juncture the Norse seem to have lost their heads too. Not realizing for the moment that the bull, with which they were all too familiar, was the cause of the sudden mêlée of running, shouting natives; and being inherently suspicious by nature, they evidently jumped to the conclusion that they had been tricked, and that this was an attack.

The saga does not offer any direct proof that this is what happened, but the indirect evidence is formidable. If the Skraelings had simply fled, having suffered no physical ill effects as a consequence of the appearance of the bull, the Norse would hardly have been so convinced that they would soon return in battle order. If, on the other hand, the panic was general and had embraced the Norse, and if they had reacted by turning on the terrified Skraelings in the belief that this was a treacherous attack, then the inevitable bloodshed would have given the Norse good reason to fear retaliation. Karlsefni, so the saga tells us, defended the door of his house against the Skraelings, and we can be sure he did not use gentle methods.

Being thoroughly experienced in the ritual of the blood feud, the Norse would have expected the surviving Skraelings to try and even up the score. But only if the Norse had inflicted serious injuries on their visitors would they have been likely to go to the lengths described in the sagas to protect themselves from a reprisal attack, even preparing an ambush against the certainty of one.

That the sagas should neglect to explain that the Norse were responsible for what followed is not to be wondered at. A glance at most modern history books demonstrates that the tendency to blame the enemy for initiating every act of hostility is still inherent in mankind. In the case of the Skraelings the Norse would have been even less likely to admit that they had brought their troubles on themselves, since they were soundly trounced in the ensuing battle.

That the Icelanders expected to be attacked is certain. They were so convinced of it that they committed their second major blunder, and thereby not only sealed the doom of their own colonizing venture, but made it virtually certain that no further attempts by Greenlanders or Icelanders would succeed.

After the flight of the Dorset trading party (presumably northward to the sealing grounds, for the Dorsets still had to pursue their livelihood even if the country was afflicted with bloodthirsty foreign devils), the Norse picked up the abandoned packs of furs and perhaps congratulated themselves on a profitable day's work. Nevertheless they felt considerable apprehension about the consequences of the incident.

When we combine the information to be found in both saga sources, a picture emerges of energetic efforts to establish a defence. Stockades were built around some of the houses—perhaps only around those near the estuary, which commanded the beached ships. A council of war was called at which Karlsefni, and no doubt Snorri and the other leaders, worked out a complicated plan whereby the attacking Skraelings would be caught off guard.

The sagas say that the Norse chose the battleground, and that it lay between the water and the wood. It may well have been on the low sandy point at the south entrance to the estuary. Ten men were posted here with orders to expose themselves and to act as bait for the approaching Skraelings, who were expected to land and pounce on this small group before attacking the main camp. The balance of the Norse warriors were to lurk in concealment in the scrub spruce fringing the southern end of the sandy point. Paths were to be cut so that they could rush to their positions unseen as soon as the Skraelings were reported in the offing. Still other paths were cleared to the seaward edge of the woods, along which the cattle could be driven onto the beach in advance of the attacking warriors.

The sagas say that nothing happened for three weeks, at the end of which time the guard (who would have been posted on the nearest high ground) came pounding into camp with the news that a group of Skraeling boats was approaching.

What followed was a compounding of error upon error. The Norse had assumed that they would be attacked. As soon as they saw a sizable group of Skraelings approaching the camp they took it for granted that this was an attacking force and put their "strike-first" plan into action. But they could not conceivably have been able to distinguish one party of Skraelings from another, particularly at a distance, and when they themselves were keyed up to battle pitch. They could not, in other words, have distinguished between friend and foe as far as Skraelings were concerned. Moreover, it probably never even occurred to them that the second lot of Skraelings who were coming up the coast might have been quite free of hostile intentions, having heard nothing about the treatment meted out to the preceding party.

It is most unlikely that the Dorsets who had been driven from Hop after the bull episode would have returned to mount a revenge attack against the Norse. It is far more likely that they fled northward at top speed toward the sealing grounds, being not the least bit anxious to try another round with the devilish strangers who apparently wished to massacre them.

In reconstructing the encounter I envisage the next party of Dorsets appearing from the south bound for the northern sealing grounds, unaware of what had happened to the earlier party. As they cleared Broom Point and struck across the shallow bight toward the mouth of the estuary they saw a number of the aliens—about whom they had doubtless heard during the winter—appear on the sandy point and begin prancing about and waving their arms in what may have seemed to the Dorsets like an invitation to land, but which was probably a display of bravado calculated to goad the Skraelings into launching an attack.

The Dorsets turned toward these men and pulled for shore. Bullroarers aboard some of the boats may have been brought into action as a normal ceremonial indication that this was a friendly visit.

The saga's statement that the instruments were whirled *anti*-sunwise as a sign of hostility carries no conviction. Even if such a thing had been done, and even if the difference in direction had been detectable by an observer on shore, the Norse could hardly have known that this was a war sign. There may in fact have been some shouting from the Dorset boats, but this was as likely to have been intended to express friendship as hostility.

As soon as the Dorset boats grounded and the people jumped out and hauled the light vessels well up on the sand and shingle beach (for this was an open shore, exposed to the swell) the Norse attacked according to plan.

There are few coherent details of what followed. The ten men on the spit presumably snatched up their weapons and charged the Skraelings while the main body of the Norse burst out of the forest, driving the cattle ahead of them and yelling fiercely in the best Viking style.

The Skraelings would have been momentarily paralyzed by surprise, but at the first flash of a raised sword or axe they would have recognized their danger and reacted instinctively. There was probably no time to launch their boats and get away, but they were not defenceless, for their sealing weapons were within easy reach.

We do not know exactly what these weapons were, but we can make an informed guess. The Norse sources say they included various sorts of missiles, slings, and something which looked like a blue-black sheep's belly that came hurtling through the air and frightened the Scandinavians half to death. Archeology has demonstrated that the Dorsets had an abundant supply of the most beautifully made stone points, of a wide variety of shapes and sizes. These were evidently used for arrow points and for the tips of several kinds of spears and harpoons. By analogy with what is known of later-day Inuit we can assume the Skraelings had three kinds of missile throwers: throwing-boards, which enabled a man to fling a spear two or three times the effective distance he could achieve by hand and arm alone; slings similar to the one with which David slew Goliath, and with which some Inuit (including the inland tribes of the Keewatin District) were very proficient; and bows and arrows. These were all hunting weapons and not primarily designed for warfare; but they could all be used just as effectively against men as against other animals.

The Norse of circa 1000 seldom made use of devices for flinging missiles. They actively disapproved of such things in warfare, considering them unmanly. Most of their fighting weapons were intended for thrusting, hacking or bludgeoning and so were most effective in close combat. Against a people who refused close combat, and who kept their distance and pelted one with slingstones, spears and arrows, the Norse armament was practically useless. Shortly after the beginning of the battle, and before they had been able to cut down more than three or four of the Skraelings, the Norse were in full and ignominious flight.

In attempting to justify this retreat the saga makes a great deal of the strange bladderlike objects which came flying overhead. It implies that these were supernatural weapons of such potency that not even a Norseman could have been expected to stand against them. Unfortunately for Norse pride there is a simpler explanation. Part of the Skraelings' hunting equipment would have been inflated bladder floats attached to sealing harpoons. When attacked, the Dorsets simply snatched up the harpoons, bladders and all, and let fly; and what the Norse saw were these balloonlike objects whirling along in the wake of the harpoons. As to the noise they made, this can perhaps be attributed to conscious exaggeration, although a tightly inflated sealskin or seal-bladder float can make quite a satisfactory bang if it is suddenly punctured, as some of them may have been by the wildly flailing swords or spears of the unnerved Norsemen.

No bladders have been found in Dorset sites, for such materials would not have survived the intervening centuries. However, all known Inuit peoples have used such things as a standard accessory to their hunting gear—their purpose being to prevent a harpooned sea mammal from sounding or diving to any great depth as well as to provide a surface marker which could be followed by the hunter in his boat.

The Norse warriors did not cease their panic-stricken flight until they reached a place where they could stand at bay with their backs to a rocky cliff. Such a cliff, about fifteen feet high, stands along the seaward face of the limestone ridge which separates St. Paul's Bay from the inlet, and it is less than a mile from where the battle probably began.

The rout of the Norse seems to have been so complete that they did not even halt to attempt a defence of their stockaded houses or of the women and children. Most of the noncombatants probably joined in the wild flight to the cliff; but it seems certain that if the Skraelings had vigorously pursued the fleeing Icelanders they would have had no difficulty in catching and slaughtering many defenceless fugitives. That they did not do so is confirmed by the saga, which states that the Norse lost only two people during the battle. Both of these were evidently warriors. Thorbrand Snorrisson seems to have been struck in the head by a harpoon point or by a sling-stone. He may have been able to run a considerable distance after he was struck, and the fact that his body was found by Freydis between the houses and the cliff is no sure indication that the Dorsets pursued the Norse for any distance, if indeed they pursued them at all. On the other hand, if this had been a preconceived attack with the object of wreaking vengeance, the Dorsets would have had little difficulty in pinning their enemies against the cliff and picking them off from a safe distance with their missile weapons.

The encounter with Freydis is of special interest. Being in an advanced state of pregnancy, she could not keep up with the other fugitives and was left far behind. The well-deserved and stinging rebuke which she flung at the backs of the fleeing men, and the way they single-mindedly ignored her scornful taunts and continued their panic-stricken flight, illustrate with merciless clarity the abject terror which had gripped the Norse warriors when their intended victims displayed such unexpected fighting prowess.

Freydis's personal reaction seems to have been of a different sort. Unable to keep up with her "protectors," she snatched up Thorbrand's sword and prepared to give the Skraelings a hard time of it. The business of dropping her shift, exposing her bosom and then proceeding to slap her breasts with the sword (some translators have it that she whetted the sword on her breasts) would have given anyone pause. Even a Skraeling might have retreated before such a bizarre spectacle. The story is really too good to spoil, yet there is a reasonable possibility that the incident may not have happened in quite the way it is described.

There is no other record in Scandinavian history of a woman attempting to protect herself in the face of armed attack by exposing her naked breasts. On the other hand this gesture was in general use among the Beothuk of Newfoundland. There are several well-authenticated accounts of Beothuk women baring their breasts when they were in danger from the bloodthirsty early Newfoundland settlers, whose hobby it was to hunt Beothuks for the pleasure of the chase. As a method of warding off death or injury from the hands of white men, it was seldom efficacious. In two of the recorded instances the white trappers calmly raised their guns and shot the women dead. But the Beothuks had a strong taboo against killing women, and the act of baring the breast was intended to ensure that the attacker recognized his potential victim as female.

One possible explanation of Freydis's otherwise inexplicable action is that the gesture of baring the breasts was known to, and used by, both the Beothuks and the Dorsets; that the Norse observed its use during the first skirmish with the Skraelings, and that Freydis made use of it herself when she thought she was in danger. Later saga men, who would not have known why Freydis bared her breasts, may have felt compelled to invent a reason and so have added the detail of the sword-whetting or breast-beating in order to make it look like a gesture of intimidation.[85]

We have no proof that the Dorsets did use the gesture, or that they copied it from the Beothuks. It is perhaps more likely to have been the other way around. For we know of no North American Indigenous cultures except the Beothuks who used the gesture, and since they were indubitably in contact (and probably not always friendly contact) with the Dorsets, they may have acquired it from this now extinct Eskimoan people.

The fact remains that the Skraelings did not attack Freydis after she bared her breasts. That they could easily have killed a lone woman with sling missiles, spears or arrows, despite her possession of the sword, if they had wished to do so seems obvious. That they were actually so terrified by her gesture that they all fled in panic to their boats seems patently absurd.

The final stages of the "battle," including the Freydis incident, make it clear that, far from being aggressors who had staged a premeditated attack, the Dorsets were themselves the victims of a surprise attack and were concerned only with defending themselves until they could make their escape. Although the saga makes it plain that the Norse warriors deserted the settlement (which would have included the houses, the ships, old people, small children, livestock and those women who could not run fast enough) the Dorsets took no advantage of this. They neither looted nor burned the buildings and ships, nor massacred the noncombatants—all of which they would undoubtedly have done had they come to Hop bent on getting revenge for past injuries.

While the Norse were in a state of complete confusion and so terror-stricken that they imagined Skraelings assaulting them from the landward as well as the seaward side, the Dorsets were retreating to their boats, anxious to get away from this fearful neighborhood as rapidly as possible.

The impression of the terrible capabilities of the Skraelings as fighting men which was indelibly implanted in the Norsemen's minds as a result of this encounter was doubtless the genesis of a fearsome myth which was to haunt the imaginations of the Greenland Norse for centuries. Later records portray the Skraelings as implacable and supernaturally formidable enemies whom it was usually impossible to overpower in open battle and who could be safely attacked only if they were caught off guard, or if the Norse had overwhelming superiority of numbers.

23

DEATH COMES TO
THORVALD ERIKSSON

The Saga Tale (c. 1006)

It now seemed clear to Karlsefni and his people that although this was an attractive country their lives would be filled with constant fear and turmoil because of the [danger from the] inhabitants, and so they immediately prepared to leave, desiring to return to their own country.

They sailed to the northward along the coast and found five Skraelings dressed in skin-doublets asleep near the sea. There were wooden containers beside them which contained animal marrow mixed with blood. Karlsefni and his people decided that [these people] must have been outlawed from their own country, and so they put them to death.

Later they found a cape upon which there was a great number of reindeer and this cape looked like one expanse of manure because so many reindeer had used it during the winter.

Then they arrived again at Straumfiord, where they found a great abundance of everything they needed.

Some men report that Bjarni Grimolfsson and Freydis remained behind here with a hundred people, and went no farther, while Karlsefni and Snorri proceeded to the southward with forty men, returning again that same summer after tarrying at a hop [there] for barely two months.

[SOURCES: Erik the Red Saga and the Thorfinn Karlsefni Saga]

[Meanwhile] Thorvald [Eriksson] went eastward in his knorr and then to the northward around Kialarness and then bore to the westward into the mouth of the fiord which lay there, keeping the land on the port side. The country thereabouts was forest land as far as they could see, with scarcely an open space anywhere.

When they had journeyed a considerable distance they came to a wooded headland which jutted out [into the fiord]. They made their ship fast to the land and put out their gangplank to the land. Then Thorvald and his followers went ashore.

"This is a fine place," said Thorvald, "I would not mind living here."

After that they returned aboard the ship [and continued on], and on the sands within the headland they saw three hummocks, and when they approached them they saw these were three skin boats, with three men under each of them.

They divided their party and captured them all except for one who escaped in his boat. Then they killed the eight they had captured.

[Afterwards] they came to a river which flowed down from east to west. They sailed into the mouth of this river and lay to along the southern bank. Then they went out on the [nearby] cape and looked about them. Some distance up the fiord they saw some hillocks, and they supposed that these were human habitations.

They were extremely weary and could no longer keep awake, and so they went to sleep.

Then a call from up above them woke them up.

"Wake up, Thorvald, and [wake] all the company if you want to save your lives. Get to the ship with all the men and sail off from the land as fast as possible!"

Now innumerable skin boats appeared from within the fiord and came toward them.

"Hang the shields [or war-boards] over the sides of the ship and [we shall] defend ourselves as best we can," cried Thorvald, "but do not carry the fight to them."

They did as he instructed, and the Skraelings shot at them for a while and then fled away as fast as they could go.

Thorvald asked if any of his men were wounded, and they replied that none of them was.

"I have a wound under my arm," he said, "an arrow flew in between the shield [war-board] and the ship's side." He pulled out the arrow and exclaimed: "Even though there is a lot of fat around my guts this arrow will be the death of me. It seems we have found a good land, but are not likely to get much profit from it. Now I advise you to get ready and go back [to Straumfiord] as soon as you can. But first you shall carry me to that headland which I thought was such a good place to inhabit. It seems I spoke the truth when I said I might dwell there for a while. You shall bury me there, and set up a cross at my head and at my feet and forever after call that place Krossaness."

Thorvald died and his men did all he had told them to do, and then they went away and rejoined their comrades [at Straumfiord]. They told the people there all that had happened, and they dwelt there that winter.

[SOURCES: Combined account from Erik the Red Saga and the Thorfinn Karlsefni Saga, and The Greenlanders Story. The reasons for combining this material, and an explanation of how it has been done, will be found in Appendix M.]

THE SHOCK SUSTAINED by the Norse as a result of the "battle" at Hop was tremendous. Not only was their intransigent pride demolished, but their sense of security and their belief in their own invincibility were badly shaken. They had also lost two men, one of whom, Thorbrand Snorrisson, was the son of the settlers' chief leader.

Their decision to abandon Hop was an admission of the extent of their loss of confidence, but they were not likely to have been able to leave as soon as they might have wished without incurring a serious risk of losing their ships if heavy westerly weather set the pack ice against the coast.

Meanwhile there could have been few pleasures left in life at Hop. The Norse would have believed themselves to be virtually in a state of siege, anticipating a new attack at any time. The cattle and sheep would have been rounded up and herded into pens close to or inside the house-stockades, which would themselves have been strengthene—if any one had had the courage to go out into the woods to cut the necessary logs. Men would have been unwilling to go hunting and fishing, except in large bands, or even to go gathering fodder for the beasts at any distance from the stockade. Supplies were probably scarce after the passage of the winter, and enforced confinement in and about the stockades would have prevented the food stocks from being replenished. A constant watch must have been maintained; but at night, or in foggy weather, the possibility of a surprise attack would have allowed no one any peace of mind.

By the time the leaders felt that the danger from the pack ice was largely past, nerves and tempers must have been strained to the breaking point. There was no lingering on the way north, but weather conditions would have been unsettled this early in the year and gales no doubt forced the ships to anchor occasionally. Near one of these anchorages—perhaps under the lee of an offshore island such as St. John or Flat Island—a party from the ship discovered five of the feared and hated Skraelings (perhaps the members of a single family in one of the skin-covered houses they used during the sealing season). These people were slaughtered out of hand. The excuse given in the sagas, that they were believed to be outlaws under sentence of banishment, and therefore (as in Scandinavian countries) outside the laws of humanity, is pitifully weak. This was a revenge killing pure and simple. Perhaps it made the Norse warriors feel a little better.

When they passed the Port au Choix Peninsula they may have seen signs of activity at the large sealing settlement there; but if they did it can be taken for granted that they steered out to sea, giving the peninsula a good wide berth. There is no evidence that the Norse ever again—even in Greenland, centuries later, after the Thule arrived there—dared make an assault upon an alert and numerous band of Skraelings.

The next landing appears to have been on the Ferolle Peninsula, where the Norse encountered a great herd of caribou. The description of a caribou wintering area is explicit, as anyone who has walked over one of their well-used grazing grounds can testify. The Ferolle Peninsula is, and presumably has long been, excellent winter range for the semi-migratory Newfoundland caribou which once roamed the island in tens of thousands. It is an area of low, somewhat boggy "caribou barrens" which stays almost snow-free even during heavy winters. A French account dating from the middle of the eighteenth century speaks of two large bateaux being laden with the skins of caribou killed on Ferolle in the course of a single hunt. [86]

So the fleeing Icelanders arrived back at Straumfiord, where they found "an abundance of everything they needed," which can be construed to mean not only food and other supplies but also the solace and the feeling of security engendered by again being leagued with others of their kind—even if these others were Greenlanders, for whom, one can safely assume, they now felt an increased measure of affection.

The return of the Icelandic ships must have been extremely welcome to the Greenlanders. There was still no sign of Thorhall the Hunter, and the forty or so Greenlanders at Straumfiord must have put in a gloomy and apprehensive winter while the conviction grew that some catastrophe had overtaken not only Thorhall but the Icelandic expedition too, leaving those at Straumfiord to face an unknown fate alone. After exchanging experiences the leaders would have called a council to decide which course they ought to follow next. Thorvald Eriksson had apparently already decided to make a ship voyage north in search of Thorhall the Hunter; but the Icelanders seem to have been divided about their future plans.[87]

From what the saga says of their departure from Hop, we gather that some of the colonists wished to give up the entire venture and return immediately to Greenland or even Iceland. Others may have been in favour of making one more attempt to find a suitable, and safe, site for a colony. Still others may have been willing to settle in the Straumfiord area, which although it had its drawbacks was better than anything Greenland had to offer, and which was apparently free of danger from the Skraelings.

As for the trader-skippers, the season was still young and they may still have been hopeful of acquiring a cargo of the invaluable hardwoods before turning for home. Perhaps with this in mind Karlsefni concluded that it would be worthwhile to make one last voyage in search of Vinland in the only direction which had not yet been explored—southward down the east coast of the Great Northern Peninsula.

Apparently it was decided that Karlsefni and Snorri, accompanied by a party of forty men, should voyage to the southward in one ship while the balance of the Icelanders remained at

Straumfiord with those Greenlanders who did not accompany Thorvald Eriksson in his search for Thorhall.

THORVALD'S SEARCH FOR THORHALL

There is no difficulty in plotting Thorvald's route. In the initial stages he followed the course that Thorhall the Hunter had intended to pursue in his search for Vinland the preceding summer, and all the accounts agree that this course lay north from Straumfiord past Kialarness to the mouth of Grosswater Bay.

This was all more or less familiar ground, but once the knorr turned westward into the foot of Grosswater Bay, she would have been entering unknown waters. Coasting the south shore ("keeping the land on the port side"), Thorvald held ever westward until the north shore of Grosswater Bay came into view. It must have seemed as if the ship was approaching the foot of a typical coastal fiord, but when she came abeam of Ticorlak Head her people would have discovered that they were opening the mouth of a narrow, steep-sided strait through which the tidal current boiled at speeds of from three to five knots. The great power of this reversing current, flowing through its mile-wide channel, would have told the voyagers that the strait must lead to a large body of water still farther to the west.

Having passed through one of the two channels which embrace Henrietta Island, they would have emerged into the head of Lake Melville.

The waters over which they then sailed, or rowed, were still salt, and the Greenlanders must have suspected that they had discovered a great inland sea lying deep in the heart of the western wilderness. They would not have been far wrong, for Lake Melville, or Hamilton Inlet as it is also called, runs for ninety miles to the west-southwest from Henrietta Island, and in places it is more than twenty miles in breadth. It is both salt and tidal and therefore, properly speaking, it is an inland sea.

Once past the mid-channel guardian rock of Eskimo Island, Thorvald steered his ship south in order to retain contact with the southern shore of this mysterious sea. He continued coasting to the westward until he reached a remarkable cape. This was evidently Reed Point, a massive headland rising to 700 feet and separated from the mainland by a broad and grassy isthmus. Thorvald and his men may not have scaled the headland to its crest—they would have had to cut and thrust their way through a solid wall of forest to have done so—but they need not have climbed more than a few hundred feet to have seen that, beyond St. John Island, the "sea" stretched out of sight to the westward, growing broader as its shores receded into the distance.

Returning to the ship, the Greenlanders cast off their lines and set their course south along the stretch of coast below Reed Point where two small and nameless points jut out to the south. Beyond the second of these, at a distance of about two miles from the great headland, there is a mile-long strip of low and level beach fringed with sand.

During historic times this beach was used as a travel camp by Hamilton Inlet Inuit en route between the salmon rivers and caribou-hunting grounds of the interior and the seal and seabird-hunting grounds on the outer coast. Finds of Dorset artifacts have been made on the shores of Lake Melville, and as the excavations of Dr. William Taylor in Ungava have demonstrated, the Dorsets sometimes ventured as much as two hundred miles away from the sea in order to winter in interior caribou-hunting camps. These facts are of importance because some authors have denied (on the grounds that Inuit would not have gone so far away from the open sea) that the Skraelings Thorvald encountered could have been Dorsets.

As Thorvald's knorr rounded the second of the small points, she would have opened the "sands within the headland" and her people would have been quick to spot three skin boats upturned upon the shore. Having heard firsthand of the experiences of the Icelanders at Hop, the Greenlanders knew what to do about this unexpected encounter.

We are not told that the three Skraelings who were under each of these boats were asleep, but this is the logical deduction. In any event they were so unwary that it was possible for the Norse to land and to surround the natives and capture eight of them, apparently without a struggle. Only one Dorset woke up in time, or was agile enough to escape capture and the subsequent slaughter. He managed to launch one of the boats and paddled frantically off to warn his fellows farther down the lake of the menace which had come upon them.

As for the Norse, they returned victoriously to their ship and sailed on past the sandy beach where the bloody bodies of the Skraelings lay sprawled.

The saga says that they then came to a river which flowed down from the east toward the west. At first glance this statement appears to be in error, since the rivers along the Atlantic Coast flow generally from the westward toward the east. However, English River in Lake Melville fits the description perfectly.[88] It flows from east to west into Lake Melville within three miles of Reed Point and about half a mile to the southward of the beach where the Skraelings were murdered. According to a trapper who lived at English River for some years, the river mouth at half tide carries about a fathom of water for a distance of a quarter of a mile inland. A supply schooner engaged to bring

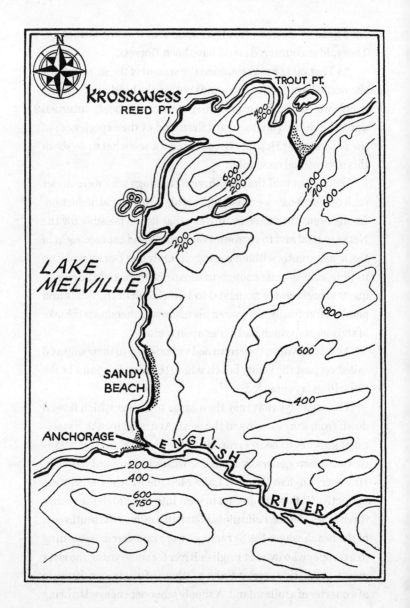

Thorvald Eriksson at Lake Melville

this trapper his winter outfit used to anchor well inside the river mouth in a cove which was secure in any kind of weather.

When the knorr rounded the low point separating the south end of the sandy beach from the river, the Norse would have been delighted to see a calm and protected stretch of estuary with sand banks on either side. Carefully they felt their way into the river mouth and anchored or moored under the southern bank.

A little more than half a mile southwest of the mouth of English River a prominent hill rises to a height of seven hundred feet, jutting out to form a headland and offering an excellent vantage point from which to survey the surrounding country. After their encounter with the Skraelings we assume that the Norse would have climbed this hill, if only to assure themselves that there were no more natives in the immediate vicinity. From its crest they saw a number of "hillocks," probably in the direction of Long Point, and for reasons which are not explained they identified these as human habitations, evidently Skraelings.

Considering the earlier events of this day, one would suppose that such a sight would have sent them hurrying back to their ship with the intention of removing themselves from the vicinity of such potentially dangerous neighbors as rapidly as possible. On the other hand they may have been so overblown with confidence after their easy victory that out of sheer bravado they refused to be perturbed. In any event they pitched their tents or shelters on the shore, made themselves comfortable, and calmly went to sleep.

Nevertheless they could hardly have been so foolish as not to have posted a guard, and it was probably a sentry on the hill who saw the flotilla of Skraeling boats appear on the southeastern horizon at dawn the next day and shouted the alarm which roused the camp.

The Greenlanders now repented of their foolhardy decision to spend the night in such dangerous proximity to the enemy. Rushing to their ship, they hauled up the anchor or cast off the shore lines, and manned the oars. There could have been little or no wind, otherwise they would have hoisted sail and made their escape before the Skraelings reached them. As things stood they realized that they could never row the big knorr fast enough to get away, and so at Thorvald's orders they prepared to defend themselves where the ship lay drifting.

On this occasion the Skraelings, alerted by the man who had escaped the slaughter, were really hostile. In their light, speedy and easily maneuvered boats they would soon have surrounded the knorr, and coming in as close as they dared, they began letting fly with slings and bows.

Sheltered behind the oaken bulwarks of their ship, and further protected by the rows of war-boards hung over her sides, the Norse were reasonably protected against missiles. They could have been seriously threatened only by a boarding party; and the Dorsets, who probably hoped only to drive the murdering strangers away from the vicinity, made no attempt to board. After spending some time firing stones and arrows at the ship with no apparent results, the Skraelings gave it up and withdrew.

They had done better than they knew. When the crew of the knorr took stock of the results of the attack, they found that Thorvald Eriksson was mortally wounded.

He seems to have died well, which was in the Viking tradition. Being great givers of death, the Norse could accept death without demur when it came to them. He was buried according to his wishes on Krossaness, the headland which had caught his fancy. Then, giving up both the search for Vinland and the search for Thorhall the Hunter, his shipmates made hurriedly for Straumfiord. Doubtless they now thought they knew what had happened to Thorhall, even if they had found no trace of him. His disappearance would unquestionably have been laid at the door of the Skraelings.

The tale that Thorvald's men had to tell when they reached Straumfiord would have increased the people's dread of the Skraelings manyfold, and they would have wondered fearfully if there was any safety to be had from them in all this hostile land.

24

LAND OF THE ONE-FOOTERS

The Saga Story (c. 1006)

Bjarni Grimolfsson and Freydis remained behind here [at Straum-fiord] with a hundred people and went no farther, while Karlsefni and Snorri proceeded to the southward with forty men, returning again that same summer after tarrying at a hop [there] for barely two months. . . .

They travelled a long distance until they came to a well-forested land. There they sailed into the mouth of a river. . . .

It happened one morning that Karlsefni and his companions saw something in an open space in the woods above them. It seemed to gleam at them and they shouted at it. It moved and they saw it was an Einfoetingr [One-Footer] and he came limping [or hopping] down to where their ship was lying . . . Afterwards he ran away to the northward with Karlsefni's men pursuing him and catching glimpses of him from time to time. The last they saw of him he was running up a stream valley.

Then they turned back [from the chase] and one of the men recited this verse:

> We men pursued, this is the truth,
> A One-Footer who came to the shore,
> But the strange man fled,
> Running swiftly over the hills.
> This we tell you, Karlsefni.

[SOURCES: Selected from the Erik the Red Saga and the Thorfinn Karlsefni Saga. The reasons why this portion of the saga has been treated in this manner are given in Appendix O.]

[Later] they [again] became aware of natives.[89] A great troop of them came out from the woods. Neither side could understand the other's language.

Their packs contained gray furs and sable. They were especially desirous of procuring red cloth. They also wanted to buy swords and spears but Karlsefni and Snorri forbade this.

In exchange for perfect pelts the natives would accept a span length of red cloth which they would bind around their heads.

So the trading continued for a while until Karlsefni and his people began to grow short of cloth, whereupon they divided [what they had left] into such narrow pieces that it was not more than a finger's breadth in width; but still the natives continued to give just as much or more in exchange for it.

Gudrid remained seated inside the door of the booth beside the cradle of her son Snorri. A shadow fell through the doorway, and then a woman entered who wore a narrow black kirtle. She was rather short in stature and she had chestnut-coloured hair and a band around her head. Her eyes were pale and so large that no one had ever seen such large eyes in any human skull.

She came up to where Gudrid sat and Gudrid asked: "What is your name? My name is Gudrid, [tell me] what is your name?"

"My name is Gudrid," said [parroted] the woman.

Then housewife Gudrid stretched out her hand indicating that the woman should sit down beside her, but at that moment Gudrid heard a loud noise whereat the woman vanished. [The noise was caused by] the killing of a native by one of Karlsefni's house slaves at this same time, because he seemed about to take [some of] their weapons.

One of the natives had picked up an axe. He looked at it for a while and struck at a tree with it and one after another the others tested it. It seemed to be a real treasure because it cut so well. But then one of their number seized it and struck at a stone with it and the axe broke. It seemed to him to be of little use since it would not cut stone, and so he threw it away.

Now there was a battle and many of the native host were slain. One man in the host was tall and fair and Karlsefni thought he might be the leader.

Then the natives ran away into the woods, each man for himself, and so ended their encounter.

Then Karlsefni and his people sailed away toward the north, believing they had seen [visited] the land of the One-Footers [Einfoetingaland] and being unwilling to risk their men's lives any longer.

They concluded that the mountains at Hop and those they had now found formed one and the same range and that they [the two places] stood directly opposite each other and were an equal distance from Straumfiord.

[SOURCES: Erik the Red Saga and the Thorfinn Karlsefni Saga]

ALLOWING FOR THE LOSS of Thorhall the Hunter and his nine men together with the deaths at Hop, the combined expedition would by now have been reduced to between 145 and 150 people. Since Karlsefni and Snorri took forty men with them, this would have left not much over a hundred people, including the entire Greenland contingent, at Straumfiord; and the saga says that when Karlsefni sailed, Freydis[90] and Bjarni remained behind in the company of one hundred people. Thorvald would hardly have sailed with less than thirty men on his expedition to the north, which makes it appear that he was still at Straumfiord when Karlsefni and Snorri got under way.

It may have been as early as mid-June when Karlsefni's ship rounded Cape Bauld and turned her bows toward the south, along the east coast of the Great Northern Peninsula.

KARLSEFNI'S COURSE

From Quirpon Island to Canada Bay, Karlsefni the trader and Snorri the would-be settler would have seen little to interest either of them in this bald and forbidding coast. Beyond Canada Bay the spine of the peninsula begins to lift higher and higher as the Long Range Mountains grow in stature. The coastal cliffs become more and more formidable, in places plunging a thousand feet into the sea below. The Norse would have sailed along this unprepossessing coast as quickly as they could. Occasionally they passed the mouth of one of the steep-sided little fiords (most of them mere slits in the sheer face of the sea-cliffs), and though they may have entered some of these in search of shelter from a storm or for an anchorage at night, they would have found nothing in them of much interest either to farmers or to lumbermen. As the voyage proceeded down this uninviting coast, Karlsefni and Snorri may at least have been heartened by the fact that they encountered no Skraelings.[91]

Up to the time they passed Great Harbour Deep they would have been sailing along an open seaboard with nothing to the east of them except a few islands—the Gray Islands—and the wide Western Ocean. But not long after passing Great Harbour Deep the lookout must have caught the loom of land to the east. At first this loom might have been mistaken for another offshore island, but as it grew into a continuous line of highlands the Norse would have realized that they were sailing into the mouth of a big sound or fiord.

This discovery (which they doubtless confirmed by going ashore and climbing the nearest cliff) may have led to renewed hopes that they had found the great fiord which ran southward into the land to terminate at Leif's Vinland.

Assuming that they entertained this hope, they would have pushed on with all possible speed. When they reached Sops Arm they may not have stopped to explore it. If they did sail into it they would have been encouraged by what they found. Although there was no hop, there was a large, sandy river delta whose myriad islands, together with the broad lowlands to the south of them, were thickly forested—and for the first time the forests contained a fair proportion of hardwood timber.

Pressing on, they would have rounded Spear Point, sailing south into what was now obviously a fiord, and moreover one which had abruptly narrowed to only three or four miles in width.

Did Vinland and its hop lie waiting close ahead? The excitement of the Icelanders must have been intense as they ran down those last few miles into Hampden Bay, passed Miller's Island and saw the end of the fiord before them.

THE HOP AT HAMPDEN RIVER

Their hopes would have reached a climax when the ship brought up on the edge of a sand and gravel tidal flat which extended out for half a mile from the river mouth, and when the lookout at the masthead called down the news that he could see a bar, and perhaps a small lagoon behind it. A hurriedly launched boat party would have rowed through the gap in the bar and into a small expansion of the river mouth which formed a tiny barasway, not much more than a hundred yards in diameter, but large enough to provide a harbour for the knorr if she was eased into it at high tide.

This was a hop, although a minute one.[92] It could have borne no comparisons with the fabulous harbour of Leif's Vinland,

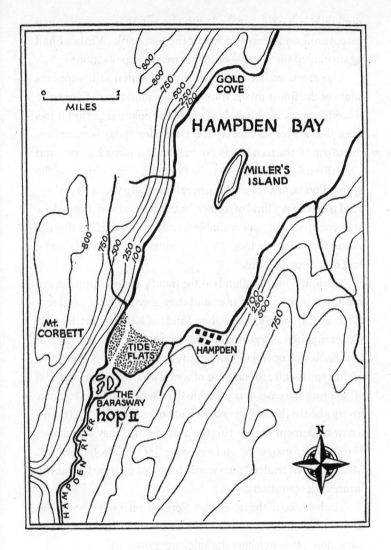

The foot of White Bay and Hop II

nor could it have compared with the hop that Karlsefni had discovered on the west coast of the peninsula. Vinland had again eluded the Norse—but there were compensations.

The steep-walled valley of the Hampden still supports some of the finest mixed forests in Newfoundland. Ever since its rediscovery in the early years of the colonial period it has been famous for its timber, and Hampden today is a lumbering town. In the past it was not unusual for birch logs two and even three feet in diameter to be floated down the river on the spring floods, and for many generations there was a busy shipyard there. Every kind of timber, both hard and soft, needed for ship construction was available locally. In Karlsefni's day the virgin forests at the foot of the bay must have been all that he had ever hoped to find.

The low-lying floodlands at the mouth of the Hampden are not forested now, of course, and they may not have been forested in Karlsefni's time either. Finds of Beothuk artifacts at old campsites suggest that the immediate vicinity of the barachois was open land and, quite probably, it was grassland of the type found around most other Newfoundland barachoix. If this was the case, it is possible that Snorri and the colonist group aboard the ship may have had hopes that they had found a new settlement site. During the next few days they would have been busy investigating and assessing the area's potentialities. Meantime the traders' men would have lost no time beginning lumbering operations.

The location of the temporary Norse camp is not given in the saga sources, but it would logically have been on the shore of the barachois, close to where the ships were moored.

My identification of the barachois at the mouth of the Hampden with Karlsefni's second hop is dictated by two facts. First, it is the only hop-type harbour in the whole of White Bay.

Second, the saga offers convincing proof that the hop must have been close to, if not actually at, the mouth of the Hampden.

They concluded that the mountains at Hop and those they had now found formed one and the same range and that they (the two places) stood directly opposite each other and were an equal distance from Straumfiord.

Since we have already determined that the western Hop was at St. Paul's Bay (or, just possibly, at nearby Parsons Pond), this statement locates the second hop in Hampden Bay. The sailing distances for a coastwise voyage from Epaves Bay to Hop and from Epaves Bay to the mouth of Hampden River are virtually identical. St. Paul's Bay lies exactly opposite to Brown's Cove, which is eight miles north of the river mouth on Hampden Bay. The Long Range Mountains fill the landscape between Hop and Hampden Bay. If there can be any objection to the use of these data to show that Hampden Bay was indeed visited by the Norse, it can only be that they are almost too exact. It may be hard for us to credit the Norse of circa 1000 with the ability to so accurately determine their position in relation to a place on the other side of the Great Northern Peninsula.

THE BEOTHUKS

If the Norse camped for any length of time in Hampden Bay during the summer months they would surely have made contact with a people they had never seen before—the Beothuk. That the party did encounter this group is established by the account of the meeting with the One-Footer. [93]

The Beothuks used to leave their wintering grounds in the interior of Newfoundland in June and begin migrating to the coasts for the summer. The Icelanders may have already been established at the mouth of the Hampden before the first of those Beothuks who wintered in the area around Grand Lake and Sandy Lake began their journey down the Hampden River in their birch-bark canoes. They would have been heading for summer camps at Sops Arm and other inlets along both the east and west coasts of White Bay, where many Beothuk sites have been located.

The Beothuks doubtless discovered the presence of strangers at the river mouth long before the Norse knew that there were locals about. The sounds of axes in the forest; the cries of men busy lumbering; the discovery of stumps and other signs of the felling of big trees along the river bank—all these would have served to alert the Beothuks, and they would doubtless have run their canoes ashore and hidden them while one of their number went forward to reconnoiter. This man may have climbed the steep western side of the valley and worked his way north along the crest as far as Mount Haggerty or Mount Corbett, from whose slopes he would have obtained a clear view of the bay shore and of the river mouth.

The sight of the knorr, of the Norse booths, and of strange men moving about would have amazed the Beothuk, but perhaps it did not frighten him unduly. Isolated as they had been for countless centuries, the Beothuks seem to have had few human enemies, and to have been a friendly and unsuspicious people. They showed no fear of the first Europeans to arrive in colonial times. On the contrary, they were so foolishly trusting that in 1501 Gaspar Cortereal had no difficulty in luring fifty or sixty of them aboard ship, preparatory to carrying them off to Spain as slaves.

There is no way of knowing whether the Beothuk scout deliberately exposed himself to the sight of the Norsemen, or whether some particularly sharp-eyed Icelander happened to spot him, perhaps through the reflection of sunlight on the numerous polished bone pendants which the Beothuks often wore around their necks and across their chests. In any event the Norse seem to have shouted at him, and the Beothuk apparently interpreted the shouting as an invitation to come down. The saga says that he limped, or hopped, down to where the ship lay, and from this we gather that he was lame, although he was still able to get along well enough.

The appearance of this lone stranger close to the ship seems to have tempted the Norse into committing an act of sheer folly. Instead of trying to make friends with him, they apparently tried to seize him. But, crippled or not, he was no easy prey. He outdistanced or outmaneuvered the Icelanders and vanished up a stream valley to the north. His winded pursuers returned to the camp, where, so the verse in the saga tells us, they made their excuses to Karlsefni for their failure.

There may have been a subsequent delay of several days before the Beothuks could make up their minds as to what to do about the Norse. Eventually they seem to have decided to confront the strangers. Since the Norse were presumably camped astride the route to the Beothuk summer camps, a direct confrontation could hardly have been avoided.

Meanwhile the Icelanders, with bitter memories of their encounter with the Skraelings before them, had doubtless given up their hopes of settling here and were making haste to complete their lumbering. Some of their number may have been told off to build some kind of defensive works around the booths, and every man would have gone about fully armed and alert to the dangers of a surprise attack.

When the day came that the Norse beheld a large company of Beothuks coming out of the woods toward them, they probably wished that they had departed while the going was good.

There must have been some frantic scurrying for weapons and for defence positions, and the atmosphere would have been explosive as the stalwart party, bodies glistening with a mixture of oil and red ochre, slowly advanced across the open ground.

By analogy with their known habits in a later time, we assume that the Beothuks made overtures of peace, probably by offering gifts to the strangers. These gifts could have included sable and other rich furs, the sight of which would have roused the natural cupidity of the Norse. In any event peaceful relations, if only of a tentative nature, seem to have been established. The Norse began trading, although the Beothuks may not have realized that this is what was happening. They probably thought that they were simply engaging in an exchange of gifts.

The Beothuks appear to have been greatly impressed by a piece of red woolen cloth which a Norseman offered them, and this material instantly became the thing they most desired to possess.

While the trading or gift exchanging (depending on the point of view) continued, some of the Beothuks seem to have been indulging their curiosity. One woman, bolder than the rest, dared to peek through the door of a booth where the Norse women had doubtless been told to remain until the danger of an attack was past, and saw Gudrid, Karlsefni's wife, sitting beside the cradle of her eighteen-month-old son, Snorri. Gudrid appears to have tried to make friends with the alien woman by asking her her name, and by repeating her own. The Beothuk woman responded by trying to imitate the unfamiliar Norse syllables, whereupon Gudrid, who seems to have been a lady of parts, beckoned the strange woman to come in and join her.

One is tempted to speculate on what might have happened if the Beothuk woman and Gudrid had managed to establish some sort of rapport. The saga literature tells us of many proud Norsemen who listened meekly to the outspoken and vigorous criticisms and suggestions of their women, and sometimes even acted on their wives' advice. It is by no means impossible that if the Beothuk woman and Gudrid had become friends, the story of the Norse attempts to plant a settlement in North America might have had a different ending.

The history of later contacts between whites and Beothuks establishes the fact that the Beothuks wanted peaceful relations with Europeans, and went to extraordinary lengths to achieve this desire. They never succeeded, but only because of the arrant stupidity and unbelievable barbarism of the whites. No doubt it is foolish to imagine that the Norse—even the Norse women— would have been more humane and reasonable in their dealings with the Beothuks than the French, English and Portuguese of five centuries later. The fact remains that had the Norse been able to keep their sanguinary instincts in check, they would have been accepted by the Beothuks and could then have established themselves in Newfoundland without opposition from, and probably with the active cooperation of, the native people who controlled the major portion of the island.

Unfortunately, the Norse knew only one way of settling differences between themselves and alien peoples, and that was by the use of sword and axe. Even as the Beothuk woman was about to enter Gudrid's house, there was a "loud noise" and the woman vanished—not into thin air as some authors have suggested, but in flight; for blood was flowing once again in a Norse camp in the New World.

We do not know what happened. Perhaps one of the Beothuks picked up a Norse axe and began to examine it; or he may have handed it about among his friends. We are told that the Beothuks first tested the axe on a tree and then, in one version, a man is supposed to have tested it on his neighbor, who promptly fell dead. In the other version a Beothuk reputedly tried to cut a rock with it, and the axe broke. Both stories are absurd. The Beothuks were fully familiar with flint hand axes and hafted adzes. The suggestions that they would have been idiotic enough to test a Norse iron axe on each other, or to attempt to cut rocks with it, is an insult to their intelligence and to ours.

What probably happened is that the Norse reacted in a blind possessive fury when the Beothuk man picked up the axe. The saga admits that one of the natives was killed "because he seemed about to take" one of the Norse weapons. There we have it in a nutshell.

With the striking of that first blow—not accidentally, or by a Beothuk, but deliberately and by a Norseman—and the death of one of their number, panic ensued among the group. The saga says that in "the battle" which followed, many of the natives were slain while the rest ran wildly for the shelter of the woods. That many of the Beothuks were slaughtered can be believed. That there was a battle, in any real sense of the word, seems dubious. The saga makes no mention of any Norsemen being killed or even wounded.

It would have been immediately after this (the first but by no means the last massacre of Beothuks at the hands of Europeans) that Karisefni and Snorri and their people got themselves back aboard their ship and hurried home to Straumfiord because, as the saga says, they were "unwilling to risk men's lives any longer" in this place. By which we are to understand that once again they were afraid of retaliation—and with the best of reasons.

25

RETREAT OF THE ICELANDERS

The Saga Tale (c. 1006)

When they sailed from Vinland [Straumfiord] they had a southerly wind which took them to Markland, and there they encountered five Skraelings. One of these was bearded [meaning he was a man], two were women and two were children. Karlsefni and his people captured the boys but the others escaped by sinking down into the ground.

They carried these lads away with them and taught them their tongue and had them baptized. The boys said their mother's name was Vaetilldi and their father was called Uvaegi. They said that kings governed their country, one of them being called Avalldamen and the other Valdidida. They stated that they had no houses [in the sense of Norse houses] and that the people lived in holes or caves.

They said too that there was a land on the other side, opposite their country, which was inhabited by people who wore white garments and who yelled loudly and carried poles before them to which cloths were attached. People believe this must have been Hvitramannaland or Ireland the Great.

And now they [Karlsefni's people] came to Greenland, where they spent the winter with Erik the Red.

But Bjarni Grimolfsson and his companions were driven out into the Greenland Sea and their ship began to sink. They did not discover until then that their ship was all worm-eaten beneath them. They hurriedly discussed what they ought to do.

They had an afterboat coated with seal-tar into which the shipworm will not bore. It was the decision of the company to transfer as many people into this boat as it would hold, but when this was done it was found that it would not take more than half the people.

Then said Bjarni: "Since the boat will not hold more than half the company it is my suggestion that those who are to go in the boat be chosen by lot; for this selection ought not to be made on the basis of rank."

This seemed to be such a manly offer that no one opposed it. They adopted the plan, and the men cast lots. It fell to Bjarni to go in the boat with half the men.

When they [who had been chosen] were in the boat a young Icelander who was still aboard the ship, and who had accompanied Bjarni from Iceland, called out: "Do you intend to forsake me here, Bjarni?"

"This is the way it must be," Bjarni answered.

"That was not what you promised my father when I left Iceland with you," he replied. "You said then that you would never desert me, and that we would share the same fate together."

"I see no other course than this one," said Bjarni. "Have you any alternative to offer?"

"I suggest we change places. You come here, and I will go there."

"So be it then," said Bjarni, "for I see you cling tenaciously to life and find it hard to die." And so they changed places.

Men say that Bjarni perished in that wormy sea together with those men who remained on the ship with him. But the boat and those who were in it went their way until they reached Iceland, where they afterwards told this tale.

[SOURCES: Erik the Red Saga and the Thorfinn Karlsefni Saga]

BY SHEER GOOD LUCK the Norse initially picked a settlement site at Straumfiord which had been abandoned by the waning Dorset population and not yet reoccupied. But although it was then free of natives, it had not always been so, and the Norse could hardly have avoided finding old camps or other signs that natives had once lived in the vicinity.[94]

Indications of prior occupancy by an unknown people might not have disturbed the Norse, secure as they were in their belief that they were a match for anyone, until Karlsefni ran into trouble with the Skraelings at Hop and discovered that they were formidable antagonists. His account of their fighting qualities must have given rise to a good deal of uneasiness among the Straumfiord settlers, even though Hop lay a long way off to the south and west.

However, the Norse would have had no reason to feel that the settlement itself was in any jeopardy until the Thorhall search party came hurrying back from Lake Melville to report that Thorvald Eriksson had been killed by Skraelings who lived to the north of Straumfiord. This alarming news would have demonstrated to the Epaves Bay settlers that they were between two fires, one of which smoldered dangerously close to the searoad linking Straumfiord and Greenland.

When Thorfinn Karlsefni returned from his second southern voyage toward the middle of August and nosed his ship into Epaves Bay, the stay-at-homes must have already been in an anxious frame of mind—a condition which would not have been eased by his report that not only had he again failed to find Vinland, but he had clashed with yet another native people.

The Norse had now conducted four separate exploring expeditions from Straumfiord: to the west, to the north, to the southeast, and to the southwest. They had not found Vinland, and what was even more discouraging, they found no country which was not already in the hands of natives. Karlsefni's return from White Bay seems to have put finis to the last prospects of finding Leif's Vinland. It also must have made it seem dismally clear that Straumfiord was surrounded by dangerous natives who, sooner or later, could be expected to appear at Epaves Bay. The combination of these two factors was doubtless enough to seal the fate of the colony as far as the Icelanders were concerned.

If the Icelandic colonists had needed any additional stimulus to persuade them to give up and go home, it would have been provided by the impending departure of Karlsefni and Thorhall Gamlisson. Having completed their ships' ladings, the two traders had no further interest in remaining in the New World. On the contrary, they had every reason to sail north and east as soon as possible, for summer was drawing to an end and they would have been anxious to avoid the possibility of being trapped at Straumfiord for another, and fruitless, winter.

Their departure would have left any Icelandic settlers who stayed behind dependent on Freydis Eriksdottir for ship transportation as well as subject to her erratic whims in other matters, since the Greenlanders, together with Helge and Finnboggi's men, considerably outnumbered the Icelandic settlers. The prospects of finding themselves at Freydis's mercy could hardly have been much more attractive to the Icelanders than the prospects of having to fight for their lives against the Skraelings. In the event we can be sure that when the ships of Karlsefni and Thorhall put out to sea homeward bound, they carried the whole of the Icelandic contingent with them.[95]

The Icelandic ships apparently did not sail for the same destinations. Skipper Thorhall appears to have taken his departure from some point not far north of Straumfiord, on course for Iceland, perhaps by way of Cape Farewell. But Karlsefni sailed for the Eastern Settlement, perhaps partly in order to sell some of his timber where it would command the highest prices, and partly to arrange for the sale of Gudrid's Greenland property, since he was intending to take his wife to live in Iceland.

The saga says that Karlsefni sailed first to Markland, and he may conceivably have retraced his outward course all the way back to Greenland. It seems more likely that he sailed north either to the unmistakable landmark of the Kaumajet, or to Bjarni Herjolfsson's point of departure near Cape Chidley, and then turned easterly across the Labrador Sea to a landfall in southern Greenland. He may even have pioneered the route between the Kaumajet and Greenland, a route which appears to have been used in later years by Greenlanders visiting the Labrador coast for softwood timber.

The account of the capture of the two Skraeling children affords us our last glimpse of the Dorset peoples before they vanished out of time.

The children were found in Markland, which could mean anywhere along the Labrador coast south of Okak Bay. They were doubtless members of a family group, and when the Norse surprised the family the three adults hid from their pursuers in crevices among the rocks.

The boys were carried off and eventually taught to speak Norse—no matter how imperfectly. They told their captors their parents' names and also the names of two personages whom the Norse took to be the kings of Skraeling Land. However, since no Eskimoan culture embraced the notion of any form of organized leadership, let alone a monarchy, we conclude that the Norse interpretation was faulty and that Avalldamen and Valdidida were doubtless pre-eminent supernatural entities in the Dorset religion—perhaps comparable to Kaila or Sila of recent

Inuit cultures. According to some ethnologists the four names mentioned by the boys show affinities to the Eskaleut language stock, which is what we would expect from a Dorset source.

The statement that the Dorsets did not have houses in the sense that the Norse did, fits with what we know of Dorset structures, which, while they can hardly be described as holes or caves, were in fact semi-subterranean.

One of the main points of interest in the account given by the children lies in what they had to say about a land on the other side, opposite their country, which was inhabited by an alien race. As we have suggested in the chapter dealing with Ari Marsson, the origin of this story evidently lies in an encounter between Greenland Dorsets and Westman settlers in south-western Greenland, during which the Skraelings observed a Celtic religious celebration or procession.

So it happens that with their own final appearance in history the Dorsets shone the light of human recognition on those forgotten Europeans whose first venturings into the dark wilderness of the North Atlantic, centuries before the time of Christ, led them on to Greenland. This is our last glimpse of the people who laid the train along which the flame of Norse audacity burned westward to reach and finally to gutter out upon that ultimate shore—the fringes of a continent which other Europeans, following after, would one day take and make their own.

It is surely a strange and moving thing that in the concluding paragraphs of the last of the sagas which tells of the westward venturing of the Norse we should briefly touch the faces of three peoples—the Greenland Norse, the Dorsets, and the Greenland Celts—all of whom were doomed to vanish utterly.

Karlsefni's ship and people reached Greenland safely and the knorr sailed up into Eriksfiord. The returning venturers were welcomed by Erik the Red and spent the winter with him there.

"But Bjarni Grimolfsson and his companions were driven out into the Greenland Sea . . ." They probably encountered strong northwesterly gales which not only set them far enough south so that they missed Cape Farewell, but which severely strained their ship.

She may have been in bad shape in any case as a natural consequence of having spent two years in the relatively warm Newfoundland waters, where the shipworm abounds and is immensely destructive to the hulls of unprotected wooden vessels. In more northern waters the worm is neither so abundant nor so voracious. Even so, it was the custom in Greenland and Iceland to coat the bottoms of sea-going vessels with seal-tar, a thick and sticky substance made by evaporating seal oil until only a heavy residue remained. In Newfoundland the Norse probably did not have the materials or the opportunity to prepare sufficient quantities of this vital bottom coating.

The saga account of what ensued when the vessel began to sink requires no commentary. Bjarni Grimolfsson was lost, but Thorhall Gamlisson survived and lived on for many years in Iceland, where he became known as "The Vinlander."

The account of the loss of the ship makes a fitting period to a brave and hopeful voyage into a new world—but one which was brought to nothing as much by human stupidity as by the ill will of those implacable fates in whose existence the Norsemen had such an invincible and unshakable belief.

26

FREYDIS AND THE BROTHERS

The Saga Story (c. 1007)

They spent the third winter at Straumfiord. Then the men began
to form into factions and to quarrel over the women. Those who
were without women tried to seize the wives of the married men
and there was serious trouble as a result.

[SOURCES: Erik the Red Saga and the Thorfinn Karlsefni Saga]

When Freydis[96] came to carry her possessions into the house she
found that the brothers [Helge and Finnboggi] had come ahead
of her and had carried their things to the house.

Then Freydis asked: "Why did you bring your belongings in here?"

"Because we supposed," said they, "that the agreements
between us would be kept."

"It is to me that Leif [Karlsefni] lent the house," said she, "and
not to you!"

Then Helge said: "We brothers cannot match your wickedness."

Then the brothers took away their belongings and built themselves a house away from the sea near a lake, and put it all in order.

Meanwhile Freydis was having wood felled [as cargo] for her
ship.

Now winter drew near and the brothers proposed that games
should be played and entertainment set afoot [between the Icelandic crew and the Greenlanders].

This was done and things went well for a while until the men began to quarrel with each other, and then their companionship broke up and the games ceased, and nobody visited back and forth between the houses; and so things went for most of the winter.

Before dawn one morning Freydis got out of bed and dressed and took her husband's cloak and put it on. But she did not put on her shoes. The weather was such that a heavy dew had fallen.

She went to the house of the two brothers and approached the door. One of the men had gone out a little while earlier and had only half-closed the door behind him. She opened the door and stood in the hallway a while without making any noise.

Finnboggi, who lay farthest inside the house, was awake and he asked:

"What do you want here, Freydis?"

"I wish you to get up and come outside, for I want to talk to you," she answered.

He did what she asked and they went to a log that lay close to the shelter of the house and sat down upon it.

"How do you like things here?" she asked him.

"I think the products of this land are good," he replied, "but I don't like the troubles between us, for they are no fault of mine."

"That is true enough, and I agree with you," she said. "But this is the reason I came to see you. I want to exchange ships with you brothers because you have a larger ship than mine and I want to go away [make a voyage?] from here."

"That can be arranged, if it is your pleasure," he answered.

Then she went home and Finnboggi went back to sleep.

She got into her own bed and her cold feet awoke Thorvard [her husband] and he asked her why she was so cold and wet.

She answered with great indignation: "I went to see the brothers to try and arrange to get their ship, since it is larger than ours, and they took this request so badly they assaulted me and roughed me up. But you! You coward! You won't avenge either my shame or your own, and here am I far away from home and Greenland. I swear I'll leave you unless you avenge this insult!"

Thorvard could not stand her jibes and so he called upon his men to get up at once and bring their weapons. The men did so, and then they all went to the house of the brothers and broke in. They surprised [the Icelanders] sleeping and took them all captive and then they bound them and led them out of the house one at a time. Freydis had each one killed as they were brought out.

This left the brothers' women, and nobody would kill them.

"Give me an axe!" Freydis cried.

Someone did so, and she slew the five women who were in the house and left them dead.

After this evil work was finished they went back to their own house and it was apparent that Freydis thought she had acted very cleverly. She said to her followers:

"If we manage to get back to Greenland, I will kill any man who speaks of what has happened. We shall say this, that they [the Icelanders] chose to stay behind when we went away."

Now early in the spring they loaded the [brothers'] ship with all the goods they could find and that the ship would hold. Afterwards they put to sea and had a good voyage, and came into Eriksfirth with their ship early in the summer.

Karlsefni was there, having prepared his ship to sail [to Norway] and he was only waiting for a fair wind before departing. It is said by many people that no richer ship than his ever sailed from Greenland.

Freydis now went to her house [at Gardar] which had stood untouched in her absence. She gave particularly rich gifts to all her companions and followers because she wished to conceal her misdeeds: and so she lived in her own home.

But not all her men kept their word to be silent about her

wickedness, and so rumors of it came out at last. Reports of this reached Leif, her brother [Erik, her father],[97] and he thought these rumors very bad indeed.

Then he took three of Freydis's men and tortured them until they all confessed what had happened and were agreed in their versions of it.

"I cannot afford," said Leif [Erik], "to punish my sister [daughter] Freydis as she deserves, but I foretell this fate for her and hers: that they [she and Thorvard] and their offspring will gain little by this act, and will not prosper as a result of it."

And so it came to pass that everyone thought ill of them from that time forth.

[SOURCE: The Greenlanders Story]

THE TANGLED WEB surrounding the slaughter of Helge and Finnboggi and their people may never be properly unraveled. In the reconstruction which follows I have attempted to make sense out of what seems like a senseless act; but, while I have taken into account all the known facts, the reconstruction necessarily remains largely speculative.

We know that Freydis came out to the new lands solely to enrich herself, as Leif had done before her, by gathering a cargo of the land's most valuable products. When Karlsefni and the Icelanders abandoned Straumfiord and sailed homeward they had ladings, but Freydis and her partners, Helge and Finnboggi, had not had the opportunity to amass a cargo of comparable value. We can believe that Karlsefni would have been willing to give Thorhall Gamlisson a share of the hardwood from Hampden Bay, but considering the hostility between the Greenlanders and the Icelanders, it is unlikely that he would have done the same for Freydis or for her allies.

With her cupidity unsatisfied (it may have been further inflamed by the wealth brought back by Karlsefni) Freydis was not yet willing to leave the new lands, nor was she willing to allow the Greenland settlers to depart even if they had wished to do so.

She was in a position to enforce her will. After Thorvald Eriksson's death, ownership of his ship had fallen to her, or she had taken it. Acting through her flaccid husband, she probably usurped the leadership of the entire Greenland contingent. It would have been difficult for the settlers to oppose her. Not only did she have the backing of her retainers, but at this stage she also would have had the support of Helge and Finnboggi and their crew. This would have given her a strength of thirty-five or forty fighting men as opposed to no more than twenty male survivors from Thorvald's group of settlers.

Freydis may well have decided to remain at Straumfiord for another winter, not because she was interested in giving the colonization plan that much longer to prove itself, but so that she could make a journey south to the land of the hardwoods early in the following spring. If this was her plan, she would have had need of the able-bodied colonists both to strengthen her fighting force and to serve as lumberjacks when she ventured into the lands of the One-Footers.

It will be remembered too that by the terms of her initial agreement with Helge and Finnboggi she was entitled to half the value of the cargo they could carry home. This agreement would no longer have satisfied Freydis now that she had her own ship. Therefore she may also have wished to keep the Greenland settlers at Straumfiord to be used, if necessary, against the Icelandic sailors and their masters. The impression we get of her character suggests that she was quite capable of playing a double game—first making use of the Icelanders to help her enforce her will on the Greenland settlers, and later using the Greenland settlers to give her an overwhelming balance of power over the Icelanders.

After the departure of Karlsefni and Thorhall Gamlisson there were about eighty people left at Straumfiord. Men probably outnumbered the women by about three to one, which would have led to tension and trouble in any isolated community. In a Norse community of those days it would have made for a violently explosive situation. The Norse were renowned for their uninhibited concupiscence and gargantuan sexual appetites, and we can take it for granted that the brief reference in the Erik the Red and Karlsefni sagas to woman trouble is a masterly understatement.

We are told that the quarrel between the two groups, which led to the Icelanders setting up a new hall some distance away from the Greenlandic settlement grew out of a conflict over possession of Leif Eriksson's booths in Vinland. Since we know that the expedition never found Vinland, let alone Leif's booths, we recognize this as an interpolation. Perhaps what really happened is that even before the Karlsefni section of the expedition departed, Freydis had begun to develop a plan whereby she would acquire the entire wealth which was to have been shared between her and the brothers. As part of this plan she may have deliberately set about rousing hostility between the remaining Icelanders and the Greenlanders.

The "house" incident may have taken place substantially as described. Possibly it had to do with the occupancy of one of the houses abandoned by the Icelandic contingent. Helge and Finnboggi may have occupied one of these houses, only to be forced out of it by Freydis on the grounds that Karlsefni had given her the use of it.[98]

What is important about this incident is that Freydis was

already breaking the agreements made between her and the brothers at the beginning of the voyage. The text establishes the fact that the brothers did everything in their power to avoid a clash. Their willingness to placate Freydis, even at the cost of their pride, is by no means typical of Norse behavior and suggests that they were fully aware of the precariousness of their own position. The withdrawal of the Icelanders to a site well away from the Greenlanders drives home the point.

It is not difficult to believe that Freydis then attempted to inflame the situation to the point where the Greenlanders would spontaneously attack and massacre the Icelanders. We can imagine some of the methods she may have used. Apart from playing on the suspicion which was evidently latent between the two groups, she may also have pointed out that the Icelanders had five women for their solace, but were selfishly unwilling to share their services with the Greenlanders. There were a score of other ways by which she could have played upon the tempers of men who were unruly at the best of times, and who, after three years of isolation in an alien land, could have been all too readily incited to mayhem.

The breakdown of the brothers' efforts to establish peace between the two camps is documented in the saga. After this failure it appears that all communications between the two camps were severed. The Icelanders must have felt themselves to be living in a state of siege.

So the winter passed and spring arrived, and Freydis's plan had not yet borne fruit. The tension between the two camps had not yet errupted into outright violence, perhaps because the spineless and incompetent Thorvard, Freydis's husband, refused to act.

Time was running out and Freydis must have felt that it was now or never. So she applied the final goad.

Superficially the account of her visit to the brothers' hall appears to make little sense. However, it must be remembered that the account of what happened presumably originated with Freydis. The Icelanders were unable to give their version, for they were dead. Perhaps some of the ambiguities in the tale were deliberate attempts on Freydis's part to confuse the issue. Freydis's claim that she went to visit the Icelanders in the middle of the night, having sneaked out of her husband's bed and having foregone wearing shoes so as not to wake the household, all for the purpose of a simple little business talk, is transparent nonsense.

What happened was probably this: on the one hand she deliberately forced her husband's sword arm by setting up a situation which suggested he was being cuckolded by one of the Icelandic brothers; while on the other she made a large, and presumably fairly public, outcry to the effect that Thorvard was not man enough to avenge an assault upon her person.

That Thorvard was a dullard is suggested by an earlier reference to him in the saga sources; but he was not so supine that he could withstand this double-edged attack. Baffled and badgered, unable to cope with the cunning of his quick-witted virago of a wife, he was finally driven in blind exasperation to play the part Freydis had prepared for him.

What actually took place when Freydis visited the Icelanders, will never be known. Perhaps she did not visit them at all—we have only her word for it that she did. In any event we can be quite sure that the Icelanders would not meekly have agreed to exchange vessels with her. They would have had to be completely spineless to agree to anything of the sort. If she did visit them it may have been merely to lull their suspicions by pretending that she had undergone a change of heart or to convince them by a concrete offer of her favours that they had nothing to fear.

The surprise attack on the Icelandic camp, which was doubtless mounted just before dawn, accomplished what Freydis desired—it eliminated the Icelanders from any share in the proceeds of the expedition and put their ship, which was larger and better than Thorvald's old vessel, into her hands. Something of the pitiless resolution which motivated her can be seen in the grim aftermath, when she personally slaughtered the five Icelandic women in order to keep their mouths shut. That she had to do this herself may have been due to some vestiges of compassion on the part of the Greenland men but it was more likely due to their desire to keep the women alive for their own use.

The saga tells us that soon after the massacre Freydis and her people loaded the Icelanders' ship and sailed home to Greenland. They seem to have made the return journey early in the season, for they arrived at Eriksfiord before Karlsefni sailed for Norway. Having taken over Helge's and Finnboggi's share of the products of the new land together with their ship, Freydis may not have made any further effort to add to the ship's lading. Possibly she never intended to visit Hampden Bay but only suggested this as a means of keeping Helge and Finnboggi at Straumfiord after the Icelandic colonists departed.

The Greenlanders would have done their best to hide the evidence of their crime, for they could not have known that there would be no more voyages to Straumfiord, and they would not have cared to risk the chance of some future expedition discovering the true fate which had overtaken the brothers, their men and their women. Perhaps the old vessel which had once belonged to Thorbjorn Vifilsson, and had made two voyages out over the western waters from Greenland, made her last voyage in the Strait of Belle Isle laden with the corpses of the Icelanders, and red with flames.

Crowded into the brothers' ship, the Greenlanders made their way home; but not even Freydis's threats could stop all mouths. Eventually somebody talked, in liquor maybe, and a rumor of what had happened reached Erik. His torturing of three of Freydis's men revealed the full story, but he himself would have had to try to hush it up because if it had become public knowledge he would have been held responsible together with Freydis and her people by the relatives of the dead Icelanders.

Karlsefni, who had wintered with his good friend Erik, probably saw and talked to Freydis and her crowd when they arrived in Eriksfiord. But apparently he heard no whispers of the bloody deed with which the last members of the great expedition to the west had sealed its inglorious and final end.

Karlsefni prepared his ship and sailed out to sea and he had a good voyage and came to Norway safe and sound. He stayed there that winter and sold his wares; and both he and his wife enjoyed the friendship of the most distinguished men in Norway.

The next spring he prepared his vessel for the voyage to Iceland. One day, when she was ready and lay at the quay waiting for a fair wind, a southerner—a native of Bremen in Saxonland—came to see him. The visitor wished to buy Karlsefni's husanotra.

"I will not sell," Karlsefni told him.

"I will give you half-a-mark in gold for it," said he.

Karlsefni thought this was a good price, and so he sold it. The southerner went away with the husanotra. He did not know what sort of wood it was [made of]; but it was mazur [birch] brought from Vinland.

Karlsefni put out to sea and brought his ship to the northern part of Iceland at Skagefiord. There his ship was laid up for the winter and he and Gudrid went to his home at Reynisness.

His mother thought he had made a poor match [in Gudrid] and would not live with them that winter. Later when she became convinced that Gudrid was a very superior woman, she came home again and they all lived happily together.

In the spring Karlsefni bought Glumboland and built his house there.

After Karlsefni was dead, Gudrid became the trustee of the property and of Snorri, her son, who was born in Vinland.

When Snorri was married, Gudrid went abroad [on pilgrimage] and to the South [probably to Rome]. Afterwards she returned to the home of Snorri, her son, and he had a church built for her at Glumbo. Later Gudrid became a nun and an anchorite and lived there the rest of her life.

Many great people in Iceland are descended from Karlsefni and Gudrid.

God be with us all, Amen!

[SOURCES: Erik the Red Saga, the Karlsefni Saga and the Greenlanders Story]

EPILOGUE

The Aftermath

THE SUBSEQUENT HISTORY of the Norse westward venturing is sunk in obscurity. There are a few fragmentary references scattered here and there in the Icelandic literature and in other ancient sources which make it plain that the Greenlanders continued to make voyages to the Labrador for timber until at least as late as 1347; but there is no indication of any further attempt to establish settlements in North America.

There were also apparently a number of accidental visits. Approximately in the year 1025 an Icelandic merchant named Gudleif Gudlaugsson set out on a voyage from Dublin to Iceland by the direct route. He encountered heavy easterly and northeast gales and was driven far off course to the west and southwest. When the summer was nearly over, so the saga[99] tells us, he found land and anchored in a convenient harbour. Here he was approached by dark-complexioned natives who spoke a language the Icelanders did not understand, but which they thought bore some similarity to the Irish tongue. That it was not Irish can be taken for granted since Gudleif or some of his men would have understood it if this had been the case.

The saga gives a very circumstantial account of this incident. It describes how the Icelanders were taken prisoner,

349.

but eventually released through the good offices of an elderly white man whom they later identified as a skald named Bjorn Asbrandsson who had disappeared many years earlier while on a voyage out of Iceland, probably Greenland bound. This castaway had achieved a position of some distinction among the natives with whom he was living and was satisfied to remain with them. Gudleif and his men managed to sail back to Iceland, where their story gained wide circulation.

Bjorn may have been bound for Erik's colony when he was lost. We know he departed from Iceland with a northeast wind, which would have been the correct wind for a voyage to southern Greenland. No doubt he was blown past Farewell and, like others before him, eventually made land to the west. There his ship seems to have been wrecked, and Bjorn was the sole survivor of the ship's complement at the time of Gudleif's visit some twenty or thirty years later. It has been suggested that Bjorn may have been the prototype of the legendary Glooscap, the mysterious god who appeared out of the sea and who lived with the Mi'kmaq of Nova Scotia for a long time. [100]

We can be sure of one thing, that during the centuries following the Karlsefni voyage, Norse ships must have continued to blunder onto the northeastern coasts of the continent from time to time. Most of the people were probably killed, or if they were lucky made their way back home again; but some may have remained alive in the New World until they and their blood were lost by assimilation into one or another of the native tribes.

In 1059 there may have been a deliberate attempt to revisit Vinland—perhaps sparked by Gudleif's experiences. There is a record of a Celtic or Saxon priest named Jon, who had at one time worked in Iceland, having gone to Vinland or Vendland on a missionary voyage. He was subsequently reported to have been murdered by the natives there.

This reported voyage is of interest, for if it is authentic it suggests that all hope of making use of the new lands may not have been abandoned, and it also seems to confirm that the chief difficulty in the way of settlement was the native population. Perhaps someone in Iceland or Greenland concluded that if the natives could be Christianized they might become more tractable. At any rate this proved to be a very efficacious method when used by later-day Europeans in their attempts to occupy "heathen" countries, and it is not yet completely in discard.

Assuming that Jon was sent to Vinland, his death should have reinforced the belief that no settlement could be established in the New World in the face of the opposition of the natives. Yet, oddly enough, the next chronological reference to the new lands is also to a missionary expedition. This one seems to have taken place in 1121, when Erik, Bishop of Greenland, is reported to have sailed for Vinland. Nothing further is known about him except that he was succeeded by a new bishop in 1124, from which we draw the conclusion that his luck was no better than Jon's.

The Vinland referred to here was not Leif's Vinland, which was apparently never rediscovered, but was the later Vinland of the Stefansson map—the Great Northern Peninsula of Newfoundland. It is an ironic thought that if Leif's original Vinland had been rediscovered by Karlsefni or later voyagers (with or without Leif's aid) the Norse might very well have succeeded in establishing a settlement in the New World. At Trinity Bay they would probably never have been involved in serious conflict with a native population. As early as the last decades of the sixteenth century parts of adjacent Conception Bay were settled by the English, and these nascent lodgments, unlike those such as ill-fated Roanoke on the mainland, never suffered from a hostile native population. If the Norse had settled Trinity Bay in the eleventh century, their offspring might be there yet.

Vinland seems to have been left to its own devices after Erik's visit, having proved too tough a nut for the Norse to crack. However, the Greenlanders continued to make voyages to Labrador and to the western coasts of Baffin Bay and into Davis Strait. In 1266 an expedition was sent from the Eastern Settlements into north Baffin Bay to find out where the Skraelings (Thule) who had recently appeared in northwest Greenland were coming from. This expedition appears to have reached Devon or Bylot Island and to have reported that this was good hunting country. By 1300 Norse hunters were wintering at least as far north as Uppernavik, where a rune stone inscribed by them was later found.

Interest in the northwestern regions seems to have burgeoned during this period, perhaps largely because exploitation and explorations of the southwestern (Vinland) regions was denied to the Norse by the presence of the relatively large and militarily effective native population.

A number of archeological finds suggest that the Greenland Norse made use of the Jones Sound district to the north of Devon Island. Beacons, cairns and eiderduck nesting shelters, all of which appear to be non-Eskimoan, have been found in some numbers in this region.

There is another ruin in this area which has not previously been mentioned in the literature dealing with the Greenland Norse. This is a stone tower which was discovered on the southern shore of Cornwallis Island by Lieutenant Sherard Osborn, R. N., during the search for Sir John Franklin in 1850–1851. Osborn describes the ruin as being a conical-shaped building, the apex of which he assumed had fallen in. It was about twenty feet in circumference and the remaining walls stood five feet six inches high. Osborn concluded that it had been constructed by someone with a good knowledge of stone masonry, and illustrated this strange building in his book.[101] Its similarity to certain Greenland Norse structures, particularly polar bear traps, is at once apparent.

The extent of Norse penetration westward into the North American arctic can only be conjectured, but it may have been considerable. Hudson Strait and Ungava Bay appear to have been known to the Greenlanders and there is no reason to doubt that sooner or later they ventured into Hudson Bay (see Appendix P). They were still active on the Labrador coast (presumably lumbering) as late as 1347, when a Greenland vessel with a crew of eighteen men was blown off course while en route from Markland to Greenland, and made port in Iceland.

Only a few years later, about 1360, it is believed that an expedition from Norway under the command of one Paul Knutsson was sent out to Greenland by royal command to try and bring the erring Greenlanders, who had reputedly fallen into paganism, back to a proper recognition of the Church of Rome. This expedition may also have had another and more important purpose—that of discovering what had happened to the inhabitants of the Western (Godthaab) Settlement, which by 1350 had apparently been abandoned without any indication of where its occupants had gone.

Although there is no documentary evidence from European sources to tell us what happened to the Knutsson expedition, there may be documentation from North America. In 1898 a stone inscribed with runic characters was found enmeshed in the roots of a tree near Kensington, Minnesota. The inscription on the stone translates as follows:

8 Goths [Swedes] and 22 Norwegians on exploration journey from [or *for*] Vinland across West. We had camp by 2 Skerries one day's journey north from this stone. We were

and fished one day. After we came home found 10 men red with blood and dead. AVM [ave Maria] save from evil. Have 10 men by the sea to look after our ships 14 day's journey from this island. Year 1362.

This stone—now called the Kensington Stone—has been the centre of bitter controversy between scholars ever since it came to light. Some insist that it must be a forgery; but others point out that, considering all the circumstances, it is more difficult to believe it is a forgery than to accept it as authentic.

One of the major reasons why acceptance of it has met such resistance is the location of the find, deep in the heart of the continent. Perhaps this difficulty is subject to a simple resolution.

The place where the stone was left by the Norse need not have been the place where it was found. It could have been discovered by Indigenous peoples and taken away by them. Considered as a cult object, it could have remained in their hands for years or even for generations, and it may have been carried a considerable distance from its original site.

At least one parallel case is known—that of an "inscribed stone" which was obtained by Pierre de La Verendrye in what is now North Dakota in 1738. This stone, which seems to have been used as a cult object, was taken by La Verendrye to Montreal and later sent to France, where it eventually disappeared. It is said to have been covered with writing which looked Tataric. Since Tataric and Runic alphabets bear a similarity to one another, this stone too may conceivably have been inscribed with runes.

If we admit the possibility that the Kensington Stone might have originated somewhere other than at Kensington, it becomes possible to link it with the Beardmore find of Norse weapons and artifacts.

This find, which is preserved in the Royal Ontario Museum of Archeology in Toronto, was made near Lake Nipigon on the north shore of Lake Superior. It consists of a broken iron sword, something which may be part of a "rattle," an axe blade and some fragments which appear to be parts of the boss of a shield. These relics are unquestionably of Norse origin; but it has been suggested that they may have been "planted." A careful analysis of all the evidence does not give much support to the fraud theory, but the very mention of the word has been enough to throw the find into some discredit. [102]

Bearing in mind the likelihood that the Greenland Norse knew Hudson Strait, and may even (as we have suggested in Appendix P) have had some sort of establishment there, it does not seem too far fetched to suppose that the Knutsson expedition may have sailed through the strait into Hudson Bay. If they then continued south into James Bay and landed near the mouth of the Albany River, they would have been able to proceed by boat to within a short distance of Lake Nipigon.

The Beardmore find might then represent either a cache made by the party after the death of ten of its men, or an actual burial. The Kensington Stone might have been carved and left in this vicinity before the surviving members of the party beat a hasty retreat toward their ships moored on salt water two weeks' boat journey distant to the northeast. Those who might later have found the stone could then have carried it to its eventual resting place in Minnesota.

If the Knutsson expedition did reach North America, it becomes the last Norse venture to the westward of which we have any record. It is true that in 1472 an expedition sailed from Europe to Greenland and evidently entered Hudson Bay, perhaps even wintering there. But this was a combined Scandinavian and Portuguese expedition which properly belongs to the age of Cabot and Columbus, of which it was the direct precursor.[103]

We have insufficient space in which to discuss in any detail the disappearance of the Greenland colonies. Essentially the breakdown of the Norse settlements was due to the steadily worsening climatic conditions between the thirteenth and sixteenth centuries. By early in the fifteenth century the Greenland climate had become so bad that it was probably impossible for a pastoral people to survive there, at least in any significant numbers. The increasing difficulty which the Norse experienced in their efforts to farm resulted in a change in the way of life of many of the Greenlanders. People turned more and more to semi-nomadic hunting to support themselves; but in this field they would have found that the Thule, who were appearing in constantly increasing numbers in Greenland, were far and away their superiors. It seems certain that some of the Norwegians, particularly in the area of the Western Settlement, began to adopt the Inuit way of life and eventually merged into the Inuit community.

Those who attempted to maintain their old manner of existence concentrated in the Eastern Settlement, but in the long run they were unable to survive the combination of a deteriorating local climate and an increasingly savage oceanic climate with a high incidence of drift ice which helped bring about a total severance of communications with Norway, and which choked off the northern supply routes.

Many of these doomed settlers appear to have suffered from endemic malnutrition. They must have died like flies whenever epidemic diseases appeared among them. Some may have escaped by going aboard Bristol, Basque and other foreign fishing and trading vessels and taking passage to Europe. A handful apparently hung on to the bitter end, and it was at or near

Herjolfsness—once the major port of the Greenland Norse—
that the last of them seems to have perished just prior to 1540.

In that year a Dutch whaling skipper took shelter in a deep
fiord which may well have been Herjolfsfiord, and "there they
found a dead man lying face down on the ground. On his head
was a hood, well made, and [he was] otherwise clothed both
in frieze cloth and sealskin. Near him lay a sheath knife, much
worn and eaten away."[104] The Dutch skipper reported having
seen habitations farther up the fiord, but the implication is that
these were empty of mankind.

The sanguinary nature which had enabled the Vikings to
overrun so much of Europe was their prime undoing in the
western continent. Instead of giving them suzerainty over
Newfoundland and Labrador, the ready hand with sword and
battle-axe cut them off from the prospects of occupying the
magnificent new world they had discovered. Nevertheless their
westward voyaging was not a sterile and bootless episode in
history, as some historians would have us believe.

It was not a dead-end venture leading nowhere and to nothing. Although the Norse failed to settle the New World, they
pioneered and established the sea routes to the west which
were followed by later waves of European venturers in the fifteenth century.

The belief that all knowledge of the Norse routes was lost
with the decay of the Greenland colonies is naïve in the extreme.
Sea lore does not pass away with the death of a single society
but is perpetuated and handed on through the members of
that amorphous guild to which all seamen, of whatever race,
automatically belong. There can be no doubt that the Bristol,
Basque, Portuguese and north European merchants, fishermen, whalers and pirates who are known to have frequented

both Icelandic and Greenlandic waters from at least as early as the beginning of the fifteenth century came to share some of the knowledge of the western waters which had been amassed by the Northmen. There can be equally little doubt that they made use of, and transmitted, this knowledge to others after the Greenlandic society had virtually disappeared.

Basque whalers are believed to have been fishing in the Labrador Sea as early as 1420 and it is inconceivable that they would not have heard about and visited Helluland and Markland and then coasted south to discover—if they were not actually told of its existence—the fabulous whaling grounds of the Strait of Belle Isle. It is equally inconceivable that British and French cod fishermen, as well as their Basque counterparts, had not found their way to the Vinland region—the Land of Baccaloas, or codfish—and discovered the Grand Banks many years, if not decades, before the first "official" discovery of this region was recorded by John Cabot.

There is good reason to believe that Columbus, who was a well-informed member of the maritime fraternity, knew about the old Norse sea routes into the northwest. About the year 1477 he visited Iceland, perhaps in order to obtain detailed first-hand information. It is true that he had no desire to sail to the Land of Baccaloas, but he did wish to circumvent it to the south, and for this reason he would have been anxious to know as much as possible about its shape, position and extent.

All through the fifteenth century fleets of European ships fished cod in Icelandic waters, and their crews had much intercourse with the Icelanders. The Iceland colony itself might very well have starved and disappeared during this fiercely adverse climatic period had it not been supported by supplies, obtained in exchange for dried cod, from English ships. The skippers of these ships could hardly have avoided hearing reports of the lands and routes toward the west. The information which in 1570 enabled Sigurd Stefansson to construct his amazingly accurate chart of the early Norse discoveries in Newfoundland and Labrador would surely have been available in some form or another to seamen visiting Iceland one hundred or one hundred and fifty years before his time.

Documents may not exist to prove the point, for merchant seamen are seldom thoughtful enough to bequeath convenient documents for the edification of future historians; but common sense and even a peripheral understanding of the sea and seamen should lead us to recognize the fact that the routes pioneered and developed by the Norse were never wholly abandoned and never lost to view. Even before the Greenland Norse colonies vanished, other men in other ships were already sailing those ancient sea routes, and they continued to sail them until eventually they were followed by the officially acceptable discoverers whose names now stand in the history books, and to whom alone accrues the credit which is due to many nameless and forgotten seamen.

The Norse westward ventures during the decade at the turn of the millennium cannot be written off as isolated and unimportant incidents out of the mainstream of North American history. It was the voyagers of those times who traced the track over the pathless western ocean—the track which became a great sea highway over which other men of Europe later sailed to seize and occupy a continent.

A NOTE ON APPENDICES

The appendices for *Westviking* are available at
https://douglas-mcintyre.com/pages/westviking.

CHRONOLOGY OF
THE WESTERN VOYAGES

A. THE EARLY PERIOD

c. 330 B.C.   Pytheas' voyages from the Mediterranean to Iceland and beyond.

c. A.D. 300   Occasional Pictish and Celtic visits to Iceland, probably to engage in summer fishing and sea-mammal hunting.

c. 450   Climatic conditions in northern waters begin to improve.

c. 500   Irish voyages to northwestern waters. Period of the St. Brendan voyages.

c. 650   Picts and Celts visiting Iceland more frequently and products of Iceland hunting expeditions finding their way to Mediterranean markets.

c. 750   Viking raids on Christian settlements in Outer Islands in full swing.

c. 770   Celtic settlements in Iceland.

c. 800   Climatic conditions much improved. Very little ice found in northern waters.

835   First papal bull referring to Christian settlements in Iceland and Greenland.

c. 860   First Viking ships appear off Iceland.

c. 870   First Scandinavian settlement in Iceland.

c. 877	Gunnbjorn Ulf Kragesson visits east coast of Greenland and discovers Gunnbjorn's Islands.
c. 880	Major Scandinavian immigration to Iceland begins.
930	Althing established in Iceland. Settlement of Iceland by Northmen completed, with little usable land remaining to be claimed.
c. 930	Herjolf Bardsson born in Iceland.
c. 940	Birth of Ari Marsson in Iceland.
c. 950	Birth of Erik Thorvaldsson (Erik the Red) in Norway, and of Bjarni Herjolfsson in Iceland.
c. 963	Erik the Red accompanies his family to Iceland, where they settle in the Hornstrandir district.
c. 970	Little Climatic Optimum established.

B. THE NORSE VOYAGES TO THE WEST

c. 970	Ari Marsson blown west from Iceland to Greenland.
	Erik the Red marries Thorhild (Thiodhild) and moves to Vatnshorn.
c. 971	Leif Eriksson born; followed by Thorstein and Thorvald Eriksson and Freydis Eriksdottir.
c. 970–977	Erik involved in a series of killings and outlawed from the Haukadale district of Iceland.
c. 975–976	Hrolf Thorbjarmarson and Snaebjorn Holsteinsson winter on the east coast of Greenland.
c. 977–978	Erik winters at Tradir. In the summer of 978 establishes a new home at Oxney.
c. 977–980	Reports of the captivity of Ari Marsson received in Iceland via Norwegian merchants in Dublin.
c. 980	Erik embroiled in a feud with Thorgest and kills Thorgest's sons.

c. 981	Erik outlawed from Iceland for a three-year term, at Thorsness Thing in the early summer. About midsummer sails for Greenland.
	First Christian missionary visits Iceland.
c. 981–982	Erik winters at Eriksey in the mouth of Eriksfiord, southwestern Greenland.
982	Erik explores the west coast of Greenland north to Cape Burnil, then crosses Davis Strait and explores the Cumberland Peninsula of Baffin Island.
982–983	Erik winters on the island of Holm near Cape Burnil.
983	Erik explores north up Greenland's west coast to the vicinity of the Steenstrups Glacier.
983–984	Erik returns south to Eriksey and again winters there.
984	Erik returns to Iceland.
985	First wave of colonists leaves Iceland for Greenland under Erik's leadership.
	In late summer Bjarni Herjolfsson sails from Iceland to join the colonists but is driven west and discovers Newfoundland and Labrador before reaching Greenland.
985–995	Early settlement period in Greenland. Eastern and Western (Ivitgut) settlements established and exploitation of the Western Obygdir in Baffin Island begun.
c. 995	Leif Eriksson determines to visit Bjarni's southernmost land, probably in order to open up a source of timber. He buys Bjarni's ship and departs in early summer, and establishes his camp in Trinity Bay, Newfoundland.
995	Olaf Tryggvason becomes King of Norway.
c. 995–996	Leif overwinters at Trinity Bay.
c. 996	Leif returns to Greenland, rescuing the trader Thorer and his men off the Greenland coast en route.

c. 996–997	Leif hears of King Olaf's exploits and determines on a visit to Norway.
c. 997	Leif sails for Norway. Visits Thorgunna in the Hebrides. In the autumn continues on to Norway. Thorbjorn Vifilsson and Thorgisl Orrabeinsfostri set out from Iceland for the Eastern Settlement. Thorbjorn arrives at Herjolfsness in the autumn. Thorgils is shipwrecked on the east coast of Baffin Island.
c. 997–998	Leif winters with King Olaf in Norway. Thorbjorn and his daughter Gudrid winter at Herjolfsness, proceeding to Eriksfiord in the spring.
c. 998	Leif returns to Greenland in late summer bringing priests and engaging in missionary activities.
c. 999	Thorstein Eriksson and Erik the Red undertake a voyage to Leif's Vinland in Thorbjorn Vifilssons's ship. Fail to reach Newfoundland and return in the autumn.
c. 1000	Thorstein marries Gudrid Thorbjornsdottir and goes to live in the new Western Settlement (Godthaab). Thorstein dies during the winter.
1000	Death of King Olaf Tryggvason in September of this year.
	Thorgunna and her son Thorgils Leifsson arrive in Iceland. Christianity becomes the legal religion of Iceland.
c. 1003	Thorfinn Karlsefni and Thorhall Gamlisson sail two ships from Iceland to Greenland. The Icelandic brother Helge and Finnboggi arrive in Greenland in their trading ship, having sailed thence from Norway.
c. 1003–1004	Marriage of Karlsefni to Gudrid Thorbjornsdottir. Preparations under way for a combined Greenlandic-Icelandic voyage to Vinland.
c. 1004	Four-ship expedition led by Thorfinn Karlsefni and Thorvald Eriksson sails for Vinland via Baffin Island and the Labrador Coast. Establish a wintering camp at the Strait of Belle Isle.

c. 1005	Icelandic contingent under Karlsefni sails down the west coast of Newfoundland and establishes a wintering camp at Hop in St. Paul's Bay. Meanwhile the Greenlandic contingent conducts two expeditions: a boat voyage, under Thorvald Eriksson, along the south coast of Labrador; and a second boat expedition led by Thorhall the Hunter, which was intended to explore Grosswater Bay, but which came to grief when the boat was blown offshore.
c. 1006	The Icelandic group abandons Hop and returns to Straumfiord in the spring. Part of the group, under Karlsefni, sails one ship down the east coast of the Great Northern Peninsula to the foot of White Bay, still seeking Vinland. Meanwhile Thorvald Eriksson leads a search expedition to Lake Melville looking for Thorhall the Hunter and is killed there by Skraelings. In late summer the two ships of the Icelandic contingent depart for Greenland. Karlsefni reaches Greenland and winters there but Bjarni Grimolfsson's ship is lost. The Greenlandic contingent remains for another winter at Straumfiord under the leadership of Freydis Eriksdottir.
c. 1007	The Greenlandic contingent returns to Greenland after murdering the Helge-Finnboggi crew. Thorfinn Karlsefni sails for Norway to dispose of his New World goods.

C. THE LATER PERIOD

c. 1025	The Norse trader Gudleif discovers the Icelander Bjorn Asbrandson somewhere on the coast of North America, both men having been driven there by adverse weather.
1035–1040	Frisian merchants make at least one trading voyage to Greenland.
c. 1059	An Irish or Saxon missionary priest named Jon is believed to have gone to seek Vinland and to have been murdered by the natives there.

1067	Adam of Bremen writes of the existence of Vinland.
1121	Erik, Bishop of Greenland, believed to have sailed for Vinland on a missionary expedition. Not heard of again, and replaced as Bishop of Greenland in 1124.
c. 1124	Islendingabok written.
c. 1200	Climate deteriorating at the end of the Little Climatic Optimum.
1261	Greenland accepts the suzerainty of Norwegian kings.
c. 1266	The Gardar priests from the Eastern Settlement send an expedition into northwestern Baffin Bay to reconnoiter the Skraelings.
c. 1300	A wintering party of Norse hunters carves a runestone at Kingiktorsuak, high up the west coast of Greenland.
	Sea ice conditions become very bad on all the major ship routes west of Iceland.
1347	"Came ship from Greenland that had sailed to Markland, and 18 men." This ship was blown off course on her homeward voyage and landed in Iceland.
c. 1350	Ivar Bardarsson finds the Western Settlement of Greenland mysteriously deserted.
c. 1360	An expedition of the King of Norway, under Paul Knutsson, commissioned to restore Christianity to Greenland and to find out what had happened to the people of the Western Settlement.
1362	Date of the Kensington Stone, memoralizing the death of a number of Northmen in the Lake Superior region.
c. 1400	Europe and the northern waters entering the Little Ice Age.
c. 1410	The Olafsson expedition makes the last recorded visit by Icelanders to the Greenland settlements. Bristol merchants fishing and trading in Iceland waters and probably trading to Greenland.

c. 1420	Basque whalers operating off the Greenland coasts and in the Labrador Sea.
c. 1476	Joint Scandinavian-Portuguese expedition to the western lands under Pining and Pothorst, accompanied by Joa Vaz Cortereal and piloted by Johannes Scolvuss.
c. 1540	Jon the Greenlander, a north European whaler, finds the corpse of the last known Greenland Norseman.
1570	Sigurd Stefansson compiles his map of Vinland, Markland, Helluland and the Northern waters.

ENDNOTES

1   For a survey of the most recent conclusions of climatologists about ancient weather conditions in the northern regions, see Appendix B.

2   Until well into the seventeenth century the word "island" was interchangeable with the word "land" and did not necessarily mean a body of land surrounded by water. Eurasia was regarded as the only continent. Any land which one reached by sailing across the sea was an "island," no matter what its size.

3   See Appendices I and J.

4   *The Northern Seas*, by A. R. Lewis (Princeton University Press, 1958). By A.D. 450 what amounted to a Celtic thalassocracy existed in the Irish Sea, extending from Dalriada in Ireland to Brittany and Spain. Lewis says of it: "Though this Celtic mar time empire owed much to surviving Roman tradition in West Britain, it seems to have owed more to the earlier Celtic maritime strength in the Atlantic. . . . ."

5   Curraghs must not be confused with the tiny, skin-covered coracles used by the ancient Britons on lakes and rivers.

6   These included the Shetlands, Orkneys and Faeroes.

7   These ships are described in Appendix E.

8   The Norse called all the inhabitants of the British Isles by this name, but it applied more specifically to the Scots, Hebrideans and Irish.

9   Sentence of exile was usually for a term of one to three years.

10 The Nobel Prize-winning Icelandic author Halldor Laxness gives a devastating picture of the nature of Icelandic Vikings in his book *The Happy Warriors*, London, 1958.

11 The best account of these conditions is to be found in Njal's Saga, which, incidentally to its blood and smoke, gives an excellent picture of Icelandic life around the beginning of the eleventh century.

A discussion of the Landnamabok and other Icelandic sources is to be found in Appendix A.

12 These sagas are identified and discussed in Appendix A. Explanations included by the author are enclosed in brackets.

13 Apart from their monetary value, which was considerable, dais-posts had a symbolic significance which made them almost price-less to their owners. They were the visible symbols of his rank and were intimately linked with his honour. They were also believed to be imbued with magical attributes, particularly when they bore the head of Thor, the Hammer God.

14 The importance of the influence of climatic conditions (particularly water temperature) on sea mammal population and distribution, and on the peoples who depend on sea mammals, is discussed in Appendix B and in Appendix H.

15 This would have been an arranged marriage.

16 The likelihood is that they deliberately sailed for Norway, both to dispose of the products of the winter hunt and to allow time to intervene before they dared return to Iceland.

17 Thorkatla's detailed genealogy occurs elsewhere in the Landnamabok.

18 See Appendix I, Part II, where the Ari Marsson story is analyzed in detail.

19 See Appendix I, Part II.

20 A detailed description of the Norse ships will be found in Appendix E.

21 The principles of Norse navigation are explained in Appendix F.

22 In the Islendingabok it is stated that Erik found human habitations in Greenland as well as stone implements and fragments of hide-covered boats. The identity of the owners of these is discussed at length in Appendix I, Part II.

23 The Western Wilderness or uninhabitable regions.

24 Not to be confused with the Narssaq in the Eastern Settlement.

25 Godthaab could never have compared with the southern fiord district as a farming country, but it had sufficient merit so that it eventually came to be the second most important Norse colony in Greenland, although perhaps this was due more to its proximity to good hunting regions than to its pastoral qualities.

26 Under exceptional conditions the mountains of east Greenland can be seen from northwestern Iceland, although the distance between these two points is more than three hundred miles.

27 The Norse of this period were accomplished whalers and could take even the larger species.

28 A proto-Inuit people who preceded the Thule culture. See Appendix H.

29 This appears to represent one of the surprisingly rare occasions when a saga clerk made an error in copying a name. On the other hand it is possible that the name Eriksfirth was also applied to the Davis Strait Baffin Bay inlet during the very early period of the Norse occupancy of Greenland. See also Appendix D.

30 This was the name by which Eskimoan people came to be known to the Norse.

31 See also Appendix H.

32 See p. 54.

33 Cf. p. 13.

34 Cf. p. 13.

35 These were the eight octants of the horizon, as explained in Appendix F.

36 A doegr was equivalent to about 120 nautical miles. See Appendix F.

37 See Appendix E.

38 The analysis of the data which establishes the identity of Bjarni's landfall as some point on the coast of eastern Newfoundland is given in Appendix K.

39 A quadrantlike instrument for measuring stellar altitudes; see Appendix F.

40 It must be remembered that, being without the compass and having no conception of our "compass rose" of 360 degrees and cardinal "points," the Norse did not think of directions as we do. North, to them, was not an absolute direction. It was that octant of the horizon lying between north-northwest and north-northeast. This matter is dealt with in detail in Appendix F.

41 Up to this point our major sources have been the three related versions of the lost Old Erik Saga; but we have now reached a stage where another of the old Icelandic manuscripts becomes important to us. This is the Greenlanders Story.

As I have explained in Appendix A, the Greenlanders Story cannot be treated as a primary source. It should be thought of as the earliest extant reconstruction of the story of the Norse western voyages. However, it is of inestimable value, since it contains passages drawn from sources which are no longer in existence.

What is required of anyone who wishes to make use of the Greenlanders Story is that he disentangle the fragments of original source material from the fabric into which the author of the Greenlanders Story has woven them.

In the sections of *The Saga Tale* which introduce the next several chapters I have used a number of such fragments. In each case specific references to this qualified use are made at the end of the quoted passages. An explanation of how and why these selections have been chosen will be found in Appendix L.

The sequence and timing of Leif's two major voyages, as I present them, are not those which are generally accepted. The reasons for believing that Leif sailed to Vinland at some time toward the middle of the last decade of the tenth century, and made his voyage to Norway a year or two later, are given in Appendix L and are further dealt with in Chapter Twelve.

42 Until sometime shortly after A.D. 1000 the Godthaab Fiord area was apparently not settled and the Ivitgut Fiord district bore the name Vestri Bygd. For a full explanation of this identification see Appendix D.

43 Although a large number of Dorset, proto-Beothuk and Beothuk sites are known from most other parts of Newfoundland, none have been found on the Avalon Peninsula, where even scattered finds of artifacts are extremely rare. There are no artifact finds at all from the foot of Trinity Bay.

44 *The Journal of James Yonge, Plymouth Surgeon*, edited by F. N. L. Poynter (London: Longmans, 1963).

45 In reconstructing this portion of the history of the voyages, the author of the Greenlanders Story has confused certain elements in the lives of Thorstein Eriksson and Thorer the Norseman.

To begin with, he tells us that Thorer brought his wife Gudrid with him on the Greenland trading voyage, and that this was the same Gudrid Thorbjornsdottir who later married Thorstein Eriksson and still later Thorfinn Karlsefni, and who played a leading role in the western voyages subsequent to Leif's visit to Vinland.

This is an error. The Erik the Red and Karlsefni sagas, supported by the Landnamabok, give an entirely different version of how Gudrid Thorbjornsdottir reached Greenland as an unmarried girl accompanied by her father. This version is so detailed and so well substantiated that its authenticity cannot be doubted.

Thorer may have had a woman called Gudrid with him, for Norse traders were in the habit of carrying women along to ease the boredom of long voyages. However, these were seldom their wives; usually they were concubines or female slaves.

The acceptable versions of the Gudrid Thorbjornsdottir story tell us that shortly after Gudrid reached Greenland she married Thorstein Eriksson and went to live with him at the Western Settlement. During the first winter of their marriage an epidemic struck that settlement, killing Thorstein. Gudrid survived to return to the Eastern Settlement, where she later married Karlsefni.

The author of the Greenlanders Story evidently knew of Gudrid's two Greenland marriages, and he had heard about an epidemic. He mistakenly concluded that it was Thorer the Norwegian trader and his crew who died of the disease, thereby freeing Thorer's wife to marry Thorstein Eriksson. He also reports that Erik died during this same epidemic, which we know was not the case, since Erik was still alive and in good health as late as 1005.

46   The original vellum of the Flateyjarbok says sixteen years. However, there are several manuscript copies extant in which the figure is given as fourteen.

47   This would have been Thor himself.

48   It will be remembered that Greenland included both sides of Davis Strait and Baffin Bay. See Appendix D.

49   Ground squirrels are not native to Greenland. However, Parry's ground squirrel is locally abundant in parts of Baffin Island.

50   This reference to what are obviously natives has usually been regarded as a piece of pure invention since it is known that there were no natives on the coasts of Greenland proper at this period. However this is actually a perfectly good description of two Inuit men dealing with a seal or walrus which they had speared at a lead in the ice. The fact that they are described as giant-sized relates them to the Tunnit, about whom there are many Inuit legends from Labrador, Baffin Island and northwest Greenland. It is now the opinion of most archeologists that the Tunnit are to be identified with the Dorsets, who at this time were still to be found on the Baffin Island, Labrador and Newfoundland coasts, but who had apparently vanished from Greenland some centuries earlier. More detail on the Tunnit-Dorset relationship will be found in Appendix H. The Norse identification of the couple as women

follows from the fact that in Inuit cultures both sexes have long hair and dress much alike. Early European explorers also frequently mistook the men for women.

51 The failure of the fiord ice to melt is important, for it should be remembered that the voyage took place near the peak of the Little Climatic Optimum. It is unlikely that this fiord could have been on the northwest Greenland coast, warmed as it was by the northward-flowing current, and in a region where in any case there are few real fiords, and none at all between Skal Island and Thule. On the other hand there are a number of very deep, very narrow fiords on the Baffin Island coast north of Cape Aston. These often remain filled with ice throughout the summer due to the chilling influence of the Canadian Current and to the fact that they are so well protected that they are not subject to much swell nor to severe wind action. These fiords also possess extensive sand and gravel beaches formed by terminal moraines from the adjacent glaciers. It is also notable that there are no fiords on the west Greenland coast which are surrounded by glaciers, while there are many such on the northeast Baffin Island coast.

52 This is a most authentic touch, for it is a typical example of the use of involved simile in ancient scaldic verse. In this case the "lazy man" is the ship herself and the head washing refers to the "bone at the teeth" or the bow wave. That such a satiric verse should be carved on an oar is perfectly in keeping with what we know about the use of runes. That the incident should be preserved in the saga, where it apparently has no particular relevance, is an example of how faithful to small details the sagas could be.

53 Shore-fast ice, producing a fixed ice-foot extending up to several miles offshore, is a summer feature of the northeast Baffin Island coast, but is not found, except in winter, on the west Greenland coast.

54 Why the natives should have brought back the boat is not explained. They may not have taken it in the first place, but may have found it after it had drifted off and brought it back in the hope of establishing some sort of friendly contact with the strangers.

55 This whole passage is obviously concerned with a sea voyage over salt water. It could describe the crossing of Davis Strait or some part of Baffin Bay. The men were evidently away from land— where fresh water would have been readily available—for such

a long time that what they carried was used up, and they were in dire straits from thirst. By accident they seem to have discovered that it is possible to get fresh water from old sea ice or icebergs.

56 It is not impossible that this may have been Herjolf Bardsson, Bjarni Herjolfsson's father. At any rate both Herjolf and Bjarni seem to have mysteriously disappeared from Herjolfsness by the time Thorbjorn Vifilsson arrived there in 997. The site of the outlawed Herjolf's stead could not have been on the east Greenland coast since there were never any farms on that coast at a distance sufficiently far north of Farewell to merit the phrase "a long and difficult journey to the Eastern Settlement." Probably the stead was on one of the lonely fiords south of Godthaab where isolated Norse farms have been discovered by archeologists. At this period the Godthaab settlement did not exist, and the name Western Settlement still referred to Ivitgut Bight, due west of the Eastern Settlement.

57 These would be the Eastern and Western settlements of those times, i.e., the Ivitgut Bight and Julianehaab Bight areas. The phrase could not possibly refer to the later Western Settlement at Godthaab, since it and the Eastern Settlement were hundreds of miles distant from one another.

58 This was in the summer of 997.

59 The first milk drawn from a goat after parturition.

60 She seems to have changed her name when she became a Christian.

61 The Landnamabok tells the story of an Icelander named Thord who wished to make a voyage to Norway with his wife in order to claim an inheritance, and who insisted on burying the family treasures so they would be safe during his absence. His wife was so appalled at this wanton throwing down of the gauntlet to the fates that she refused to sail with him, and sure enough Thord and his ship were lost at sea.

62 Norse traders of this period had learned that it was advantageous to at least profess Christianity, since they often had to visit ports in Christian countries where to be both Norse and pagan would weigh doubly heavily against them.

63 The text says Vinland but for reasons given in Appendix M it appears that the original must have been Iceland.

64 No mention is made of this vessel or its owners in either the Erik

the Red or Karlsefni sagas; however, the Greenlanders Story
speaks of them in connection with what is reputed to have been
an independent voyage to Vinland conducted by Freydis, Erik's
bastard daughter, and her husband Thorvald after the Karlsefni
expedition had returned to Greenland. But that this voyage did
not take place independently is established in Appendix M.

65   Karlsefni's and Thorhall Gamlisson's ships carried approximately
forty people each. According to the general agreement with the
Greenlanders, it would appear that thirty of those aboard each
ship were men, of whom about fifteen belonged to the permanent
crew. The fifteen male colonists would have included three or four
heads of families and some adult dependents and male thralls.
The remaining ten people would have been women and youths—
young children were probably not counted.

The composition of the group aboard the ship skippered by
Thorvald Eriksson would have been a little different, since the
whole party apparently planned on remaining in Vinland as
settlers. This conclusion is supported by the fact that Freydis, who
had no intention of settling but went along only "for honour and
wealth," had to make arrangements for a ship of her own to bring
back her booty. She would not have needed to do this if the plan
had called for Thorvald Eriksson's ship and crew to return
to Greenland after disembarking a party of colonists.

Thorvald's vessel would therefore have carried thirty Greenland men, all of whom were colonists, and a considerably larger
number of women and children than did the Icelandic vessels.

The Helge and Finnboggi ship would have had a full Icelandic
crew of about fifteen sailors together with five women who, in
accordance with the normal practice of those times, had been
brought along to look after the crew's needs in a variety of ways.

Freydis and her husband Thorvald would have been accompanied by male retainers and thralls at least equal in number to the
Icelandic crew, both to guarantee against treachery on the part of
Helge and Finnboggi and to do the hard work involved in gathering
a lading for the ship in Vinland.

66   See Appendix P for details of the Norse penetration into
Hudson Strait.

67   Some of the extant copies of the Erik the Red and the Karlsefni
sagas tell us that the ships sailed to the Vestri Bygd, which was

the Western Settlement, and thence to Bear Island. However, other recensions say Vestri Obygd, the Western Wilderness. Most authors have taken the Vestri Bygd reading as the correct one, but this interpretation leads to almost insoluble difficulties. Bear Island must then be looked for on the coast of Greenland, and it has consequently been supposed that it must be identified with Disco Island. However, the sagas say that Helluland lay two doegr south of Bear Island, and in order to make Disco fill the bill the saga direction must be altered to read "southwest." This would then mean that Helluland was the Cumberland Peninsula, which leaves us with the problem of how to get the expedition to a forested country (Markland) in two more doegr on a southeasterly course, as specified in the sagas. This course and distance from Cumberland Peninsula would have taken the ships into the middle of the Labrador Sea as well as leaving them several doegr northward of timberline. Quite apart from this difficulty, the choice of Disco as Bear Island is absurd, since Disco lies nearly seven hundred miles north of Eriksfiord; and it is quite clear from all the sagas that Karlsefni was intent on finding Vinland and was not engaging in a polar expedition. A more detailed discussion of this matter will be found in Appendix D, Part II.

68 At the present time the line of demarcation between the almost completely barren mountain region of north Labrador and the forested coastal plains of the southern region reaches the sea just south of the Kiglapait Peninsula. In historic times it extended north to take in Okak Bay, where in the late eighteenth century Moravian missionaries still found stands of large spruce trees which were abundant enough to justify the installation of a sawmill.

69 Although Belle Isle probably had few nesting eiders, it was a breeding ground for vast numbers of seabirds of other species, which fact may have helped to confuse the saga scribes.

70 Champlain's map of 1632 still calls the northeast section of the Gulf of St. Lawrence "La Grande Baye."

71 The Epaves Bay site is discussed in Appendix N.

72 The English translation is Wreck Bay, and the name is derived from the fact that the bay provides no shelter for ships, several of which have driven ashore here during northwesterly storms.

73 Epaves Bay lies 240 nautical miles north of Tickle Cove Pond and,

apart from this increased northing, its climate is so much worse that wild grapes could probably not have survived there.

74   Deer, moose and elk were not found in Newfoundland. Moose have since been introduced.

75   Thorhall may have scaled the prominent coastal cliff at nearby Cape Ardoise.

76   An analysis of the data on which we have based our reconstruction of the events of this first summer will be found in Appendix M, together with an explanation of how, and why, we have combined certain conflicting information from the various sources.

77   Meaning Leif's Vinland.

78   See Appendix H.

79   The evidence demonstrating that this voyage was made south-westward from the Straumfiord Camp is given in Appendix M, Part II.

80   Although there is a break in the bar at Parsons Pond now, it was apparently not in existence in Karlsefni's day. See Appendix M— The Location of Hop. For a Description of the type of haven known to the Norse as a hop, see Part II of Appendix L.

81   I made an estimate of the amount of pasturage in the immediate vicinity of St. Paul's Bay, using aerial photographs checked against ground reconnaissance. I found that three types of pastureland were available: (1) Tide grass pasture (mud flats covered with salt water at spring tides only, and supporting a growth of salt-grass), amounting to approximately 180 acres; (2) Hay meadows (light, well drained, sandy land), approximately 450 acres; and (3) Bog pasture (wet, swampy, but well covered with tussock grasses), approximately 4000 acres.

82   The evidence identifying the Dorsets with the people encountered by Karlsefni is to be found in Appendices H and O.

83   The eleventh-century meaning of the name Skraeling is in doubt. Sigurd Stefansson, writing late in the sixteenth century, tells us that it meant cowardly weakling, but this was a late usage. In the thirteenth century it implied a dwarfish people, but this was in reference to the Thule and not to the Dorsets, who appear to have been singularly robust in build.

84   More likely milk products such as cheese and skyr.

85   See also Appendix O.

86   This saga passage is a further indication that Hop could not have

been in a country to the south of Newfoundland since the race of woodland caribou which was found throughout the forested regions of the eastern seaboard of the mainland did not form large herds, but lived dispersed in small groups in forest cover.

87   An analysis of the data justifying the reconstruction of two voyages subsequent to the return of the Hop expedition will be found in Appendix M.

88   According to Gwyn Jones in *The Norse Atlantic Saga* (Oxford, 1964), Jorgen Meldgaard has also reached the conclusion that this is the river that Thorvald discovered.

89   Throughout the remainder of this section of the saga story (taken from the Greenlanders Story) the word "Skraeling" is used in the original text. This usage evidently resulted from the fact that the author of the Greenlanders Story confused this second battle between the Norse and Newfoundland aborigines with the battle fought at Hop between the Norse and the Dorsets. I have therefore substituted the word "natives" in order not to perpetuate the error. This matter is fully explained in Appendix O.

90   The adventurous Freydis did not accompany Karlsefni this time, presumably because she was in such an advanced state of pregnancy.

91   See Appendix H.

92   There is no longer even a small barachois at the mouth of the Hampden, due to alterations in the topography made by a pulp-wood company. However, British Admiralty charts show that a tiny 'hop' existed there as late as 1897. The charts also show a narrow approach channel over tidal flats through which a vessel of a knorr's draft might have been rowed. The barachois may well have been slightly larger in A.D. 1000, if we accept the hypothesis that the land has risen a few feet since then (see Appendix C). The Hampden River itself is not much more than a good-sized stream, except during periods of heavy rain. It is navigable only by canoes.

93   For a detailed evaluation of the evidence supporting this conclu-sion, see Appendix O.

94   In 1963 the Ingstad expedition found Dorset artifacts at Epaves Bay. These predate the arrival of the Karlsefni-Thorvald party, as does a Boreal Archaic cultural site at the same locality.

95   The Erik the Red and Karlsefni sagas tell us that after the return

of Karlsefni's second southern expedition, Greenlanders and
Icelanders settled down together to spend a final winter at
Straumfiord. The unstated corollary is that the entire flotilla
sailed for Greenland as a unit in the spring of the fourth year.
The Greenlanders Story, on the other hand, concludes its
account of the western voyages with a description of a separate
voyage by Freydis Eriksdottir to Vinland—a voyage which, as
we have shown in Appendix M, could not have taken place.
We are also told that the survivors of the Greenland contingent,
led by Freydis, returned to Greenland the summer after Karlsefni
and his Icelanders arrived there. This being the case, we need have
no difficulty in resolving the conflict between the two accounts.

 I conclude that the Icelanders departed toward the end of
the third summer, with sufficient time in hand for a voyage back
to Greenland before the autumnal gales began. But for reasons
which I will discuss in the next chapter, the Greenland contingent
chose to remain behind for one more winter.

96 The short portion of the Greenlanders Story which describes
the purportedly independent voyage of Freydis to Vinland has not
been reproduced here. We begin the narrative with a description
of a quarrel between Freydis and the brothers Helge and Finnboggi
over possession of a house.

97 The author of the Greenlanders Story had disposed of Erik prior
to the Karlsefni-Thorvald-Freydis voyage to the western lands.
Consequently he was forced to substitute Leif for Erik as head of
the family when he wrote his account of what happened to Freydis
after her return to Greenland. We conclude that it was Erik who
discovered the true facts about what had happened at Straumfiord,
and who forecast a black future for his wayward daughter.

98 A mile and a half west of Epaves Bay a good-sized lake lies close to
the coastline. Its north end is 175 yards from the bottom of Rudder
Cove, and its western side is the same distance from the bottom of
Pond Cove. Pond Cove offers an excellent small harbour and it may
well be that the brothers moved, with their ship, to Pond Cove and
built their hall just inland from it, on the protected lake shore.

99 Eyrbyggja Saga.

100 There can be no doubt that Bjorn Asbrandsson actually existed.
He was forced to leave Iceland because he had become the lover
of Thurid, the daughter of the renowned chieftain, Snorri Godi,

who was also one of Ari Thorgilsson's most reliable sources in the compilation of his famous history, the Islendingabok. Unfortunately for Bjorn, Thurid was already married and her husband took a dim view of the affair. In the ensuing mêlée Bjorn wounded the husband and killed two of his friends, for which he was exiled. Upon Bjorn's return to Iceland three years later the frightened husband persuaded the powerful Snorri Godi to prevail on Bjorn, by threats or bribes, to stay out of the country. Bjorn then seems to have set sail for Greenland.

101   *Stray Leaves from an Arctic Journal* (London, 1852).

102   Johannes Brøndsted, director of the Danish National Museum, has examined this find and the Kensington Stone, and can discover no good reason for doubting their authenticity. See Smithsonian Report for 1953, Washington, D.C.

103   For details see Appendix P.

104   Grönlands Historiske Mindesmærker III.

INDEX

Einarsfiord, 83

England. *See* British Isles and Britons (England and English)

English Channel, 5

English River, 268

Epaves Bay, 252, 254–257, 262, 325, 333–334, 376n71, 376n72, 376–377n73, 378n94, 379n98

Erik, Bishop of Greenland, 351, 366

Erik the Red (Eric Thorvaldsson), 154–155, 223–224, 331, 341, 379n97, 347; appearance and character, 28, 42; attempted voyage to Vinland, 190, 196, 197–198, 199–200, 201–202, 203, 223–224, 318, 364; birth, family, childhood, 28–29, 362; conflict with Leif Eriksson, 159, 161, 166, 193–196, 200, 214; Greenland settlement, 55, 64–65, 66, 69, 78–79, 81–82, 83–87, 87–88, 88–92, 93, 98–99, 124–130, 153, 162, 167–168 *passim*, 180, 183, 187, 190, 195–196, 199, 211–213, 213–215, 218, 372n45; Icelandic career and exile, 30–32, 181, 190, 363; marriage and children, 29, 84, 188, 362; relationship with Thorgisl Orrabeinsfostri, 177–178, 180; religion, 189, 193–194, 214; saga tale, 26–27, 32, 43, 52, 66, 77, 83–84, 155–156, 188–190, 197, 210–213; voyages to Greenland, 32, 33, 36, 38, 41–42, 43–46, 46–48, 48–50, 52–53, 54–55, 57–58, 59–61, 66–67, 67–69, 69–71, 71–72, 72–76, 77–79, 79–80, 80–82, 101–104 *passim*, 363

Erik the Red Saga, 144, 371n45, 164, 180, 204, 214, 224, 230, 236, 293, 343, 374–375n64, 375–376n67, 378–379n95

Eriksey, 52, 62–64, 64–65, 77, 78, 82, 363

Eriksfiord, 52, 54, 57, 59, 63, 66, 67, 77, 83, 84, 89, 126, 155, 158, 177, 189, 197, 202, 203, 206, 207, 210, 214, 217, 226, 336, 346, 347, 363, 364, 376n67

Eriksfirth, 77, 340, 370n29

Eriksholm. *See* Holm

Eskaleut language, 336

Eskimo Island, 312

Eurasia, 368n2

Europe, 1–2, 4–5, 9, 13, 15, 38, 41, 75, 76, 98, 101, 128, 198, 202, 208, 267, 355, 366, 367

Eyrbyggja Saga, 163

Eyjolf of Sviney, 27, 32, 43

Eyjolf the Foul, 26, 30

Eykarstad, 137, 146

Eyrar, 97, 98, 100, 101, 103, 104

Eyvind, 96

Eyvind Cheekrift, 162

Eyvind Eld, 96

FAËROE ISLANDS, 2, 6, 10, 11–12, 14, 17, 101, 368n6. *See also* Outer Islands

Fair Haven, 140

Famish Gut, 140

Farewell, Cape, 18–19, 38, 49, 52, 88, 99, 104, 106, 334, 337, 350, 374n56

farming, 10, 11, 12, 18–19, 28–29, 30, 50, 63–64, 91, 127–128, 144–145, 218, 243, 279, 280–281, 356, 369n25

Faxafiord, 169

Ferolle Peninsula, 309

narwhals, 35, 74, 75, 215

navigation, 5–6, 39, 46–47, 60–61, 70–71, 71–72, 103–104, 111–112, 120–121, 131–133, 197–198, 199–200, 201–202, 223–237 *passim*, 369n21, 370n35, 370n40

Neolithic Age, 1, 9, 285

New Brunswick, 146–147

New England, 98, 146, 147, 236

New Harbour, 254–255

Newfoundland, 1–2, 5, 97, 98, 106, 246, 337, 359; animal and plant life, 107–108, 115, 147–149, 258, 280–281, 309, 37774; Bjarni Herjolfsson voyage, 109–122, 363; climate, 138, 140, 144–145, 148–149, 281; European discovery, 108, 109–118; Karlsefni expedition, 210–337, 364, 365; latitude, 146; later expeditions, 148, 189, 195–196, 197–198, 199–200, 201–202, 203, 364; Leif Eriksson voyage, 132–134, 136–140, 140–144, 363; "natives," 143–144, 272–273, 273–275, 283–288, 290–304, 305–309, 318, 325–330, 331–333, 334–336, 351, 352, 372–373n50; post Karlsefni activity, 349–353, 357–358; resources and products, 60, 94, 142–143, 147–149, 149–153, 363; topography, 110–111, 140, 142–143, 279–280, 377n81; trade, 293–294; Vinland controversy, 140–144, 144–146, 146–149; whaling and other industry, 151–153

Nidaros, 156

Nipigon, Lake, 355

Njal's Saga, 96, 368n11

Norman, Cape, 247, 249, 257, 263, 268, 273–274

Norse Atlantic Saga, The, by Gwyn Jones, 378n88

Norsemen, 150–151, 337; characteristics and appearance, 20–23, 195, 294–295, 327–328, 337, 343; early Icelandic activity, 13–16; emigration, 9–12; fishing and whaling, 149–151, 279; Greenland exploration, 32–33, 33–37, 37–41, 41–42, 47; Greenland settlement, 55, 64–65, 66, 69, 75–76, 78–79, 81–82, 83–87, 87–88, 88–92, 93–94, 98–99, 102, 124–130, 153, 157–159, 159–160, 162–168 *passim*, 176–177, 180, 183–185, 188–194, 356, 366, 370n29, 372n45; Icelandic settlement, 13–14, 16–17, 17–19, 19–20, 20–23, 362; later western activity, 349–356, 366, 367; maritime activity, 7–9, 168; New World value and errors, 357–358; North American discovery and settlement, 109–122, 252; religion, 374n62; sea routes, 101, 357–359; ships, 7–10, 12, 13, 44–45, 48, 85–87, 105–107, 129, 255–257, 336–337, 369n20; superstitions, 195, 284; Viking raids, 9–11, 11–13, 13–16, 41–42; weapons, 299–300. *See also* Bjarni Herjolfsson; commerce (trade); Erik the Red; Leif Eriksson; navigation; Newfoundland; Thorfinn Karlsefni

North Atlantic. *See* Atlantic Ocean

North Dakota, 354

North Sea, 5

North Star. *See* Pole Star

Northern Seas, The, by A. R. Lewis, 368n4

THE DOUGLAS & MCINTYRE
FARLEY MOWAT LIBRARY

People of the Deer

A Whale for the Killing

And No Birds Sang

Sea of Slaughter

Born Naked

The Snow Walker

My Father's Son

Westviking

Please visit www.douglas-mcintyre.com
for upcoming titles in this series.

FARLEY MOWAT (1921–2014) began writing upon his return from serving in World War II and wrote 44 books, which have sold nearly 25 million copies in more than 60 countries. He spent much of his youth in Saskatoon and lived in Ontario, Cape Breton and Newfoundland, while travelling frequently to Canada's far north. Throughout, Mowat remained a determined environmentalist, despairing at the ceaseless work of human cruelty. His ability to capture the tragic comedy of life on earth has made him a national treasure in Canada and a beloved storyteller to readers around the world.